The Body Leads the Way

The Body Leads the Way

Ritual, Liminality, and Imagination

Mary Lane Potter

A Collection of Essays

The Liminality Press

The Liminality Press

510 West Walnut Street
#552
Columbia, MO 65205

www.liminalitypress.com

ISBN: 979-8-9891640-2-8

ePub ISBN: 979-9891640-3-5

First published by The Liminality Press, 2025

Cover Photo and Chapter Photos: Mary Lane Potter

Book Jacket design: Carolyn Dyess

For Ruben and Naomi

Is not the Body more than Raiment?

William Blake, *To the Christians*

In everything, in everything your body will be an asset.
Our body is ever at our side. It is the one thing which stays with
us to the end.

Clarice Lispector, *Fair Tidings for a Child*

Sacramental words and gesture are not simply the embodiment of
some thought. Like tangible things, they are themselves the
carriers of meaning, which is inseparable from the material form.
They do not evoke the idea of God: they are the vehicle of His
presence and action. In the last analysis the soul is so little to be
separated from the body that it will carry a radiant double of its
temporal body into eternity.

Maurice Merleau-Ponty, *Faith and Good Faith*

Gratitude

It takes a community to write a book, and I am grateful to belong to such a generous, thoughtful, and lively one. Thank you to:

Thomas A. Byrnes, American empirical moral philosopher, H. Richard Niebuhr scholar, and treasured friend, for sending me the Tim Ingold, Alva Noë, and Hans Joas books (among *many* others!), for responding to a draft of the introduction and Chapter 1, and for engaging me in countless thought-provoking conversations, from pragmatism to mysticism, history to poetry, biology to metaphysics. How would I think without you?

Mary Farrell Bednarowski (Big Mary), scholar of American religions and the religious imagination, inestimable colleague and treasured friend, who generously and graciously read and responded to drafts of every chapter in this book, who revives my flagging spirit, who expands my field of vision, my reading list, my joy—and always makes me wiser. How would I think without you?

Kelly A. Malone, writer and editor extraordinaire and treasured friend, who graciously and generously read and responded to drafts of all these chapters, who helps me become a better writer—and always makes me laugh.

Rabbi Anson Laytner, writer and theologian, dear friend and conversation partner, for his insightful comments on a draft of the Introduction and Chapter 1.

Richard I. Gordon, spiritual psychology therapist and writer, dear friend and conversation partner, for his judicious edits to a draft of the Introduction and Chapter 1.

Timothy L. Carson, co-founder of the Engaged Liminality Guild and The Liminality Press, who invited me to join the Guild after reading my essay "Standing on Moonstones." The presentation on ritual, liminality, and creativity I gave to that gathering became an essay that morphed into two chapters in this book and prompted the idea for this book.

Lisa R. Withrow, co-founder of the Engaged Liminality Guild and The Liminality Press for her support and her shepherding of the manuscript.

All my teachers at the Divinity School of the University of Chicago, who showed me that rigorous thinking could be creative and fun, and to all my friends who introduced me to thinkers and writers over the years. Without Susan E. Shapiro, I would not know the work of Gaston Bachelard and Edmund Jabès. Without Vítor Westhelle (z"l), I would not know the work of Clarice Lispector.

And thank you with all my heart to my family, Sam, Marisa, Ruben, and Naomi, and Miriam and Tarik, with whom I've shared so many rituals and liminal experiences over the years and without whom I would not know who or where I am in the world.

Table of Contents

Acknowledgements

Gratitude to the publishers listed below for granting permission to revise and reprint these essays in this volume.

"Between Chaos and Light: Calvin, Card Playing, Comic Books, Sex, God, and Dancing." *Spiritus: A Journal of Christian Spirituality* 16 (2016): 78-98.

"Because We Are Bodies: Bread, Wine, Rice, Water." *The Other Journal* 30 (Fall 2021): 134-44.

"When Bones Are Not Bones." *Bearings Online* (November 2, 2020): https://collegevilleinstitute.org/bearings/bones-are-not-bones/

"The Story of a Hollowed-Out Bone." *Still Point Arts Quarterly* 39 (Fall 2020): 92-101.

"The Liminal Work of Sacred Clowns." Published as "The Sacred Clown." *Parabola* 48 No. 3 (Fall 2023): 85-87.

"A Gathering of Different Lights." *Bearings Online* (November 21, 2019): https://collegevilleinstitute.org/bearings/a-gathering-of-different-lights/

"Feeding the Spirit." *Tablet Magazine* (November 10, 2022): https://www.tabletmag.com/sections/belief/articles/feeding-spirit-rituals-luang-prabang

"Ever Becoming, Never Being: Dwelling in the Sukkah." Published as "The Shelter of Your Peace" in *Parabola* 48 No. 1 (Spring 2023): 44-49.

"By the River of a Thousand *Lingas*." *Parabola* 48 No. 2 (Summer 2023): 62-67.

"On Sam Mountain." *River Teeth: Beautiful Things* (February 22, 2021): https://riverteethjournal.com/blog/2021/02/22/on-sam-mountain

"Between the Dead and the Living." Published as "This Too Is a Practice." *Leaping Clear* (Fall 2021): https://www.leapingclear.org/mary-lane-potter-essay-1

"On the Way to the Woods, a Detour." *Labyrinth Pathways* 11 (November 2017): 13-16.

"Stepping into the Between." Published as "Stepping onto the Path." *Leaping Clear* (Fall 2019): https://www.leapingclear.org/mary-lane-potter-essay?fbclid=IwAR090SxGt42-WL485hmPtpow4xzc10W6t2y-YERnA32IabRBfd8yIUlKoS8

"Standing on Moonstones: The Art of Dwelling Between." *ARTS: The Arts in Religious and Theological Studies* 31 (November 2019): 26-37.

"Playing in the Fields of Between: Art as the Realm of the Possible." Portions of this essay were published as "The Body Leads the Way: Ritual, Creativity, and Liminality," in *The Liminal Loop: Twelve Tales of Transformation.* ed. Timothy L. Carson. (Cambridge: Lutterworth Press, 2022): 41-55.

"Strange Tools: Fiction as Holy Possibility." Published as "Stories to Think With: Fiction as a Mode of Inquiry." *IMAGE Journal* 119 (January 2024): 115-22. +https://imagejournal.org/article/stories-to-think-with-fiction-as-a-mode-of-inquiry/]

"The Body Leads the Way: Ritual, Liminality, and Imagination." Portions of this essay were published as "The Body Leads the Way: Ritual, Creativity, and Liminality," in *The Liminal Loop: Twelve Tales of Transformation.* ed. Timothy L. Carson. (Cambridge: Lutterworth Press, 2022): 41-55.

Coda: "*Minyan*, or How To Wear a Prayer Shawl." *The Ekphrastic Review* (October 1, 2020): https://www.ekphrastic.net/the-ekphrastic-review/minyan-or-how-to-wear-a-prayer-shawl-by-mary-lane-potter

Introduction: A Holy Between

This book was born of dancing. One Sunday morning, while dancing in a gathering called "Sweat Your Prayers," I suddenly found myself transported. The ordinary world of cause and effect, visible and invisible, I and not-I, had fallen away and everything—my mind, my body, my spirit, the other dancers, the music, the light, the air, the shouts and blares from the street below—was moving as one, caught up in a dance without beginning or end. I had crossed a threshold into another way of being, entered a state that was neither wholly outside everyday reality nor wholly inside it, but between the two. A deep, calming joy spread through me and radiated from me. When the music ended, we stopped dancing and packed up to go our separate ways. But that experience lingered in my body and mind as I walked home, and for weeks afterward. Something powerful, something sacred, had happened that I wanted to understand.

Then, one day, sociologist Emile Durkheim's account of ritual dancing in a tribal society flashed into my mind. Durkheim had described those dancers as being in a state of exaltation. They had left the everyday world behind and were caught up in a feeling of oneness, a transformative experience in which the profane became sacred. Recalling that description electrified me. Until that moment I hadn't considered my weekly practice with a handful of other barefoot dancers dressed in rumply clothes, all of us moving our bodies freely in an old Seattle ballroom with scuffed floors and faded curtains, a ritual. Ritual, I assumed, was a solemn, sacred practice found in synagogues, churches, mosques, and other holy places. Nor would I have named my experience *liminal*, for I associated liminality with the kind of threshold experiences that occurred in rites of passage like initiation, coming of age, and wedding ceremonies—not the kind of holy between I had experienced. While Durkheim hadn't used the words *liminal* or *liminality* in his description of the dancers, in a flash of insight I saw that in bodies moving, ritual, liminality, the sacred, and art were all connected. That intuition dogged me until I wrote what became the first essay in this book, almost a decade ago.

The question behind that exploratory essay on dancing—What does the liminal look like when we approach it through a broad understanding of ritual?—sent me on a journey of discovery. I found myself time and again attending to what had happened in a specific experience of ritual I had been invited to participate in or I had stumbled upon, particularly as it gave rise to liminality and creativity. Alert to the nexus of embodiment, ritual, liminality, the sacred, and creativity, I encountered it wherever I turned, in surprising places like bones, hand-carved riverbeds, temporary dwellings, and writing habits. Intrigued, eager to deepen my understanding of these experiences, I turned again to the page, for writing is the way I pay attention, the way I think.

Those investigations became Chapters 1 through 17, each of which attends to a particular personal or cultural ritual and the ritual space in which it occurs. The earlier chapters focus on ritual practices as sanctifyings of time or space, reflecting that we live in "the all-embracing stuff of Space-Time."[1] The final chapters focus on the power of ritual as a "holy between" in the creation of art. Throughout, I look closely at how the holy between is related to our corporeality, and the essential role of the physical in creating and inviting us into liminal moments or spaces, whether specific gestures, concrete objects, or built spaces. The role imagination plays in ritual as a liminal activity and the way ritual opens a space between where things can collide and meet, lose focus to discover new forms, disintegrate to reintegrate in order to be reimagined, is also threaded throughout, though the final chapters treat this subject more directly in terms of art and artists, particularly writers and writing.

The view of ritual and liminality that emerges from these essays is the fruit of a lifelong fascination with ritual and many years of observing, reflecting on, participating in, and creating rituals, sacred and profane, those of my own tradition and those of others. Though I hadn't realized it before embarking on this journey, I am built for ritual. Growing up in a Dutch immigrant Calvinist community, I was formed by a constant stream of communal rituals—praying before and after every meal, reading the Bible after dinner, singing Psalms of praise in unison, hearing the Word of God read and interpreted several times a week, and witnessing the solemn ritual of Communion once a month. We had our dramatic rites of passage as well—baptism, confirmation, marriage, burial—but it was the rhythm of the everyday rituals that sculpted my inner landscape and made me a ritual-dependent person.

I don't feel whole without ritual. I don't feel truly alive. This is why wherever I find myself in the world, it is not museum or temple art that draws me, but the living art of rituals—speaking in tongues in a Chicago church basement, Sundancing on Rosebud Reservation, raising the cone of power in a social hall in Minnesota, worshipping *Kumari Devi*, The Living Goddess, in Kathmandu, sacrificing goats to Kali in a sacred valley in Nepal, burning offerings to ancestors on the streets of Hanoi, floating burning boats down the Mekong during Lai Heua Fai in Louangphrabang, Laos. And why two mornings a week I would wake up with my infant grandson, wrap us together in a blanket, and step outside to recite *Modah ani*, a Hebrew prayer of thankfulness for the soul being restored to the body, ending with our own song-dance, *boom boom boom boom*. If I waited too long, Ruben Zev would crawl to the door we always stepped through and put his hands on the threshold. At 12 months, he already knew the deep joy of sharing a repeated sequence of acts.

Ritual or ritualizing, I have come to believe, is one way that we *intentionally* enter a holy between, a liminal space where transformation can occur. By situating our bodies in space, by moving, alone or together, in time and in intentional sequences of actions, we sanctify space and time, we enter the realm of imagination or the possible, and open up space for new ways of perceiving, acting, and thinking.

This broad view of ritual and liminality as the body leading the way to transformation underlies all the essays in this book, whether they focus on traditional communal religious rituals or private rituals, on time-based rituals or built ritual environments, on religious practice or the creation of art. This understanding emerged gradually, organically, from the writing of these essays and the experiences and reflections on which they were based; it did not precede them.

While this view underlies each of the concrete explorations in Chapters 1 through 17, in Chapter 18 I have articulated more directly how I understand the nexus of embodiment, ritual, liminality, and imagination. Ritual, I argue there, is a unique embodied thinking activity. It is an intentional sequence of acts or gestures or body movements, performed individually or in community, privately or publicly, that *enacts meaning* by sanctifying space and time; it carves out a moment from the endless flow of time and erects a temporary shelter in the vast expanse of our world, a holy between, a moment and a shelter that we can step into to cross over from the profane to the sacred. Rituals can create liminal spaces or moments that give rise to creativity and help us make our human existence, this created world of becoming, more habitable.

In that final chapter, I also make an argument for the power of ritual in contemporary life and suggest how ritualizing corresponds to the liminal nature of human existence. Along the way, I offer metaphors—inspired by biology, a medieval Islamic mystic-philosopher, a Jewish *midrashic* tradition, and a contemporary American philosopher—that point to the often-perplexing experience of liminality: a littoral or intertidal zone; *barzakh,* or isthmus; the twilight creation; and a state of perception called *metainstability*. These four complement the architectural metaphor of moonstones developed in Chapter 14.

Understanding ritual in this broad and dynamic way is a clear departure from common assumptions about ritual. In popular culture, ritual is often seen as a *mindless* habit, a routine set of actions we perform automatically, whether it's shaking hands, brushing our teeth, doing yoga, or preparing our morning tea or coffee. There is nothing creative about these actions. They're practical, utilitarian. Like the greeting rituals of dogs, the mating rituals of flamingos, the boundary rituals of wolves, the location rituals of bees, the soothing rituals of pigeons, and mourning rituals of elephants, they're rooted in our biology, and primarily serve our physical and psychological survival.

Since the Protestant Reformation, with Zwingli's interpretation of the presence of the Lord in the Lord's Supper as symbolic rather than real, religious rituals such as baptism, bar and bat mitzvahs, and ordination, have come to be seen by many as symbolic expressions rather than transformative acts. Secular ceremonies like graduation, marriage, and citizenship are interpreted this way also. For many modern anthropologists and sociologists, religious and cultural rituals are symbolic expressions of actual social relations, social status, or the role of individuals in a society. They are structures that organize our individual social experiences and regulate our emotions and group processes. In other words, ritual as symbolic expression of sanctioned orders or beliefs is often assumed to be socially conservative: they reinforce a community's identity, cohesiveness, structures, and worldview.

To limit our fundamental human need to create and participate in ritual in these ways is to miss the liminal nature of ritual, its creative, transformative power. While ritual does not distinguish human beings from other animals, it does operate differently in *homo sapiens* because of consciousness, our unique mode of being as body-mind. And while ritual does play a role in our social organization and harmony, it also offers more than that. Far from being empty routine, ritual interrupts the routine of daily life. Rather than functioning as a deadening habit, ritual can disrupt our habitual ways of organizing our lives, inviting us to reflect on those habits. Instead of operating only to regulate existing social structures, ritual opens a space that enables participants to imagine and perceive the world in new ways, to act in new ways. Neither mindless nor passive, ritual is enactive, embodied thinking. Ritual need not be rigid; ritual can be creative.

Ritual in this sense, as a way to nourish the spirit and make way for new life, permeates our way of being in the world, both within and beyond religious communities, in contemporary societies as well as ancient ones. *Homo sapiens* has been characterized as *homo faber* (humankind the maker), *homo sciens* (the knower), *homo symbolicus* (the symbol-maker), *homo aestheticus* (the artist), and *homo ludens* (the player). Each of these terms points to one aspect of our way of being. The characterization missing from this list is the one that captivates me: humankind the ritualizer.[2] Our lives as ritual makers and participants depend on our being *homo liminalis*, an unstable creature poised between two ways of being, the corporeal and the spiritual, and the profane and the sacred. Though ritual may be fundamental to flourishing, not everyone will feel the need for it in the same way or to the same degree. However, in the chaotic, disorienting, isolating world in which we find ourselves today, with the demise of religious institutions and increasing skepticism of traditional rituals, we may need such transformative ritual more than ever.

Evolution of the Study of Liminality and Ritual

Over a hundred years ago, ethnographer Arnold van Gennep forged a link between liminality and ritual in *The Rites of Passage*. In analyzing rites of passage rituals or "life crisis" rites, he identified three phases: separation from the community; transition, during which the participant crosses a *limen* or threshold; and incorporation back into the community with a new role or status.[3] Anthropologist Victor Turner explored van Gennep's liminal phase in his classic work *The Ritual Process: Structure and Anti-Structure*. He describes the necessarily ambiguous attributes of "threshold people," emphasizing their passage from structure into *communitas*, an anti-structure that he explores in detail, and their "return to structure revitalized by their experience of *communitas* [a shared experience of equality in which customary social differences are temporarily eclipsed]."[4]

  While the study of ritual was once the domain of ethnographers and cultural anthropologists, as well as sociologists and historians of religion, it has been steadily expanding over the last fifty years beyond a focus on rites in religious or ritual contexts, both ancient and contemporary. Turner himself, in his later work, signaled a shift to looking at ritual more broadly, as a contemporary cultural activity, investigating it in relation to play, theater, sports, and performance.[5] With the advent of Ritual Studies in the late 1970s, pioneered by Ronald L. Grimes, ritual became a field of study, a wide-ranging interdisciplinary conversation for exploring ritual events, acts, spaces, and time.[6] In 1992, religious studies scholar Catherine Bell, in *Ritual Theory, Ritual Practice*, critiqued theories of ritual that bifurcate thought and action, and developed not a new theory of ritual but "a new framework within which to reconsider traditional questions about ritual." In that framework, ritual activities are put in their rightful context as purposeful human activities. For her, "ritualization" is seen as a strategic way of acting in specific social situations, with the power to facilitate acceptance of, consent to, or resistance to social structures.[7]

Recently, neurocognitive scientists, kinesiologists, psychologists, theologians, and philosophers, recognizing the significance of ritual for human behavior and culture, have begun studying the experience of ritual and the act of ritualizing as they occur in a wide variety of cultural activities: in sports, business, education, athletics, theater, politics, and the military.[8] These investigations offer welcome views of ritual in terms of anxiety reduction and performance enhancement, meaning-making, social cohesion, embodiment, the somatic ground of knowing, and more. Few, however, speak of liminality in relation to ritual, and even those who do usually have not pursued further study of this relationship.[9]

To pursue the relationship between the liminal and ritual more broadly, we can take a cue from Turner's later work, when he turned his attention to the liminal beyond threshold experiences in rites of passage. Emphasizing the importance of lived experience, he began speaking of how the dynamic ritual process and the experience of liminality take place in the contemporary world in art, play, and sports. In order to restrict the meaning of the term *liminal* to small-scale tribal, early agrarian or pre-industrial societies, on which his previous research was based, he coined the word *liminoid*, which he used to refer to experiences not necessarily tied to a ritual context or a *rite de passage*, such as a festival, pilgrimage, or other public celebration.

Turner's verbal distinction was intended to highlight four additional differences he saw between liminal and liminoid experiences. According to him, liminal phenomena are collective; liminoid phenomena, though they may have a "mass" effect, are "individualized." Liminal phenomena are integrated into a total social context, while liminoid phenomena take place on the margins of social processes or in the interstices of institutions and are more fragmentary and experimental. Liminal phenomena appear to have a common or shared meaning for members of a group; liminoid phenomena are idiosyncratic, generated by groups that compete with one another in a culture. Finally, liminal phenomena tend to facilitate the social structure, whereas liminoid phenomena are "often parts of social critiques or even revolutionary," such as books, plays, films, or other arts works that expose injustices. Though both types exist in modern societies—the liminal in religious institutions and initiation rites of clubs and sororities, the liminoid in leisure activities like art, sports, and games—he believed the liminoid was "felt to be freer"than the liminal, "a matter of choice, not obligation."[10]

Because of these differences, for Turner, the use of *liminal* to describe phenomena in complex societies is metaphorical. Though, as will become clear, I do not accept Turner's restriction of the word *liminal* to pre-industrial societies, or his strong contrast between liminal and liminoid experiences, I have found his turn toward a broader understanding of ritual and liminality a fruitful one, as well as his persistent emphasis on ritual as a *process* and its generative power for a society, as opposed to common Durkheimian views of ritual as socially conservative.

A Word on My Approach to Ritual and Liminality

My approach to ritual and the liminal follows this broader line of inquiry. While it draws on insights from classic anthropological, sociological, and history of religion viewpoints, it is fundamentally phenomenological. Specifically, it is inspired by the work of three phenomenologists, Max Scheler, Gaston Bachelard, and Maurice Merleau-Ponty. Scheler turned his insightful eye on complex experiences of feeling, including sympathy and *ressentiment*, and on religious acts such as repentance and rebirth.[11] Bachelard explored our lived experience in the world, attending to the poetics of space, water, and fire. Merleau-Ponty investigated our experience of perception, focusing on the body.[12] I am also indebted to the work of the American philosopher Alva Noë on perception, which continues the work of Merleau-Ponty but ranges farther to explore art and philosophy of mind.

My approach is perhaps closest to the "home-grown phenomenology" of anthropologist Tim Ingold. In the introduction to his essay collection *Correspondences,* Ingold says that as an amateur, not a trained philosopher, he does not engage in textual exegesis. That approach, he suggests, may not be the best way "to get to the bottom of our experience as beings in a world." Perhaps "the best way to fathom the depth of human experience" he counters, "would be to attend to the world itself, and to learn directly from what it has to tell us. This is what inhabitants do all the time, and we have much to learn from them."[13]

Attending to a broad array of ritual experiences in different cultures, using an interdisciplinary approach, and focusing on ritualizing as a unique embodied thinking activity creates a dynamic picture of ritual and liminality as we experience them in our lives. This cumulative approach is similar to Ingold's in *Making: Anthropology, Archeology, Art, Architecture, Anthropology.*[14] In that book, he follows a thread of *making*—understood as a unique embodied *thinking* activity in which participants collaborate or "correspond" with active materials—and uncovers what making means by focusing on examples, including basket making, housebuilding, watchmaking, and drawing.

By following a thread of ritualizing as a unique embodied thinking activity in different contexts, I hope to convey a *feel* for how we *experience* the liminal in the world and a sense of the power of ritual as a way of enacting meaning, an opening to creativity, and a path to transformation. I explore in these essays how liminality occurs in a wide variety of ritual actions and spaces, focusing on the way that embodiment, imagination, art, and creativity enable transformation of individuals and groups, both within and between cultures, within and between religious traditions, and in secular contexts.

I also hope these essays encourage an approach to ritual grounded in a spirit of discovery, attuned to ritual as an embodied thinking activity, wherever and whenever it may occur in our individual and shared lives. I intend to disclose the power of ritual to open up liminal spaces, nurture creativity, and transform lives, with hopes that experimentation in the form of play, even sacred play, emerges. To that end, I invite readers to enter wherever they are drawn and to attend to whatever is most provocative, to dancing (Chapter 1), food rituals (Chapter 7), walking rituals (Chapters 11-13), prayer rituals (Chapters 9-13), traditional religious rituals (Chapters 2, 3, 5, 6, 7, 8, 10, *Coda*), personal experiments with rituals (Chapters 4, 10, 11, 15, *Coda*), ritual objects (Chapters 3, 4, 7), ritual spaces (Chapters 8-14), or the power of ritual, liminality, and imagination in writing (Chapters 15-17)—all discoveries that emerged in an experience of a holy between. The presentation of the concepts and metaphors underlying my approach in Chapter 18 can be read first, as an orientation to the other essays, or last, as a weaving together of ideas that appear in the other essays. Or it can be skipped altogether.

Ingold suggests that perhaps "all true scholars…are amateurs," people who study a topic "for the love of it, motivated by a sense of care, personal involvement, and responsibility."[15] I am such a person. I come to this inquiry as one for whom ritual is breath and water, food and fire, home and wonder, joy and peace. I come as one who marvels at the mystery of our existence as entangled body-mind-spirits, and one for whom ritual is essential to that bodily-spiritual being. The mystery of our corporeality, our embodiedness, stands at the center of all we do, feel, and know—

including our practice of ritual, which depends on physical objects and spaces as well as the near environment of our bodies. And the path I have found to explore this tangle of body-mind-spirit is through ritual and liminality, creativity and art.

In these essays, I look toward the spirit through the body and toward the body through the spirit, in and through the places they meet—in ritual objects, actions, roles, movement, and places, and in the power of imagination and creativity to transform our lives. By practicing a home-grown phenomenology of body-mind-spirit, working toward a concrete poetics of body-mind-spirit, I hope to point the way to a corporeal spirituality, spiritual corporeality that depends on the liminal, especially as it occurs in art and ritual. These essays, in pursuit of the connection between ritual and liminality, are also gestures toward making peace with our enfleshment-enspiritment. They are, in part, love letters to the body and to the power of the imagination.

Amateur study for Ingold includes "*rigor* and *precision*," a kind of thinking that "joins *with* things "rather than "joining things *up*," that is "continuously in touch with feeling, with lived experience." To practice theory as a "mode of habitation" means staying "close to the grain of things." Following Ingold, I have tried, with rigor and precision, to join with our experience of the liminal in ritual, to attend to those experiences with "practiced care and attentiveness in the ongoing relation of conscious awareness and lively materials."[16] These essays, therefore, are offered not as a set of definitive concepts or a new theory of ritual or liminality. They are an attempt to think *from* rather than think *about* ritual and liminality, to "think *through* observation rather than *after* it," as Ingold says.[17] The path followed here is not a straight line heading toward a fixed destination. It is an emerging understanding. To paraphrase the opening of Paul Klee's *Pedagogical Sketchbook*, "An active line on a walk, moving freely, without goal,"[18] this book is an active intuition going for a walk. These chapters, written over many years, are *essais*, trials, offered in a spirit of inquiry into our habitation in the world. They explore ways in which ritual invites us to enter liminal moments and spaces, *because we are bodies*.

Ritual as Invitation
to the Liminal

Chapter 1

Between Chaos and Light: Sex, Card Playing, God, Calvin, and Dancing

I was born for dancing, into a Calvinist community that outlawed dancing.

This sounds like a story of belonging. But it's not. I'm not interested in pitting society against the individual or glorifying the artist as rebel. Though I admire Chaim Potok's *My Name is Asher Lev* for its rendering of the conflict between tradition and the individual, religion and art, that's not what I'm after here. I'm no rebel, no artist—more a wondering spirit, eager to taste and see that the world is good. I'm also not interested in bashing John Calvin for banning dancing in Geneva as part of his campaign against the libertines and their love of all dissolute pleasures. I'm no Calvin hater. In fact, I'm one of Calvin's few admirers—a gargantuan task in an age when Calvin figures as a favorite "whipping boy" for intellectuals and people on the street alike. Total depravity? Anathema to liberals. Double predestination? Heresy to the New Age law of attraction: Manifest your desires! And then there's the matter of burning Michael Servetus at the stake for denying the trinity and infant baptism—offensive to a host of sensibilities and stances. No, I do not rail against Calvin, or Calvinism, as the Great Repressor who did not permit me to dance. I'm after something different here.

What I want to understand is what dancing *is*. What kind of act is it? Physical? Symbolic? Secular? Spiritual? What makes dancing necessary to my existence? What does it do in my life, for my life, that I cannot live without? That's my inquiry. And it's pursuing these questions that leads me into the experience of growing up a dancer in an anti-dancing community, formed by the clash of two commands.

Flowing

"Dance!" a voice commanded. "Dance," I heard, whenever a joy so profound overtook me I felt as if I could not bear it. Before there was I and Not-I, before language was mine, the urging was there, neither inside nor outside me, just there, suddenly, rousing my spirit-flesh—wordless, insistent, irrepressible, undeniable. When the sun warmed my bared belly or lips brushed the fine hairs on the crown of my head. Once self and words had emerged, I heard it still: "Dance!" When I was swimming in Lake Michigan or the Atlantic Ocean. When I sat on a branch in our maple tree and watched the light and shadow playing through the trembling leaves. When I picked up a twig and it crawled across my palm— the wonder of a stick that was alive! When I was singing with the congregation in church, my sister's voice resonating with mine. When childhood left me, the voice did not. "Dance!" it whispered. When I heard John Coltrane playing "Welcome," or a choir singing Handel's Messiah in a cathedral, or a stream rushing over rocks. Backpacking through forested mountains. Standing on a cliff gazing at the ocean. Gazing into the face of my newborn son, the face of my newborn daughter. Meditating. Whenever joy threatens to shatter this earthen vessel, "Dance!" a voice says. And I do, quite without willing it, as if my body had a fail-safe mechanism. In those moments, all my cells straining with the pressure, eager to explode, I am, suddenly, without thinking, without willing, dancing. Not on the ground or any surface. In space, in the dark, among the stars, moving freely, in every direction. No up. No down. No East, West, North, or South. No in, no out. No origin or destination. No pattern and variation. No here or there. Just moving, freely, moving in joy, out of joy, into joy. Spinning, leaping, jumping, tumbling, whirling, whirling, whirling with the music of the spheres. And when I have danced the joy into a bearable state, I return to the earth, my body holding the joy for a glorious moment, until it dissipates and I am clay once again, breathing, moving, animated—but no longer enspirited.

Staccato

"Don't dance," the chorus of voices outside me commanded—father, mother, *dominies* (as we called the ministers in our Dutch immigrant community), elders, grandmothers, grandfathers, aunts, and uncles. "Don't dance," they chanted. A single voice, dispassionate, persistent, inescapable, like a heart beating out the rhythm of life. "No dancing. No dancing. No dancing." As I grew, the chorus grew louder. First a shake of the head. No. Then a whisper. No dancing. Then sober instruction. Dancing is *verboten*. Then a shout and a slap. No dancing! No!

But how could I keep from dancing? And not just in my imagination.

I first danced in my body in the living room of my aunt and uncle's cottage by Lake Michigan. It was the summer of 1960 and I was nine. Cherrie, one of my older cousins, put Chubby Checker's "The Twist" on her portable record player one afternoon and started hula-hooping to the beat. In the middle of the song she let the hula hoop slide to her feet, kicked it across the room, and started twisting. "It's exercise!" she said, grinning mischievously. "Come on, try it!" If my aunt, Cherrie's mom, caught us, she'd harangue us and sentence us to memorizing Bible chapters. She was even stricter than my mother about Sabbath observance, never allowing her kids to watch TV or to swim on Sunday, even when the heat was unbearable. She was vigilant about all the other rules of our denomination too, though once a summer she turned a blind eye while her husband and my other uncles sipped a beer on the screened-in porch. But my aunt was still down at the beach with the little kids, and we'd hear that noisy troop coming up the boardwalk in time to jump back into our sanctioned hula hoops. I climbed out of my hoop and started twisting too. I can still feel myself in that front room, working my legs and hips, shoulders and arms to the beat, now to the right, now to the left, now down low, now back up again. Breathless. Sweating. Happy.

Not until I was fifteen did I dance again. Uxbridge High had regular dances, which was all anyone talked about for months, before and after—"Are you going? Anyone asked you yet? Did you go to the quarry after? Did he kiss you?" But dances were for "the other kids," the Catholics, the Presbyterians, the Jews, the Who-Knows-Whats, the Nothings. We Christian Reformed—CRC—kids were not allowed to go. No exceptions. Not for prom. Not for the graduation dance. Dancing wasn't the only issue. We were forbidden to fraternize in any way with the unchosen. Our church was "counterculture," meaning it prided itself on being separate from the dominant culture, against it. We took seriously the rule derived from the Gospel of John: Be in the world, but not of the world. We weren't permitted to play with the Catholic kids in the neighborhood or enter their houses, which were awash in idols. We couldn't join the Boy Scouts or Girl Scouts; we had our own youth organizations, Calvinettes and Calvin Cadets, that sponsored car washes in the summer to raise money for missionary trips, hayrides in the fall, and sledding parties in winter. So there was no way our elders and parents were going to allow good Christian Reformed boys and girls to mingle with worldly boys and girls. Certainly not at a dance. What if one of ours fell for one of theirs, or the other way around? The horror of "marrying out" loomed large and dancing was the slope we were bound to slip down, landing outside the church, which meant hell, for "outside the church there is no salvation." For years I obeyed this prohibition against exogamy, more by circumstance than by choice: I danced only with other CRC kids. I wasn't a rebel. I just needed to dance.

That's how I danced for years—on the sly, but among my own. The summer I was fifteen I went on a church youth group trip, traveling by train from eastern Massachusetts to Edmonton, Canada, to mingle with other CRC teens. The highlight of that trip was not seeing the Canadian Rockies or horseback riding around Lake Louise or being kissed when the train passed through a long dark tunnel. It was dancing. After our host parents went to bed, we gathered in the girls' bedroom, locked the door, and threw open the windows to see if we could hear Herman's Hermits, who were performing in an outdoor stadium a few blocks away. We had walked past the stadium after dinner, climbing on one another's shoulders to catch a glimpse of the stage. Now we were stuck inside, but we could hear them. "Something tells me I'm into something good." We lip-synced the words along with them. When they started singing, "I'm Henry the Eighth I am," the crowd screamed its pleasure, so we shoved the rug under the bunk beds, took off our shoes, and danced.

When I was sixteen, my parents went away for the weekend, leaving my older brother Steve and me in charge of our three younger siblings. Sunday evenings after church the youth group gathered at one house or another, and that Sunday evening they came to ours. It was mostly our regular high school group, but a few kids home from college showed up. All from our church. Not one outsider. Boys wearing their Sunday dress pants and shirts, girls their Sunday dresses and, as always, no make-up. We sat in the living room of our old farmhouse, on velvet-covered antique love sofas and chairs, talking and laughing. No one cursed God's name or used foul language. No one smoked. No one drank alcohol. No one made out. No one sneaked off to an upstairs bedroom for sex. Steve went upstairs to his room and came down with The Beatles' Sgt. Pepper's Lonely Hearts Club Band. The album had just come out and everyone just had to hear it. He put it on the record player and suddenly the furniture was up against the wall and we were in our stocking feet, sliding across the smooth, wide planks of the floor, our bodies jerking and spinning, our arms carving the air around us. We danced to every song. It was glorious! After helping us put the furniture back, everyone left—at a decent hour—and Steve and I went to bed. But I was too stirred up to sleep. In my mind I was still dancing.

Our parents returned after midnight, none the wiser, and all was well. Until word leaked out—how, we never found out. The minister and two elders made a house visit to inform my parents and us of our sin—dancing, compounded by lies and deception and disobedience. *Decry it, confess, and repent!* After that, Steve and I were branded as troublemakers in the church community, and we were punished by our parents, though I can't remember how. I remember only how it felt, arms circling over my head, feet tapping the smooth pine of the floor, shoulders, torso, and hips undulating, all of me moving to the rhythm, carried away into an eternal moment of joy in which body and heart and mind—always warring within me—were one. It was an ecstasy—standing outside (*ek-stasis*) the everyday reality of a divided self—that returned me to those moments of joy as a child, an ecstasy that I sought again and again. Had I known then about Friedrich Nietzsche, I would have taped these words of his to my Smith & Corona: "I would believe only in a God that knows how to dance."[1]

Dancing was forbidden at Calvin College when I arrived there in 1967. That spring, a senior invited me to the Graduation Banquet, which meant "Formal Wear for a Dinner Not Followed by Dancing." A queen was chosen for the event, and I was one of the "ladies" in her court. But it was not a prom; it was a dinner eaten "decently and in good order" (1 Corinthians 14:40). Once or twice a year, though, certain unnamed individuals hosted an off-campus dance party for Calvin students—school ID required. The hosts' names were well-guarded secrets. Attending the dances was almost as dangerous because representatives of the college raided them. They didn't take photographs of the crowd, as they did in chapel at seven every weekday morning, to record who and who wasn't occupying their assigned seat. But if they caught us at one of those dances, we would be suspended or worse. Those illicit dances were very well attended, which comforted and disturbed me. If so many "good Christian kids" risked not only their souls but their reputations and their futures to dance, how could dancing be so bad? And what, exactly, was wrong with it?

Chaos

Dancing Leads to "Other Things"
Why was dancing anathema to my Dutch Calvinist community? I never understood. Not as a child, not as a college student, not as a Calvin scholar, not as a professor in Reformed and other seminaries. I still don't understand, even now as an adult who decades ago became a Jew, a member of a community that danced its deliverance from slavery on the far shore of the sea and has been dancing ever since, the Hasids dancing their prayers, whole communities dancing with the Torah on Simchat Torah, in the synagogue and in the streets. I don't believe my ancestral community's prohibition against dancing was simply an unexamined carryover from Calvin's Geneva. Our community was far too analytical and reflective on matters of doctrine, and we relished theological debates. The only explanation ever given for why dancing was forbidden was this: "It might lead to other things." What these "other things" were, they never said, which meant they were acts so horrible as to be unspeakable, or that they were so delicious that the mere mention of them was enough to lure both speaker and hearer into temptation, away from God. But my young mind was hooked. Other things! Those eviscerated words, cleansed of the concrete, stripped of specifics, purified of all flesh—how those gutted words fascinated me. Like the *mysterium tremendum et fascinans* of Rudolph Otto in his book *The Idea of the Holy*, they caused in me a *frisson* of attraction and repulsion. How tantalizing—to gain the knowledge of good and evil, to gain the world! How frightening—to lose one's soul!

I still wonder today. Why this horror of dancing? What were the theological grounds for it? Our community prided itself on its theological acumen and doctrinal purity. At the Sunday dinner table, one was as likely to hear an argument about why the sixteenth-century Dutch theologian Arminius was anathema for declaring man had free will as to hear a diatribe against Duncan Littlefair, the local minister preaching the Norman Vincent Peale gospel of optimism—"Duncan Littlefaith" they called him. So there had to be reasons for the prohibition against dancing, in spite of the fact that no one offered me any, if not for strictly theological reasons, then reasons of faith. "The heart has it reasons, which reason does not know," says Pascal. What were the reasons my faith community abhorred dancing?

Card Playing?

Is dancing like card playing? We were strictly forbidden to use playing cards. This meant "face cards," a distinction I wasn't aware of until second grade, when the *dominie*'s daughter invited me to her house after school to play games. We sat around the dining room table with her older brothers and their friends, waiting for the *dominie* to join us. He came in smiling, sat down, pulled a deck of cards out of his pocket, and said, "I'll deal first." He split the deck in two and began shuffling the cards, face down.

Fear stiffened me, robbed me of words. The only card game we were permitted to play was "Authors," and these cards looked nothing like those. These shiny-backed cards looked adult, forbidden. I knew I should turn away, say "get thee behind me, Satan," and run home. But I sat transfixed, staring at the cards flipping up and down, up and down, intermingling again and again in his long, delicate fingers. Well worn, with nicked corners and frayed edges, the cards yielded easily to his hands. I could not grasp what was happening—a minister of God tempting me to sin!

"It's okay," the *dominie* said to me, his face and voice softening. "These aren't *verboten.*"

His kids and their friends sniggered, their contempt of my naiveté obvious.

He shot them a look, and they sat up straight and composed their faces. "Look," he said, spreading out the cards on the table. "It's just numbers and colors and a bird. The bird's called a 'rook.' These aren't face cards. There are no Jacks, Queens, or Kings. No Jokers either. That means these are not the kind of cards people use in gambling, so it's not forbidden to play with them."

I didn't like the look of that bird. Its steely eyes and sharp beak were menacing. And it was black, black as sin. I remembered my dad talking about "getting rooked" by someone, which meant something like being cheated or lied to. How did I know the *dominie* wasn't lying to me? *Dominies* weren't infallible. Hadn't I witnessed my grandfather on the church steps accuse his *dominie* of preaching falsehoods about God's grace? I played one round of "Rook," ran home, and never stopped at the *dominie's* house after school again.

Comic Books?
Playing with face cards was *verboten* because it led to gambling, a terrible waste of the gifts God has given and faithless reliance on chance instead of trusting in God's providence. But what does that have to do with dancing? Dancing does not lead to gambling. What then? Is dancing like another of those verboten "other things"? Is it like reading comic books? Reading material of this ilk was not allowed because it led to another kind of sin: idleness, the most fertile ground for the Devil.

The first time I saw a comic book was at my friend Betty's house. I went home with Betty after school one day when we were in third grade. We walked from our Christian school, past our red-brick church with the white pillars and steeple, and just beyond the *dominie's* house, which was across the street from hers. After a snack of Ritz crackers and Hawaiian Punch, Betty pulled out something from under her bed and thrust it in my face as she put her finger to her lips to silence me. It was a Donald Duck comic book. A banned book! I was scared. What would happen now? Would the Devil appear and snatch us away, leaving the comic book behind for our parents to find?
Betty rolled up the comic book, stuffed it under her sweater, and headed outside. I followed. We climbed high in the maple tree in her back yard and read the book, stealing glances at her house to see if her mother had returned from the grocery store and across the street to the *dominie's* house to see if we were being watched. Betty turned the pages, giggling here and there, either because she thought the story was funny or out of nervous delight at our

daring. I didn't care much for the book. The story and the drawings didn't impress me. It was Betty's calm, lighthearted defiance of a command that shocked me. Hiding in a tree to furtively read a comic book was not idleness. It was flagrant disobedience of the commandment to "honor thy father and thy mother," which meant disobeying God. Which meant not a few whacks on the butt with the "Board of Education" and being sent to bed without supper, but eternal punishment.

But if reading comic books, or indulging in other "guilty pleasures," as people today call frivolous, brainless pursuits with no redeeming social value, like watching melodramatic television series and reading romance novels, does contribute to the sin of idleness, what does that have to do with dancing? I can't find a connection. There must be something else that made dancing objectionable to my community.

Sex?

Perhaps it was the association of dancing with the body and sex that led to its prohibition. If the body is bad or dangerous, a fount of temptation and lust, or a descent into flesh and away from spirit, as it is for some religious traditions, and sex is only redeemable by marriage ("Better to marry than to burn," says Saint Paul), then dancing as a physical pleasure and as a first step toward sex has to be off limits. But this doesn't make sense for my ancestral tradition. In my experience, the Christian Reformed Church wasn't riddled with hatred of the body and repression. Quite the opposite. Perhaps it was the Dutch heritage, but sex was referred to frequently and positively in my extended family and in the community. "Hotter'n Dutch love" was a phrase my mother and aunts said often, with a gleam in their eye. And it was common knowledge that on Sunday afternoons children were to make themselves scarce, because the parents would take a nap and "take their pleasure." It wasn't the body or sex that were to be avoided at all costs; it was dancing. The classic Christian Reformed joke says it well: Why can't Christian Reformed people make love standing up? Because it might lead to dancing!

No, the body was not the problem. We were far from being gnostics, of the ancient or contemporary ilk. We didn't believe the material world was evil, the creation of an evil god, who stood in opposition to the true God, a God of light and spirit. We didn't believe the body was a prison of darkness, from which the soul must free itself through gnosis, saving knowledge of its true condition, a disembodied spirit that once fell into the world. We didn't believe we had to escape from this evil world by acquiring gnosis and refraining from all material acts, especially sex and the evil consequences thereof: plunging one's spirit back into ignorance and darkness and generating new bodies, new prisons for other souls. No, we were no gnostics. We were Calvinists. For us there was one God and only one: God, the Giver of Every Good Gift, the creator of the world and the redeemer of the world. That meant the created world was good, "a theater of God's glory," as Calvin has it. And we were Dutch—a people less spiritually or metaphysically inclined and more prone to practicality and action in the material world, the temporal realm—reclaiming land from the sea, colonizing the world to make our food tastier with exotic spices, etching and painting the beauty of the world, teaching the humanism of Erasmus and the ethics of Spinoza. No, for my childhood community the body was not the reason dancing was forbidden.

Freedom?
What then? If dancing is not a gateway sin, a sign of rebelliousness, or a giving way to the flesh, what is it? What makes religious communities—not only the one I grew up in but others as well, with different traditions, different histories, different ethnicities—recoil from it and set limits around it?

When I moved beyond the Christian Reformed community, first to liberal Protestantism and then to Judaism, I continued to dance. Denied this pleasure in my youth, I seized every opportunity to dance I could: parties, weddings, outdoor festivals, solo sessions in my living room to Aretha singing "Spirit in the Dark." In those years I danced secularly, by which I mean free-form, non-partner dancing in which I could creatively express myself. If that's what dancing is, I can understand why some religious communities prohibit it. Freedom of expression, through speech or art, appears threatening to communities that value tradition over change. They fear that if individuals do not submit themselves to the inherited ways and thoughts and practices, the tradition will become corrupted. If individuals give free reign to their thoughts and actions, heretical ideas and ways will undoubtedly surface and the faithful will be tempted away from the true path. Better, for the good of all and the honor of the tradition, to suppress freedom of expression.

It's not only religious traditions that perceive dancing as a threat, though it may seem that way to us in the United States, with our Puritan (read "Calvinist") beginnings, tradition of separation of church and state, radical individualism, and our own version of the generation wars—the Footloose version, in which lively, dancing teenagers triumph over the moribund ways of religious elders. But China's recent crackdown on the "dancing grannies" reminds us that political systems, too, are alert to the dangers of dancing, especially when those systems value cultural unity over individual expression.

In the 1990s, tens of thousands of women in China who had been forced into retirement started dancing in parks and plazas. They chose their own music and styles of dancing—Western music and styles included. They danced freely, each group the way they chose, each woman the way she chose, to music broadcast over speakers. "When I dance," one woman told an interviewer, "I forget all my cares. And I can also hike up mountains with little effort."[2]

In early 2015, when non-dancers objected to the noise and railed against the women's dancing as a disruption, the Communist Party stepped in to restore harmony. Henceforth, the government announced, public dancing would be regulated to transform it from a counter-revolutionary activity (one that varied from place to place and caused social disharmony) to "a nationally unified, scientifically crafted new activity that brings positive energy to the people."[3] Currently, guidelines are being developed on when and where the dancing should occur, how loud the music is, what kind of music may be played, and what kind of "scientifically crafted" dancing is acceptable. The Chinese government choreographed twelve model routines for the women, to ensure that the women got a proper fitness workout. And they formed a national outdoor dancing association to "strengthen management and promote healthy development" of dancing.

For certain religious and secular systems, dancing means trouble. It encourages free movement, free thinking, and freedom of expression in individuals. Of course, this form of freedom can lead only to dissent and strife. For the health of the society, therefore, dancing must be prohibited or strictly controlled.

But that is not all dancing is—an example or symbol of free expression of an individual or group. I learned this late in my life, during the 1990s, when those thousands of Chinese women were discovering dancing. One spring my sister and I attended a week-long drumming workshop at Omega Institute in upstate New York. On one of our nights off, as an extracurricular activity, I happened on Gabrielle Roth and her son Jonathan leading a "Sweat Your Prayers" gathering. Sometimes called "5Rhythms dance" or "ecstatic dance." "Sweat Your Prayers" is a form of moving meditation, a meditative practice in which people move to music, alone or occasionally with a partner, in a sequence of rhythms: Flowing, Staccato, Chaos, Lyrical, Stillness.

I was not prepared for what I experienced. I was familiar with liturgical dance in the Lutheran Church and the United Church of Christ, but had never been drawn to it, in spite of my love for all things danced-related. The examples of liturgical dance I had been exposed to seemed to be a translation of a concept into movement instead of an invitation to a different experience in community. This Sweat Your Prayers dancing was different. It wasn't sacred dance as much as it was sanctifying dance. I saw men and women of all ages, from teens to elders in their seventies and eighties moving with grace, out of grace, in grace. It seemed to me they were praying, entering into a space of attentiveness in which their bodies and spirits were integrated, united, all through movement and rhythm. Watching their bodies and spirits communing reminded me of the Sufi whirling dervishes I had seen in their white robes and tombstone hats, circling and circling around the one still point as they moved together like planets in the solar system, their bodies prayers. It reminded me, too, of the Native American Sundancers I witnessed one August at a private Sundance on Rosebud reservation in South Dakota. For a week I stood under the pine-bough arbor from sunrise to sundown, doing the two-step in place with other "supporters" while members of many tribes in beautiful regalia danced their prayers inside the sacred circle, around the sacred pole, the *axis mundi*, danced to the rhythm beaten out on animal skins and sung by groups of drummers and singers. They were praying with their bodies. Their bodies had become prayers. They were living out the words of the Baal Shem Tov, that dancing mystic: "I am prayer."

That night as I watched Gabrielle Roth and a room full of dancers sweating their prayers—dancing in a windowless room, dressed in street clothes, moving in no recognizable circle, with no *axis mundi* in sight—I saw that they, too, were praying with their bodies, they too had become prayer. For these dancers, like the Sundancers, dancing wasn't a symbol of something else— freedom of expression, freedom of the individual, creativity, the non-rational. It wasn't a language into which they translated feelings or ideas. It wasn't a way to something else; it was the way. It was a communing, of one's body and spirit, of the self and the world, of the self and the One—it was a spiritual act.

Lyrical

I didn't join Roth and the other dancers sweating their prayers that evening. I'm not sure why. Perhaps my head was so intent on learning the drum rhythms of the workshop I was attending with my sister that I couldn't hear the rhythms they were dancing to. Perhaps I didn't trust that the grace with which I saw people moving, the ease they had with their bodies and one another—

people old and young, slender and rotund, shy and flamboyant—
was possible for me. I returned home and continued dancing in
my secular, devil may-care way. A decade went by. I moved from
the Southeast to the Northwest. My son and daughter grew up. I
went through a divorce, spent a year meditating, danced alone in
the dark, hung out with Sufis (meditating, not whirling), and
started a new life.

Then, one Sunday morning I happened upon a Sweat Your
Prayers group in Seattle. For two hours I moved in and among a
room full of dancers, moving to music arranged in a carefully
selected sequence of rhythms: Flowing, Staccato, Chaos, Lyrical,
Stillness. The rhythms take one on a journey, if one is willing, and
I was, finally, twenty years after that first arresting encounter with
Roth and a room warm and alive with body-spirits journeying
through the rhythms. For Roth, the dance journey is a path to the
soul or true self. As she writes in *Sweat Your Prayers: Movement as
Spiritual Practice*, "The soul can only be present when body and
spirit are one."[4]

"When body and spirit are one." That is what I had been
seeking all my life, the world I had experienced as a child when I
danced in my imagination, the world I had tasted and had been
looking for ever since—the oneness of body and spirit, space and
time. Not flesh warring against the spirit. Not spirit escaping the
prison house of the flesh. This—enspirited body, embodied spirit.

And that is what I experienced that first Sunday morning
when I danced the five rhythms in that community. Enspirited
body. Embodied spirit. Home coming. Joy. A calm presence that
breathed the words of Julian of Norwich, the fourteenth century
anchoress and mystic, through me: "All shall be well, and all shall
be well and all manner of thing shall be well." Not every moment
of those two hours did I experience this, but enough to taste that
union and want more. I started dancing with that community
almost every week.

Over the next two years, dancing changed for me. It became a
communing, of body and spirit, self and world, self and the One,
communing with that which is beyond, a world beyond the

ordinary world we experience in our everyday life. It became a
spiritual act.

In the act of dancing or by the act of dancing, I entered
another way of being. I moved through the rhythms—Flowing,
Staccato, Chaos, Lyrical, Stillness—with eyes sometimes closed,
sometimes half-closed, my awareness not centered in my mind or
heart or body, but in all of them at once. The rhythms caught me
up and I surrendered to them, let them move me. I felt
part of the whole and I sensed the others in the room as part of
that whole too. I moved easily into and through the spaces
between those bodies-hearts-minds-spirits—no thought to what
they were doing, how they were dancing, or how I might look to
them or to anyone. There was no "anyone" outside to look at me,
no "me" to look at. We were all caught up in the rhythms, in a
whole beyond ourselves, with a different kind of awareness and a
different way of being than we experienced in ordinary life and
that refreshed our spirits and sent us home changed—at least for
several hours, if not the rest of the day or week.

The sociologist Robert Bellah, in *Religion in Human
Evolution,* calls experiences like these "unitive events," events that
bring an "experience of the felt whole," enactive events "in which
the whole body participates, along with mind and spirit, again
without a sense of bifurcation."[5] Unitive events are more vision
than feeling, "vision that puts reality in true perspective, with the
focus not on the individual or group or the transient world, but on
the majesty of the eternal." And they are often accompanied by "a
profound sense of wholeness"[6] and well-being.
Unitive events often occur during rituals, which frequently
include dancing and singing. Rituals, for Bellah, are summed up
best by the anthropologist Clifford Geertz: rituals are not
representations of religious events but religious actions, actions
that create worlds; rituals create the world as imagined, which is
joined to the world as lived, which in turn leads to the
transformation of one's sense of reality. Bellah also says, following
the sociologist Emile Durkheim, that unitive events were
primarily and originally collective, with rituals leading to

"collective effervescence," in which people together experience "a different and deeper reality" in a way that changes them. Here is Durkheim's description of what happens during rituals, especially ritual dancing, as this experience of a different reality disrupts the experience of the lived world.

> One can readily see how, when arrived at this state of exaltation, a man does not recognize himself any longer. Feeling himself dominated and carried away by some sort of external power which makes him think and act differently than in normal times, he naturally has the impression of being himself no longer. It seems to him that he has become a new being. . . . And as at the same time all his companions feel themselves transformed in the same way . . . everything is just as though he really were transported into a special world, entirely different from the one where he ordinarily lives, and into an environment filled with exceptionally intense forces that take hold of him and metamorphose him.[7]

Durkheim's point, argues Bellah, is that "the world of ritual is quite different from the one 'where his daily life drags wearily along.' It is the world of the sacred in contrast to the profane everyday." Ritual is "a break with the rhythm of everyday life" in which one is transformed.[8]
This notion of ritual as a break with the rhythm of everyday life that arises out of an experience of a different and deeper reality, creates a sense of well-being and leads to transformation is as close to describing what I experienced dancing, week after week, as I have found. Dancing bumped me into a unitive event in which ordinary reality with its separation between self and world, between this world and that which is beyond this world, did not apply. It was an integrating event in which the ordinary distinctions between body, mind, and spirit were suspended.

Giving myself over to the rhythms, I experienced a deeper and wider world that broke the rhythm of everyday life, created in me a profound sense of wholeness and well-being, and in so doing, changed me. During those two hours, as I experienced a communing of body-heart-mind spirit, a calm and calming joy flowed through me. Joy, not happiness. Not a passing feeling or emotional response, but a steady state of relaxed attention and appreciation that lasted for many hours afterward, coloring everyone and everything I saw, heard, thought, said, and did. I left the dance hall and stepped outside on the street, breathing deeply and unable to stop smiling. I had become joy.

Dancing in this way, experiencing a different way of being, became for me a different way of knowing, and so a path to transformation. By dancing, in dancing, being present to another world beyond the assumptions and patterns of my everyday world, discoveries came to me, from body to spirit, and from spirit to body. The kind of knowing that happens during this kind of dancing feels similar to the way one knows through meditation: by opening awareness to a realm larger than the intellectual or psychological alone, you become aware of "more," and that "more" transforms everything you knew before. It was like discovering an "answer" when you didn't even know what the question was, like being reintegrated when you couldn't see or name the pieces that had broken apart from one another. In dancing, through giving myself—body-heart-mind-spirit—over to the rhythms, I became aware of changes I needed to make, longed for, was undergoing. I moved out from the limits of subjective feeling to an expansive vision that put everything else, myself, this daily world we experience, in perspective, that illuminated what could be and made it possible. Dancing became my preferred way to pray, to meditate, to commune with the One, to be made whole, to become a new being, to be made new.

Once I discovered this way, I used dancing intentionally as a path to transformation. At first, I would just let myself feel whatever it was, sorrow or pain or discouragement or hope—feel it in my heart-self and my body-self and move through it. Other times I would dance out my heart's deepest desire, such as for a true companion. Sometimes I would ask a question and let my dancing self-lead me to an answer. For example, one of my greatest challenges has been how to be a full self in an intimate relationship with a partner. Like most women, I'm other-directed, too quick to give away my freedom or give up my desires for the sake of another. On the other hand, I'm fiercely independent and an unapologetic feminist. This wasn't an issue with my children. I knew the joy of dancing with my infant son and infant daughter held close to my heart and dancing with my children when they were young in the living room or at outdoor concerts with wild abandon and joy. Dancing with my son at his wedding outdoors on Lopez Island, overlooking glorious Puget Sound, the two of us moving easily from the traditional slow first dance to a faster free-form dance, overjoyed me. But I was constitutionally unable to dance with a partner—What? Me follow someone else's, a man's, lead? Conform my "free-form" moves and position to his?

Through dancing in this new way, the puzzle of how to reconcile these pulls in opposite directions—to other, to self—a puzzle that had eluded my body, heart, and mind for decades, was somehow solved. It was a transformation that occurred beyond rationality. It wasn't that I received a solution to the problem, a resolution of this issue that had troubled me for so long, or even a reconciliation of the conflict. It ceased to be a conflict. It was as if whatever had been the problem or had troubled me dissolved. I don't believe I would have married again, taken the risk of intensely living out being an individual in-relation, if not for this transformation by and through dancing.

As dancing in this way changed me, week after week, dancing itself changed for me. I came to think of dancing not as a secular activity but a spiritual act. For spirituality, like religion with its rituals, opens up another world to live in, if even for a moment; a world that puts the ordinary world in perspective and makes possible a different way of living, a transformation of self that lasts not just for the moment of dancing, but endures beyond that moment and bears fruit in one's life.

I also came to think of dancing as a sanctifying act, a sanctifying of space by moving in time, a sanctifying of time by moving through space. When you are dancing, moving your body in time, from one moment to the next, you are sculpting the physical space around you into a unique form, an invisible, time-bound sanctuary that holds and lifts you. And as you create this sacred space with each movement, as it takes shape and you begin to dwell, to move within that space, time seems to cease—you enter a time beyond time, a sacred time.

The language of "another world" and "being transported" during rituals focuses on space and thus tends to obscure this dimension of time, which is also fundamental to ritual. Rituals in many traditions open up another world beyond the everyday world by sanctifying time as well as space. This phenomenon can be seen in Judaism, which distinguishes clearly between the holy and the everyday, marking off every seventh day as Shabbat and the holidays during their season as sacred time, time beyond time. The community enters those times to break with the rhythm of everyday life and be present to the Presence. One may speak of holy places—Mt. Sinai, the Wailing Wall, Jerusalem, the Holy City and Israel, the Holy Land—but, for me, there is no holiness inherent in place, unchanging, for all time, without human beings moving through it. The ground on which Moses stood was holy not in and of itself for all time, but because Moses encountered the Presence there: Space was transformed in that moment in time when he took off his shoes and stepped close. Synagogues are not sacred spaces in and of themselves for all time. They are sacred spaces only when a living community is moving through them in the dance of prayer and praise, open to a different and deeper reality, ready to encounter the Presence. When a community dies and its building is no longer a place of ritual, that space is decommissioned, desanctified. *Moving* through time in space, moving through space in time—that's when sanctifying occurs.

Dancing can become a sanctifying act when one moves through space in time, moves through time in space, in a way that invites an experience of a world beyond the ordinary world, an encounter with the One, the Presence. Neither the sanctifying nor an experience of a world beyond is guaranteed. It's a gift when it happens. You enter a dancing session just as you enter a place, a synagogue or church or temple or sacred circle, or you enter a moment, Shabbat or Christmas or Diwali, in hope for such a meeting, such a communion, such a sanctifying, and the transformation that can result. Out of that praying, ritualizing, and dancing, all moving through space in time, moving through time in space, something new is created. The opening verses of Genesis point to this. Genesis 1:1-2: "At the beginning of God's creating of the heavens and the earth, when the earth was wild and waste, darkness over the face of Ocean, rushing-spirit of God (*ruach elohim*) hovering (*merachephet*) over the face of the waters." The Spirit of God was moving (brooding, trembling, fluttering, whirling) over the face of the waters. Spirit was in motion, moving, in space, over time. Over chaos, over what was not whole. And what was the result? Genesis 1:3: "God said: Let there be light! And there was light."[9] Between chaos and light comes sanctifying movement.

This creative, transformative movement between chaos and light is how I think of dancing now and it is the way I have come to dance, on Sunday mornings in a group, sweating our prayers, and by myself, at home. I dance a movement of the body through space in time, through time in space, that unites space and time, body-heart-mind-spirit, the self with the Whole. It is an event that breaks the rhythm of daily life and bumps me into a deeper, wider reality, opens me to Presence. A communing. A sanctifying. A spiritual act.

Because I experience dance in this way now, views of dance that relegate it exclusively or primarily to one or the other, body or spirit, this world or that world, don't make sense to me. If you think of dance as gesture, for example, as merely the expression of self or an expression of desire, it appears to be separate from the spiritual realm. The Swiss theologian and philosopher, Max Picard, defines gesture this way, asserting that it belongs to the physical world, emerging from the passions and the desires of the body. As such, it is "unfree, unredeemed, still completely mixed with the material it uses."[10] Within this view, though dancing may not be "evil," it is definitely caught in the material world and therefore lower than language, which for

Picard is a different category altogether. For him, gesture
expresses a desire, while language expresses a being, a whole, not
merely a desire that is only part of a being and not a whole being
in itself.

Even thinking of gesture as a kind of language, like sign
language, doesn't strike me as adequate now. That dancing is not
gesture in this sense became clear to me one morning during a
recent Sweat Your Prayers gathering. The leader that morning
was a substitute and, wanting the group to meet before the
dancing journey began, asked us to stand in a circle and introduce
ourselves. "Say your name," the leader said, "and make a gesture
to show who you are or how you are feeling today." As we spoke
our names and translated our inner states into a gesture to
communicate to the group, it became obvious that this was not
dancing. The gestures were drawn from a limited set of stock
movements; they shared little of the creativity of our bodies in
motion during dancing. And they were created for the benefit of
representing ourselves to others. They were not a unitive
experience or spiritual act.

This suggests to me that viewing dancing primarily as an
expression or representation of the non-corporeal world is no
more adequate for understanding what dancing can be than is
conceptualizing dancing as gesture. Dancing is not simply
symbolic—of ideas, feelings, or "higher" realms, or even events—
though it can be used that way and beautifully so.

My favorite playwright for decades, Athol Fugard, uses
dance as a metaphor in many of his plays. The metaphor runs
throughout "Master Harold and the Boys," culminating when the
two male characters dance together in harmony for the first time,
overcoming oppositions. It also plays a central role in "Boesman
and Lena," when Lena counsels the man who has taken out his
oppression on her to dance his sorrows into the ground. This
metaphorical understanding is a beautiful and moving way to
think of and use dancing. But, given my experience of dancing as
a unitive event that transforms one, it is not enough. Like ritual,
the kind of dancing I am trying to speak about is not a
representation of anything. Like ritual, it is a spiritual act. An

action in which one's experiences of an imagined world fuses with the ordinary world in such a way that you are changed. A way of being. A way of knowing. A path to transformation. A way of ecstasy. A sanctifying. A hovering over the waters of life, moving from chaos to light. Joy.

Stillness

Dancing in this way has opened for me a new understanding of why I was so attracted to Judaism over twenty years ago and why I feel such a kinship with the Hasids of the eighteenth century. They know this creative encounter. They know this joy. They dance. When Rabbi Israel Baal Shem Tov (1698–1760), the founder of the Hasidic movement known as the Besht, was asked by one of his disciples why some of his opponents criticized the Hasids for their excessive joy and their dancing, saying this was not the behavior of healthy, sane individuals, he responded with this story of collective effervescence:

> Once, a talented fiddler stood in the street playing in an ecstasy of passion. Many people stopped to listen and were so enchanted by his music that they began to dance, lost to the world. A deaf man happened to pass by and, since he couldn't hear the
> ravishing music, was utterly astonished at the bizarre scene before his eyes. Not knowing why the people were dancing, he was certain the people were actually madmen! The truth is, if he heard the music and experienced the tremendous joy and ecstasy, he would have danced with them. 'My disciples,' said the Besht, 'hear and see the song that emanates from each and every thing that God, blessed be He, has created. If so, how can they keep from dancing?'[11]

Perhaps this story is what inspired the creation of this common modern proverb, often attributed to Nietzsche but not found in his works: "Those who dance are thought mad by those who hear not the music."

Deaf. Hearing. Sane. Insane. Secular. Spiritual. No dancing. Dancing. Dancing in the imagination. Dancing in the body. Before words. After words. What do these divisions among us matter? What matters is to be moving, whirling with the music of the spheres, trembling with creation—from chaos to light.

This is why I dance.

To enter that space between chaos and light, a liminal space.

To become a new being, to be made whole, made new.

This is why I dance.

For the joy of it.

Chapter 2

Because We Are Bodies: Bread, Wine, Rice, Water

"They're animists, you know," my preacher friend said on one of our bike-and-talk-theology rides. "Not even Buddhists. They believe spirits are alive in everything—plants, rivers, rocks, wind, fire, places, people, anything. They don't have a concept of one God, let alone any idea of the Trinity or what's going on in the Eucharist." Tyrone was talking about the Hmong refugees he had befriended and invited into our Presbyterian church community—our church suppers, gospel concerts, square dance evenings, and worship services. Every Sunday about twenty women and small children sat silently in two pews near the front, just under the elevated wooden pulpit. They had come to Saint Paul in the late seventies from the hills of Laos, refugees from our war with Vietnam. They were fleeing the landmines we planted in their rice fields and teak forests, the bombs we rained on their villages. They were also running from the Viet Cong and Pathet Lao, communist soldiers who hunted them down as traitors for cooperating with the United States, captured women and children to use as bait, and then slaughtered the husbands, brothers, and fathers who came out of hiding in the jungle to free them.

They were a tribal people. They arrived in Minnesota without a written language, having lost it long ago to the Qing Dynasty of the seventeenth and eighteenth centuries C.E., or the Tang Dynasty of the eighth century C.E., or the more ancient Chinese invasions that forced them, according to legend, to eat their books or throw them in the river as they fled. They built three-stone hearths on the floors of their public housing apartments to steam their rice in a basket over an open fire. They prayed to the spirit of their ancestors. They sought the help of shamans to heal the spirits of those who fell ill or lost their way in this strange new land. For them, the world was alive with spirits who were always present, acting for good or for ill, and who needed tending.

But each Sunday morning, here the Hmong were, present among us, women and children who didn't speak English, nestled together in the hard oak pews, alert and still, their eyes fixed on Tyrone as he preached. And here they were, once a month, taking Communion with us. Lifting a small square of crustless white bread from the plate offered to them, cradling it in their palms until we had all been served, and eating it in unison with us when Tyrone said, "The Lord Jesus, on the night of his arrest, took bread, and after giving thanks to God, he broke it, and gave it to his disciples, saying: Take, eat. This is my body, given for you. Do this in remembrance of me." Lifting a tiny cup of grape juice from the clattering tray, holding it solemnly while the rest of us were served, and drinking it in unison with us when we heard, "In the same way he took the cup, saying: This cup is the new covenant sealed in my blood, shed for you for the forgiveness of sins. Whenever you drink it, do this in remembrance of me. Every time you eat this bread and drink this cup, you proclaim the saving death of the risen Lord, until he comes."[1]

It was a bold move to invite "the unbaptized" to partake of the Lord's Supper, even for Tyrone, whose way was to challenge the comfortable ways of the church. "Open the doors of the church," he would call out from the pulpit. And doors and hearts were opened. I loved the welcoming congregation he nurtured. Black, Brown, White, rich, poor, old, young, wheelchair-bound, lifelong Presbyterians, agnostics, skeptics—all sat together, all took turns reading Scripture and serving Communion. When someone cried out wordlessly or grunted or let out a loud slow groan during a sermon, no one shushed them. When a woman missing both her forearms lifted the heavy tray of communion cups onto her stubs and walked among the congregation delivering the tray to the person at the end of one pew and stepping to the end of the next pew to receive it and pass it on, no one thought it odd. Everyone belonged. It was the kingdom of God on earth.

According to the U.S. Presbyterian tradition, any baptized person who comes "in faith, repentance, and love" may share in the feast. The official doctrine states that "even one who doubts or whose trust is wavering may come to the Table in order to be assured of God's love and grace in Christ Jesus."[2] But my friend had opened wide the doors of the church, inviting to the Lord's Table not just the unrepentant, not just the unbaptized, not just the lapsed or unchurched or agnostic or atheist, not even Jews or Muslims or other monotheists, not even adherents of a polytheistic religion like Hinduism or devotees of an ancient philosophy like Buddhism. He had welcomed animists, people who inhabited a world teeming with spirits they interacted with daily, a world so unfamiliar to us that we could barely conceive of it, a world for which we had no language.

I passionately believed the sacrament of Communion, as "a visible sign of an invisible grace" (the classic definition, derived from Augustine and often attributed to him),[3] should be welcoming and inclusive. In the denomination I was raised in, even baptized members in good standing in their home church had to be examined in their faith by the minister and elders of any sister church they visited if they wanted to take Communion with that congregation. With this requirement, the church leaders were protecting the honor of the sacrament and the name of the Lord and also their members from "eat[ing] and drink[ing] damnation" to themselves, for to take Communion in an unrepentant state meant spiritual death (1 Cor. 11:29 KJV). But this gatekeeping seemed to me a travesty of Communion; it turned a ritual of love given and shared into an instrument of exclusion. I judged just as harshly denominations that would not serve Communion to people with intellectual disabilities or dementia because they deemed that such persons could not understand what was happening in the ritual and thus, could not eat and drink in remembrance of Jesus Christ. I believed that Communion was an invitation to the love of God through the loving sacrifice of Jesus Christ and should not be sullied with "No Trespassing" signs, should not be enclosed in barbed wire fences, and should not require participants to pass through moral or intellectual or doctrinal metal detectors.

But here my friend was, serving the body and blood of Christ to Hmong refugees, farmers and weavers and fishers who didn't have a concept of a personal god or gods, or any other way to help them grasp the meaning of the one God in three persons of Christianity and the sacrificial death of this one God's Son. Did being inclusive mean that faith communities have no boundaries? No identity that mattered? That religion was a free-for-all—anyone could participate in any ritual of any tradition, regardless of what they believed or where they stood in relation to the community, simply because they showed up? And what did this mean for the doctrine of the sacraments and the church as the body of Christ?

Purity of doctrine wasn't on Tyrone's mind. Nor did he seem to be worried that he might be disciplined by the Presbyterian synod. He, like one of his favorite theologians and mystics, Howard Thurman, was in search of a new interpretation of the sacraments, whose practice had united and separated so many. While in seminary, Thurman discovered the pre-Christian origins of Communion: To eat the body and drink the blood of the sacred totem of the tribe in special ceremony meant sharing the life and partaking of the essence of the sacred object—in so doing, one became like the object. Thus, one became what one worshipped. This made structural sense of the Communion service. As applied to Jesus, it became symbolically an experience of total surrender to or a taking into one's self of His spirit and His life.[4] Based on this understanding, when he founded the Church for the Fellowship of All Peoples in San Francisco in 1944, an interfaith, interracial, intercultural community of seekers, Thurman decided that "in keeping with the spirit of the Master, participation in the service would be open to all who wished to become one with His spirit." The Communion service in his church became, in his words, "a high moment of dedication and commitment."[5]

I don't know if Tyrone had the practice of the Church for the Fellowship of All Peoples in mind when he invited the Hmong to the Lord's Table. It's possible that he was inviting people who were familiar with spirits to open themselves to the living spirit of Jesus, that he believed there could be a communion of spirits in love even in the absence of a shared language and understanding. I do know my friend stood firm on the Bible: "Welcome the stranger, for you were strangers in the land of Egypt" (Deut. 10:19, my paraphrase of KJV). "Think about it," he said to me once. "If we invite these people into our community and they see us share a meal, without offering them the food or the drink, what can they think? Communion is an act of communing with the spirit of Jesus, the one who identified with the disinherited. It's sharing the love of Christ—with the widow, the orphan, the refugee."

*

"They're animists, you know."

I didn't know.

I could conjure up a halfway decent definition of animism based on my graduate school history-of-religions readings in "primitive religions" and indigenous tribal peoples: from *anima*, Latin for "breath" or "spirit," animism is the belief that souls or spirits exist not only in human beings but also in certain creatures, places, natural phenomena, and objects. In animism there is no separation of the physical and spiritual worlds; it's a way of living in the one, undivided world.

I could also boast of having encountered animism in practice—or at least beliefs and practices that sounded or seemed animistic to my untrained ears and eyes. The Midwestern seminary where I taught had a longstanding relationship with the Native American Theological Association and welcomed Native American students from tribes in the surrounding region. In class discussions, some of the Ojibwe and Winnebago students insisted that trees were alive, like the four-hundred-year-old Spirit Little Cedar Tree, known to some as the Witch Tree, on the shores of Lake Superior near Duluth, where people still left tobacco offerings. Rocks too were alive, they said, passing us a smooth gray stone they had warmed in their hand. In sweat lodges, Lakota medicine women prayed to *Wakĥáŋ Tȟáŋka*, the Great

Mystery, and prayed for *mitákuye oyás'iŋ*, "all my relatives," invoking the spirit of all forms of life joined as one in the sacred circle, rocks, rivers, mountains, plants, trees, winged ones, four-leggeds, two-leggeds.

In a healing ceremony at the home of a friend, a Choctaw Presbyterian minister, I sat cross-legged on the floor in the pitch-dark with my eyes closed, sensing, almost seeing, bright flashes of light across the room and inches from my face as a Lakota medicine man performed the ritual. When I felt the person to my left offer me a rock, a rock pulsating with energy, radiating the warmth of all the hands and bodies that had touched it before me, I cradled that rock in my palm and held it on my body where I needed healing, before passing it on to the next person in the sacred circle. Later that evening, eyes now open, I watched and prayed with the others in the circle as the medicine man did battle with an evil spirit and drew it out of a person suffering from a mysterious illness.

At a weeklong Sundance on the Rosebud Indian Reservation, I watched as pemmican and tobacco were buried in the earth at the center of the dance circle, offerings for the spirit of the freshly felled cottonwood tree to be erected there, and as the tree itself, the *axis mundi*, was adorned with thousands of prayer ties, bits of colorful cloth wrapped around sacred tobacco. One evening, stirring a pot of venison stew in an outdoor kitchen, I heard a Lakota medicine man speak of the spirit of the deer that guided him. During the days, as I stood in the arbor for supporters that surrounded the sacred circle, I heard many prayers to *Tunŋkášila*, Grandfather, and frequent talk of the spirit of the buffalo, the spirit of the drum, the spirit of the ancestors.

No one in these Native American communities called their ideas and practices animism. The people I met weren't concerned about labels and categories; they were committed to living their worldview of the harmony of the world, nature and spirit as one. But brushing up against this honoring of spirits taught me that this way of life—in which everything is alive, the natural world and the spiritual world continually weaving into and out of each

other, spirits abounding in the land—was no relic of a bygone
past, nor a mere curiosity of primitive peoples. This was a living
reality for people now, people here in Minnesota and South
Dakota, a reality I had tasted and admired but didn't understand.
So when Tyrone said of the Hmong, "They're animists," I didn't
know what he was saying.

Getting to know several of the Hmong women in our
congregation didn't help me understand. Over rice and tea, with
one of the women's older sons translating for us, I heard stories of
how they escaped, how they ran over mine-seeded mountains and
rice fields and across bloody rivers, how the bodies of family
members and friends fell around them, shot by Pathet Lao and the
North Vietnamese, how others were captured and dragged back
to captivity. I admired the intricate textiles they created and sold
at the local farmers' market alongside the vegetables they grew:
red and green Christmas ornaments, bright-colored quilts with
geometric designs in reverse appliqué, cloth hangings
embroidered with colorful scenes of monkeys in trees, dragons,
rice plants, rivers, and battalions of soldiers carrying rifles and
ammunition belts. One day they brought over the traditional
clothes of one of the women and dressed me up in them after
lunch—the indigo and batik skirt, the embroidered sash, the
heavy silver necklace that covered my chest, the tall headdress—
giggling about my long bare legs sticking out from under the skirt
like two saplings.

I never learned which of the many hill tribes they belonged
to. Black Hmong? Striped Hmong? White Hmong, Green Hmong,
Blue Hmong? Flower Hmong? I never saw inside their homes,
those intimate spaces where altars reside and acts of devotion are
performed daily. I never visited the agricultural plots that the
University of Minnesota Agricultural Extension Services and the
Lao Family Community of Minnesota helped them establish nor
the fields where they grew the tenderest green beans and baby
spinach sold at the market, the envy of the other farmers. I never
asked them about spirits. Or about their experience of eating those
small squares of bread and downing those tiny cups of grape juice

in church with Brown and Black and White North Americans, some with whole bodies, some broken. All I had was the testimony of my friend—"They're animists"—and my love for their radiant smiles and their gentle, still spirits, baptized by the fire of suffering.

*

When I left Minnesota in the early nineties, I lost contact with the Hmong people and the Native Americans I had come to know. I landed first in South Carolina, a decidedly Christian state, and then in Washington, one of the most unchurched states in the nation. Animism was not a living presence in either place, and it slipped from my consciousness easily, remaining hidden until the fall of 2016, when I trekked with three others in the hills of northern Laos, in the province of Louangphrabang.

In Nong Khiaw, hours north of the city of Louangphrabang, we boarded a small boat to travel up the Nam Ou River toward China. Along the way, we visited several villages, then disembarked to trek to a remote village higher in the mountains. After a riverside lunch of fried fish, smoked eggplant, sticky rice wrapped in banana leaves, and fresh chilis dipped in salt, we set off. We climbed steadily for hours, passing through river brush and wet fields of rice, teak forests, dry fields of rice, and jungle. The vistas amazed. The mist, *mok bang*, winding through the mountains, now revealing, now concealing the blue-green hills, often blurring the line between earth and sky, was redolent of spiritual mysteries. It stirred me, that diaphanous veil, drew my heart toward the unseen, the unnamable, the unknown. But what pulled harder at my heart was something lowlier. At the edge of a rice field, hidden among luxuriant rice fronds, atop a pole sunk into the wet earth, stood a shrine, an A-frame about 16 inches high and 12 inches wide at its base, with a woven bamboo roof and a scrap-wood floor.

At first glance, the miniature hut looked more like a birdhouse than a shrine. In Louangphrabang City, as well as in Vietnam and Cambodia, we had seen many shrines for ancestor devotion. Some were simple boxes of bare wooden planks topped

with a corrugated aluminum roof, each box holding an offering of
rice balls and a plastic bottle of water. But most were miniature
pagodas, ornately carved and painted a gaudy gold, lavished
inside with marigolds and lotus blossoms, dragon fruit, brimming
bowls of the ancestors' favorite foods, fake money, bottles of
expensive whiskey, smoldering incense, and glinting candles.
Modest or magnificent, those shrines were at least four times
larger than this meager shelter hidden in the field, and they stood
in a place of honor outside or inside the house or restaurant or
business or Buddhist temple. This makeshift structure at the edge
of the rice field was far smaller and lowlier than the poorest
ancestor shrine we had seen, and there was no house or temple in
sight, just a sea of rustling rice fronds, the forest beyond, and,
beyond that, the mountains veiled in the mysteries of the spirit.

I stopped and looked inside the little house. Small rice
balls lined the floor and a small clay pot of water sat at one end.

"Is that a shrine?" I asked our guide.

Joi nodded, still humming the song he'd been humming
off and on all day as he walked ahead of us on the trail.

"Way out here?"

"It's for the spirit of the rice field," he said.

"Are the people here animists?"

Another nod.

"Are you?"

Joi nodded and went humming up the trail, and I
followed. The Vietnamese and Cambodians we had talked with
had told us that their families, like most people they knew,
combined ancestor devotion and Buddhism, and we had seen the
two kinds of shrines in use in almost every house and pagoda we
entered. No one had said anything about animism.

As evening fell and we climbed higher toward the village
where we would spend the night, I couldn't get the image of that
little house for the spirit out of my mind. So beautiful, so moving.
Rice was life to the people living in these hills, and this shrine was
a visible sign of that. That sign stood as a remembrance of that
gift, and it showed their gratitude for it. The wonder I felt at this

act of devotion was steady and whole. No intellectual objections to naïveté or primitivism shook it. No theological condemnations of polytheism beat it down. No dismissal of this shrine as self-serving superstition, the propitiating or bribing of spirits to ensure a good crop and hence health and prosperity, shattered it. Not even worries that I, an outsider, unfamiliar with animism, completely misunderstood this sign tainted that wonder. Nothing clouded my joy in the presence of this beautiful gesture of the human spirit, one bearing witness to the giftedness and miracle of existence. From that moment, whenever we walked through rice fields, I looked eagerly for another such sign. And when one appeared, my heart bowed toward it, brimming with thanks and love, for its presence, for the fecundity of the earth, for the human spirit, for the miracle of existence.

The next day, after trekking down from the village to the boat, we traveled farther up the river, to a small landing where a herd of water buffalo was lounging in the water and on the banks. In an open-sided shelter overlooking the river, we lunched on sticky rice wrapped in bamboo leaves, fish steamed in banana leaves, bamboo shoots, pomelo fresh from a tree, and sweet, sweet bananas. Fortified, we began another trek, this time to what a small hand-painted sign near the beginning of the trail called a holy cave. Why holy? I wondered. Had a monk lived there? Had a special revelation or ceremony occurred there? We started on the path. Just before it angled upward, we passed a shrine on our left. The floor of this shrine was a piece of rough-hewn tree trunk strewn with the drippings of candles, its roof a single piece of tin folded in half. Inside were balls of sticky rice and a cup of water. A shrine to the spirit of the cave. What was the gift of this cave? Joi had already started up the steep path that cut through dense vegetation, too far away for questions.

The climb was steep and slippery, with stairs fashioned out of roots and rocks and an intermittent handrail made of bamboo lashed to tree trunks. We climbed and climbed, pulling ourselves up, breathing heavily. The entrance was small and unremarkable except for the hand-lettered sign that read "Cave is

here." Not "Please remove shoes before entering the temple,"
words we were familiar with from slipping into Buddhist temples
and pagodas. Not "Take off your shoes, you're standing on holy
ground." Ordinary words, with no pointers to or echoes of spirit:
cave is here. We snapped on our headlamps and followed Joi
inside, ducking and twisting to fit ourselves in.

The daylight disappeared, and the air grew dank. Joi
walked steadily into the darkness, shining his light on stalagmites
and stalactites. About one hundred feet in, his light shone on a
ceiling blackened with soot from fires. During the American
carpet bombing of northern Laos, the villagers nearby had used
this cave as a bomb shelter. At the first sound of plane engines
they would gather their families and run up the long path to the
cave. They lived together inside, cooking and sleeping, until all
was quiet again.

Joi walked deeper into the cave. After another one
hundred feet, a sour, acrid smell greeted us. He shone his light
upwards. On the ceiling hung hundreds of bats. At Joi's request,
we stood still, silent, so as not to disturb them. Joi kept us there,
motionless, his light fixed on the black creatures, a long time. He
loved bats, the way he seemed to appreciate and respect all things
in the jungle—the sesame bushes, flowers, medicinal plants, and
the ants and snakes—he stopped to point out to us along the way.
At last, his light left the bats, and he began walking, deeper into
the cave. We followed. The air grew danker, cooler, heavier,
denser, sucking the breath out of me. The darkness blackened and
the walls closed in on us. The cave was 450 feet long. We were
only a little over halfway to the end.

"Is there a way out the other side?" I called to Joi, who had
disappeared into the darkness ahead of me.

No answer.

We kept walking. Finally our way was blocked. The cave
narrowed too much for our bodies to continue. We turned around
and headed back the same way we had come.

A straggler on the trek into the cave, I was first on the way
out, eager for fresh air and sunlight. And eager too, for the

lightness and innocence of the open sky. Inside the cave there was a pressure, a presence. Of something. Something living. Heavy, threatening, fearful. An odor of sorrow and death. Suffering. Perhaps it was just the lack of oxygen and light that I felt. Or the leapings of my imagination. But it was palpable. When we emerged into full daylight, I was relieved.

When we exited the cave, we didn't climb back down the path to the shrine near the river. We took a different path, the one on the ridge of the hill that the villagers had used during the bombings. It was a long walk, and I imagined the women carrying babies and small children, the older children and men carrying rice and pots for cooking and firewood, everyone hurrying, the planes throbbing above them, all of the villagers running for the refuge of the cave. The cave that had sheltered them, held their community together. The cave that had given them the gift of life and brought them out alive from their suffering. This cave for which they were grateful and for whose spirit they daily brought offerings of thanks, rice balls, water, and burning candles, placing them in the shrine at the bottom of the path from the river, offering food and drink in remembrance. A holy cave.

A holy cave. No holy men or women had meditated there. No special revelations had been received there. No miracles or supernatural wonders had occurred there. The cave was sanctified by the sheltering presence the village encountered there, by their recognition of that sheltering presence and the gift given to them, by their daily acts of remembrance and their thankfulness. All of this bound them to the spirit of the cave and to one another.

*

A visible sign of an invisible grace—this classic definition of sacrament is common shorthand for Augustine's discussion of sacraments in his treatise "Catechizing of the Uninstructed." Augustine's own phrasing in that treatise may be translated this way: "the signs of divine things are, it is true, things visible, but . . . the invisible things themselves are also honored in them."[6] By either the common definition or this translation of Augustine's

words, the shrines of the Hmong and other hill tribes in Laos—
shrines to the spirit of the rice field, the shrine to the spirit of the
cave, other shrines to other spirits—are sacraments. The invisible
thing, the spirit, the gracious gift of fertility or shelter, is visible in
the concrete houses of remembrance and devotion and in the
physical acts of offering food and drink in thanks. By means of the
concrete object in the physical word, the spirit is honored.

Such a claim need not shock. Augustine himself, in his
Reply to Faustus, says that every religion, true or false, has its
visible signs or sacraments. John Calvin repeats this view and,
building on another of Augustine's definitions of sacrament, as a
"visible word," offers several metaphors for understanding why
"visible words" are essential to the spiritual life, why we cannot
live by words alone.[7] The final-metaphor Calvin offers is a mirror:

> Or we may call them mirrors, in which we may
> contemplate the riches of the grace which God bestows
> upon us. For then, as has been said, he manifests himself to
> us in as far as our dullness can enable us to recognise him,
> and testifies his love and kindness to us more expressly
> than by word.[8]

The misunderstood and much maligned mystic Jonathan Edwards
experienced these mirrors, this harmony of the natural and the
spiritual, not only in the sacraments of baptism and the Lord's
Supper, but in all of the natural world. As he recorded in his
astounding testament of presence and attentiveness, *Images or
Shadows of Divine Things*, everywhere he looked in nature he saw
the beauty of the world and, like the Israelites at Sinai, he saw the
voice of God present there, in lanced wounds and vanishing
shadows, in spiders sailing through air in delight on wind-borne
web strings, in the intimate union of a branch grafted onto a fruit
tree.[9]

We need not call these visible signs "sacraments." That is
the term used by Western Christianity. The Eastern church never
adopted that language; the Orthodox choose to speak instead of

mysteries, which they understand, following the "treasure in earthen vessels" language of 2 Corinthians 4:7 (KJV), as earthen vessels that convey divine grace to humankind, vessels that allow human beings to experience the mystical presence of divine grace and to commune with it. I find mystery more evocative of what happens in those moments of encounter between the unseen spirit and the things of this world. But whether we speak of sacrament or mystery, real presence or mystical presence, mirror or image or shadow, the goal is the same: to bring human beings and the divine into communion with one another by means of something in our everyday world that can be seen, heard, touched, smelled, tasted.

Seeing balls of sticky rice and water in a humble wooden shrine on the edge of a rice field or at the bottom of a path to a cave, like seeing the bread and wine in Communion, enables us to remember and meditate on the beauty of the world and the gift an unseen presence or reality bestows. We're human beings, not disembodied spirits. Every one of us—Native American, Hindu, Buddhist, Jew, Christian, Muslim, Goddess devotee, agnostic, atheist, animist—is human, akin to *humus*, Latin for earth. We speak of "my body" and of ourselves as "embodied" and as "having a body," but that smacks of a hard and fast separation between body and spirit that doesn't do justice to our experience as unified selves who do not exist outside of our bodies. It may be truer to our experience to say we're body-mind-spirits or to simply say we are bodies. Not that we are our bodies, a biological organism and nothing more, but that we are bodies. We don't have any experience of what it means not to be a body-self. Our consciousness depends on our being a body. Even an out-of-body experience depends on being a particular body, before and after that experience. Our being, human being, arises from the constant interweaving of our unique visible organism and our unique invisible consciousness. One does not exist without the other. We do not exist without both, as Maurice Merleau-Ponty makes clear:

Sacramental words and gesture are not simply the embodiment of some thought. Like tangible things, they are themselves the carriers of meaning, which is inseparable from the material form. They do not evoke the idea of God: they are the vehicle of His presence and action. In the last analysis the soul is so little to be separated from the body that it will carry a radiant double of its temporal body into eternity.[10]

Not merely symbolic expressions, sacramental acts or rituals are events that mediate between human beings and the transcendent, the visible and the invisible, and in so doing shape our understanding of who we are in the world.

Because we are bodies, we cannot escape the physicality of our existence, its distractions and seductions. We're easily dazed by the demands of the physical world, and we forget there is more than what we see, more than what we know. We're lulled into taking the gift of existence for granted. We deem it our right, get lost in the power of our will, our needs, our desires, and we forget there is a world beyond ourselves.

Because we are bodies, we cannot bypass the corporeal world on our way to a spiritual world. We need concrete objects to help us remember there is more than what our eyes see and our ears hear and all our senses perceive. We need visible signs to point us beyond what is visible, to expand our perspective, open us to gratitude for all that we depend on, all that sustains us, all that we are given. We may be naive Cartesians, unrepentant Cartesians, post-Cartesians, or animists who never separated the natural and spiritual worlds, but whatever our philosophy, we need visible signs to call our attention to invisible things, that we may remember and give thanks. To commune with the spirit, we need objects from our material world—bread, wine, sticky rice balls, water. Sacraments and sacramental objects, then, may be seen as liminal realities, places where spirit and matter meet, invitations to a holy between.

The Hmong came to Minnesota seeking refuge and a new home. They came with no written language of their own and no understanding of English words, but they were fluent in the interweaving of the natural and spiritual worlds and familiar with spirits of many kinds. In inviting them to eat bread and drink grape juice in Communion with other human beings, to partake in the Eucharist, the Sacrament of Remembrance and Thanksgiving, Tyrone gave them a visible word, a concrete mirror in which to contemplate the riches of grace, to encounter the spirit of Jesus, his love and kindness—whether they named it that or not—and to experience in a strange new land the invisible world of the spirit through visible signs in the natural world.

However anthropologists may categorize the worldview of the Hmong; however scholars of the history of religions may define animism; however theologians and other church authorities may interpret and circumscribe the mystery of the Lord's Supper, this much I know: in Saint Paul, Minnesota, Hmong and non-Hmong, with no words in common, communed in spirit, with the spirit, by means of bread and grape juice. Because we are bodies.

Chapter 3

When Bones Are Not Bones

"Bones are bones, not gods," the sixteenth-century reformer Martin Bucer wrote, railing against relics.[1] To Bucer's charge of idolatry, John Calvin added—almost gleefully—superstition, fraud, absurdity, and religious and political power plays.[2] Bucer's own bones confirm their judgments. Five years after he died, Queen Mary of England, fearing the power of his bones to incite Protestant rebellion, had them exhumed and burned at the stake. Four years later, Queen Elizabeth, defender of Protestantism, restored Bucer's tomb *ad majorem Dei gloriam*, to the greater glory of God. No wonder Calvin insisted on being buried in an unmarked grave!

As a Calvinist-Evangelical-turned-Jew, I'm inclined to agree: Relics are a dangerous business, ripe for abuses of all kinds, by individuals and institutions. Yet I can't condemn preserving and venerating relics—from the Latin *reliquiae*, remains, from *relinquere*, to leave behind—either body or first order relics like bones and ashes or second-order relics, objects worn or used by a dead person. Revering bodies or belongings of the dead is so widespread, even today, that it seems more an irrepressible need than a vestige of primitive religion or a hoax.

Examples are not hard to find. On *Dia de Los Muertos*, a household *ofrenda* or altar holds images of Jesus, saints, and deceased members of the family. Spirit tablets of Chinese ancestors are housed on family altars, the zither and writings of Confucius in his family mansion in Qufu. The ashes and bone-pearls of the Buddha were spread among eight, then 84,000 stupas; his tooth resides in a temple in Sri Lanka. Nails and splinters of the cross, Mary's breast milk, St. Peter's brain, bone fragments of St. Kateri Tekakwitha, pieces of St. Bartholomew's skin, severed heads of saints and martyrs, St. Paul's chains, St. Moninna's hoe and badger-skin garment, and other relics are cared for in Roman Catholic communities. A hair from Mohammed's beard, his footprint, and a signed letter are kept in Topkapi Palace; the bones of Rumi and Isaac Luria rest in shrines built over their tombs; Lenin's body in a mausoleum in Moscow, Mao Zedong's in a crystal case in Beijing, and Ho Chi Minh's on ice in Hanoi; the remains of Bruce Lee and Denise Levertov in Seattle's Lakeview Cemetery, Jimi Hendrix's in Renton, Washington. All of these are pilgrimage sites.

It's too easy today to cast relics as "trash" as Calvin did, and foreclose inquiry into them by claiming, as he also did, that it's "no use to discuss the point whether it is right or wrong to have relics merely to keep them as precious objects, without worshiping them, because experience proves that this is never the case."[3] It's precisely our experience of relics I want to explore. Why do we hold on to the leavings of those we love or seek to emulate? Visit their remains? Buy letters written and signed by Abraham Lincoln, Gandhi's gold-plated glasses, Prince's "angel cloud" guitar? Keep close the ashes of loved ones, or things they wore or used? Here's my inventory of my own personal relics:

> A petrified camel bone from the Sinai wilderness
> My grandparents' Dutch Bible
> My dad's two-handled tin lunch pail
> His Helix engineer's ruler
> His *Complete Works of Shakespeare*
> A sampler my sister held on her lap, stitched with her
>   hands
> Two terry cloth dish towels from her kitchen
> Her ashes, in one of her canning jars.

We're drawn to what those we love or admire leave behind because we, still-bodied presences, want to keep their now-un-bodied presence close, touch them, body to body, spirit to spirit. Their ashes, clothes, tools, these physical leavings of their life in our world, keep them present to us in their absence. Calvin's admonition to put aside relics and all that is "carnal" to focus on the "spirit" isn't helpful today, when we're countering dualisms and investigating the body's ineluctable role in our lives as "the knowing animal," to use philosopher Raymond Tallis's term.

We need to reclaim the body and its knowing, in all human activity, including spirituality. We need a spirituality that can help us understand our experience of conserving and honoring chosen objects.

By "corporeal spirituality," I don't mean the incarnational theology of Western Christianity, or the "religious materialism" of Eastern Orthodox theologian Sergius Bulgakov, in which the corporeal is transfigured like the resurrected body of Jesus. I envision a spirituality that affirms human being as body-mind-spirit-being and acknowledges the body and the material world as integral to all our experience, including the sacred. Theology aside, what do we make of living intimately with objects left behind by those who once lived among us in the flesh? Why do we wear a watch or necklace once warmed by the skin of another, cradle a book or kiddush cup once held by another, or caress prayer beads once rubbed by another?

Because objects are not necessarily objective; they can contribute to who we are. That's what Mihaly Csikszentmihalyi, a behavioral scientist, and Eugene Rochberg-Halton, a sociologist, found in their study of household objects. Objects selected to have "close at hand," they argue in *The Meaning of Things: Domestic Symbols and the Self*, "create permanence in the intimate life of a person, and therefore…are most involved in making up his or her identity." We make order in ourselves and retrieve our identity by first creating and then interacting with the material world, and the nature of that transaction determines "the kind of person that emerges."[4]

The things we choose to live with are "inseparable from who we are." And because they reflect as well as shape "the pattern of the owner's self," cherished objects can, potentially, represent "the endogenous being of the owner," being that arises from within. They can become "containers for the being of the person." More than simply representing the potential energy of a person or her power to affect others, however, "they bring that actuality about." They produce power, "like the sound of a trumpet, not the trumpet itself, is a concrete manifestation of the communal spirit of a tribe."[5] The objects we charge with psychic energy by tending them, cherishing them, also act on us, and what is exchanged is real energy.

We're comfortable seeing objects as expressions of ourselves, Csikszentmihalyi and Rochberg-Halton argue, but it's "more difficult to admit that the things one uses are in fact part of one's self: not in any mystical or metaphorical sense but in cold, concrete actuality."[6] This doesn't mean their aim is to disenchant objects; their goal is to "unlock the magic of things," by "seeing them objectively and subjectively at the same time," a process they identify as "the basic symbolic act—*sym-ballein*, to 'throw together.'"[7] Our ability to freely create meaning, to change the meaning of goods and energy we possess, is a weapon against the deadening, fragmenting (*dia-ballein*, "to throw apart") force of what they call the "terminal materialism" of our day, in which everything is measured by utility or an expected pleasure and we are dominated by mere things—mere objects.

Objects, then, can become reservoirs of meaning, conduits of energy, a locus of power in which the subjective and objective are brought together, and the profane becomes sacred—a description not far from Peter Brown's definition of religious relics as a locus of power joining heaven and earth in the body.[8] Objects that were *loci* of power for the loved one can become *loci* of power for the survivors. When we cherish objects that made a person who they were when they were alive, and allow those objects to shape who we are, we multiply that joining of subjectivity and objectivity, creating a meeting of endogenous beings through a material object, the dead and the living.

The remains of our loved ones we keep near us, then, are not objects to be worshiped or venerated. But neither are they mementoes, mere memory jogs. They are not abstract symbols that point to someone not present. They are a "throwing together," a physical place where energy is exchanged, a tangible moment of meeting, a palpable aid in becoming who we are. As such, they may serve as a holy between, an invitation to enter a space of communing that is neither absence nor ordinary presence. One might even say they generate real presence. Is this so far from the Buddhist concept of the power of relics to bring the "living presence" of the Buddha near? Or from the Confucian language for relics as "traces" or "tracks" or "a footprint" of a human being who walked the earth as we do, and who can thus inspire us to live a similar life?

Body to body, spirit to spirit, the touchstones we treasure release energy for our lives. They bring the living presence of our loved ones near, to comfort, heal, form, and guide us. Miracle enough.

Chapter 4

The Story of a Hollowed-Out Bone

In 1986, while visiting a Tibetan refugee village outside
Kathmandu, I came upon a hollowed-out bone lying in a glass
case heaped with ritual objects. It was old, worn smooth and
burnished to a golden caramel. Here and there, delicate carvings
rose from the foot-long shaft. I longed to hold it.

"It's a femur," my doctor-husband said. "Strongest bone in
the body. See the ball joint? Where it attached to the hip? And
how it tapers toward the knee? Probably female."

The shopkeeper nodded. "From a young girl. A virgin."
Seeing me recoil, she quickly added, "No killing. If a girl dies,
maybe disease, maybe accident, they take her bone and make this
trumpet."

"It's like a shofar!" I said to my husband, thinking of the
hollowed-out ram's horn curled on our shelf back home, the
trumpet blown on Rosh Hashanah and Yom Kippur to wake
sleeping spirits, call them to face death and live anew. Bending
closer, I saw the bone lay nestled among other thighbone
trumpets. But unlike the bone that captivated me, these were all
sheathed in silver or copper at each end, the casings intricately
carved and studded with turquoise and coral. On some, a braided
silver chain linked the two casings. On others, a silver girdle
encased the middle as well. These trumpets were exquisite. Great
care had been taken to adorn them. But my bone, brown and
humble, shone with a darker beauty.

The shopkeeper reached in the case to show me the bare
bone trumpet. Waving her to stop, I escaped to the other end of
the shop, where I busied myself testing hand drums, spinning
prayer wheels, and dragging a wooden mallet around the edge of
singing bowls to see if I could make them sing. In one corner I
discovered *malas* whose skull-shaped beads were sculpted from
bone, *khatvangas* or staffs made from a long bone and carved with
skulls, and *kapalas* or skullcups, bowls crafted from human skulls,
lined and bordered with silver and inlaid with coral and

turquoise. I didn't need to know how these objects were used to understand that they were tokens of impermanence, bodily reminders to face death so one will know how to live.

I returned to the display case. The shopkeeper removed the bone and laid it in my open palms. It felt strangely heavy, solid, and it grew warm as I held it, the thighbone of a young woman, a woman who had once walked the earth, whose dead body had become a sign signifying how to live, a sign I couldn't comprehend but was holding in my hands, my body touching hers.

Here and there, Buddhist symbols rose out of the bone, each no more than an inch or two across. A conch shell. A dharma wheel. A swastika. They looked like they had grown out of the bone, like leaves budding from a branch. I ran my fingers over the carvings, lingering over each raised symbol—the shell, the wheel, the swastika—as if I were reading Braille, hungrily searching for meaning. As I turned the bone over, the largest carving appeared, a six-pointed star woven into an endless knot. A *magein David*, a star of David! That bone seemed marked for me, and I wanted it.

"What's this used for?" I asked the woman.

"To drive away evil spirits."

Now I really wanted that bone-become-trumpet. I desperately needed help countering forces of destruction in my life. Hoping to keep evil spirits at bay, I'd been wearing eighteen Navajo ghost-berry bracelets on my left wrist for several years. I told myself the elasticized bracelets, all different colors, all bought at powwows in Minnesota, were arty, fun, a tangible link to the Native American students and colleagues I worked with at the seminary where I taught. But I was wearing them for protection. I never took them off. And now this bone-become-trumpet appeared, offering a stronger defense. I imagined putting my lips to the narrow end and blowing hard, watching my breath expand and leave the wide end full and powerful, pushing away all that would harm me and creating a space around me in which I felt safe.

I wanted that bone.

Still, I hesitated. I was afraid of that bone. Cradling that young woman's dead body in my hands made me uneasy, and I didn't understand why. Superstition? Repulsion? Fear, certainly. But of what? My life being extinguished? Used for another's purpose? Hoping to escape its grip on me, I asked, "Is it okay to buy a sacred object like this?"

The shopkeeper nodded.

"I'm not a Buddhist," I explained. "I'm a Jew. I wouldn't want anybody to come and buy one of our ritual objects as a souvenir or art object. It seems wrong to make a sacred object part of a money transaction."

"It's good," she said, nodding. "It helps us."

Since 1959, when China annexed their country and restricted their religious practices, many Tibetans had chosen self-imposed exile over submission to Chinese control. My people, the Jews, had been forced into exile also, thousands of years before by the Babylonians and not so long ago by England, France, Spain, Germany, Russia, and other nations. Tibetan Buddhists and Jews were both an ancient, spiritual people struggling to keep their way of life, their people, alive, as the Dalai Lama would later publicly acknowledge, when he met with a group of Jewish scholars in New York in 1989, to learn, as he said, "the Jewish secret technique" of survival.

Who was I to question what Tibetan or Jewish refugees deemed necessary for their survival? And where was all this pious worrying coming from? In most religions, no thing is sacred in and of itself. Any object marked as sacred by a community can become secular, when necessary, by an act of that same community. How many menorahs have, by violence or assimilation or poverty, become candelabras sold in shops? How many amulets sold as jewelry? Tewa pots and Lakota pipes as art objects? Bibles as rare books? *The Sarajevo Haggadah*, carried out of Spain to the Balkans during the expulsion of the Jews, was, after centuries of family seders, sold by its family to keep them alive, and it now lives behind a bomb-proof glass wall in the National Museum of Bosnia and Herzegovina.

The bone rested in my hands as if it belonged there. My left palm slid over the ball joint, feeling its rough knobs and the sharp edges of the wide opening where sound emerged, and my right hand closed around the smoothed circle of the narrow end, the opening so many lips had touched. My fingertips settled on the hollowed-out shaft that so much warm breath had passed through, creating sound out of emptiness, deliverance from evil. Dead girl or not, I needed that bone.

I bought it for one hundred dollars.

*

I slid the bone in my daypack for the long flight home, along with a copy of Alexandra David-Neel's *Magic and Mystery in Tibet*, hoping to learn more about how to use my strange new companion to drive away evil. When I found her description of the "mystery" of *chöd* (cutting off), "the dreadful mystic banquet," the ritual in which the thighbone trumpet or *kanglang* is used, I devoured her words and quickly fell rapt to the scene she depicts. The celebrant goes alone to a cemetery "or any wild site whose physical aspect awakens feelings of terror."[1] He goes to such wild places because it's there that violent or evil forces may be stirred up, either by deeds that took place there or by the concentration of many people's minds on imaginary events at that spot. It's at such spots that one is most likely to encounter demons, spirits of those who habitually harbored hatred and ill will, who delighted in cruelty during their lives, and who are still trapped in their viciousness. Once there, the celebrant blows the *kanglang*, "calling the hungry demons to the feast he intends to lay before them."[2] At those words, the hairs on the back of my neck stood up and my scalp tingled. The trumpet was to summon demons? Could the shopkeeper have gotten it so wrong?

Hoping I'd misunderstood, I read on. The celebrant imagines that a goddess, a personification of his own will, "springs from the top of his head and stands before him, sword in hand. With one stroke she cuts off [his] head...Then, while troops of ghouls crowd round for the feast, the goddess severs his limbs, skins him and rips open his belly. The bowels fall out, the blood flows like a river, and the hideous guests bite here and there, masticate noisily...."

I put the book down. When my breath and heart caught up with this gruesome scene, I resumed reading. While the demons are chewing his flesh and bones, feeding on his blood, the celebrant excites and urges the demons on with liturgic words of unreserved surrender:

> *For ages...I have borrowed from countless living beings...all kinds of services to sustain my body, to keep it joyful in comfort and to defend it against death.*
> *Today, I pay my debt, offering for destruction this body which I have held so dear.*
> *I give my flesh to the hungry, my blood to the thirsty, my skin to clothe those who are naked, my bones as fuel to those who suffer from cold. I give my happiness to the unhappy ones. I give my breath to bring back the dying to life.*
> *Shame on me if I shrink from giving my self!*[3]

My mouth went dry. I glanced at the overhead bin, where the trumpet was safely stowed in my pack. I no longer wanted to touch it or be near it. I had seen in it a powerful ally and protector, promising relief from my suffering. But it had quickly shown its true and terrifying face, an adversary challenging me to offer my self—my flesh, skin, bones, blood, happiness, breath—to relieve the suffering of others.

Without reading how the *kanglang* ritual ends, I closed David-Neel's book, stuffed it in the seat pocket, and tried to escape into sleep for the rest of the flight.

When we got home, I hid the trumpet in our Judaica cabinet, blocking it with our silver Shabbat candlesticks, *menorahs*, *kiddush* cup, *havdalah* set, and *shofar*. I wanted to make sure no curious person picked it up and blew it, unwittingly unleashing demons in the *mikdash ma'at*, little sanctuary, that was our home, to wreak God-knows-what destruction.

*

The bone stayed safely hidden for twelve years—through the birth of our son, the birth of our daughter, a move to rural South Carolina, and another to Charleston, South Carolina. But one morning, after the kids had left for school, I took it out of its hiding place, sat down on the living room floor, and prepared to blow it.

My life had become a "wild site" that "awakened feelings of terror," a place where violent and evil forces had been stirred up, where a person who delighted in cruelty made frequent visits—my mother. As my father slipped into the darkness of Alzheimer's, my mother descended into a kind of moral Alzheimer's, forgetting how to act lovingly and justly toward others, taking vengeance on those who didn't agree with her or do her bidding. She railed at my sister for questioning her care of our father. When my sister refused to be our mother's factotum any longer and to stay quiet about her neglect, if she did not get help for our father, our mother's anger descended into rage. She stalked my sister and her husband, broke into their house, threatened to disinherit her and her family. Trying to mediate, I called her to remind her that she could never be that cruel to her own daughter and grandchildren, that it wasn't loving or Christian, which she professed to be. "You're just mad right now," I said. "You don't really want to do this."

"Oh, I do. And I will. I have every right."

"May God have mercy on your soul," I spat out before she hung up.

My mother rarely spoke to me after that. When I joined the rest of the family for Christmas that year—all of us except my sister and her family, who chose self-imposed exile over submission. My mother barely tolerated my presence. She accused me and my sister of lying about my father's dementia. "There's nothing wrong with him!" she insisted. She threatened to bring legal action against us for plotting to kidnap him. She told lies about me to my brothers, undermined me to my children, and locked me out of the room when she called the whole family together to announce the changes to her will.

It was the week after that Christmas that I picked up the thighbone trumpet to call the demons. Though desperate to run from the pain and anger that were choking me, I remembered the lesson my Baha'i self-defense teacher had taught me. When an attacker chokes you from behind, don't try to pull away. That only strengthens their hold. The way to break free is to raise one arm fast while turning to face them. I had to turn and face the forces of destruction and violence. I had to call them to me. For what I wasn't sure. I hadn't opened David-Neel's book since the flight home from Nepal, and I had only a vague memory of the *chöd* ritual she described. Something to do with going to a place, real or in the mind, where violence or evil had occurred and calling the destructive forces so they could devour you. A kind of sacrifice, I seemed to remember, offering oneself to ravenous demons so they could be satisfied at last, their suffering ended. I didn't believe in *ad hoc* syncretism, individuals assembling a pastiche of ritual beliefs and practices from diverse traditions. I didn't believe in cultural appropriation—Christians celebrating Passover seders focused on Jesus, Whites holding sweat lodges or Sundancing or going on vision quests. I didn't believe in performing a ritual one didn't understand: It could be dangerous. Dabbling in another's tradition was like breaking into a Lotus or Lamborghini or Rolls Royce on the street, hotwiring it, and taking it for a joyride: you ended up crashing the car, taken to jail, or both—maybe shot dead in a high-speed chase. Yet here I was. Breaking all my rules. Courting disrespect, desecration, disaster.

Sitting cross-legged, holding the trumpet in my open palms, I began to call the demons that had been tormenting me, the destructive forces set in motion by my mother, a restless, unhappy soul whose only pleasure seemed to be telling lies, sowing mistrust, stirring up jealousy, inciting violence—an Iago in drag. "Come and consume me," I called. "Devour me."

I put the thighbone to my lips and blew. A sound sputtered out, like someone gagging. I took a deep breath and blew harder. This time a clear blast pierced the room. I held the bone with both hands before me, the way a snake charmer holds his flute, and waited. Silence. "Here I am!" I called. "Come and destroy me! Finish me off! Leave nothing behind."

I waited. Nothing. I think I expected to see my mother appear. Like the goddess of the *chöd* ritual, springing forth from me, sword in hand, ready to cut off my head, sever my limbs, and disembowel me—the skills she had used so effectively on me since I was a child. Or like one of the demons in Buffy the Vampire Slayer, a shapeshifting, growling-and-grunting horror of a beast, chained to her habit of hurting others, thrashing about, lashing out in her misery, beside herself with the desire to destroy. Or a hissing, fanged snake. Or a black hole that swallowed all joy.

She didn't show up. No one did. I could hardly breathe. My spirit wanted to burst the bonds of my body. Something had to happen. Even if I had to take that virgin's thighbone and splinter it against the light streaming through the window or crack it over my skull. Something had to happen. I couldn't carry all that pain and horror and righteous indignation and raw anger inside me anymore. It was eating me alive, hollowing me out.

And then I saw the demons. They had been there all along. They weren't out there, in my mother or the harm she worked in the world. They were in me, living in the cemetery of my heart, that stony, blood-soaked battleground where so many family dramas of violence had been played out over the years—all the lies, treachery, terror, woundings, beheadings, dishonorable surrenders, amputations, retreats, routs, banishments, exiles. The evil I had to face was not hiding in a dark and dank ether outside me. It was not them I had to defeat. It was not her, my mother, I had to overcome, whether by an indomitable spirit or psychic courage. It was my heart I had to sacrifice, the withering demons that lived in that wild place—my rage, my grief, my suffering, so comfortingly familiar and not altogether unenjoyable. I had shrunken into a pinprick self, a pinprick that cast a shadow that eclipsed the world. Who was I if I remained withered by my own suffering and did not give my self for the suffering of others?

It was time to let go of my unhappiness and make room for the world once more, my mother in it. She was an unhappy soul, and I hadn't made life easier for her. I was the "little devil" that dared to question her, the child who told her No! to her face. Now I wished her peace, an end to her suffering, true satisfaction of her desires so she would no longer hunger for chaos, thirst for power: love so boundless it would heal her shame and self-loathing. "May God have mercy on your soul," I said out loud to her, this time without sarcasm.

My hands tightened around the bone of that young Tibetan woman and I rested it over my heart, while I let the demons eat my flesh. With each mouthful they ripped from me, my spirit became lighter and lighter, until I was almost nothing, a heap of bones.

Hardly the *chöd* ritual of intentionally and nobly sacrificing oneself to relieve the suffering of all other beings. But stumbling into compassion for my mother was magic and mystery enough. Twenty years later, in an op-ed on overcoming hatred by the Dalai Lama and Arthur Brooks, I would read these words of the 8th-century Indian Buddhist master Shantideva in his *Guide to a Bodhisatva's Way of Life*: "Unruly beings are as unlimited as space. They cannot possibly all be overcome. But if I overcome thoughts of anger alone, this will be equivalent to vanquishing all foes."[4] Somehow in that plundered ritual, the illusion of my mother as my enemy had been destroyed, long enough for my hatred to die.

I kissed the thighbone trumpet and put it back in our Judaica cupboard, this time beside the shofar, not behind it. Two trumpets to wake deadened hearts to forgiveness and compassion. Two bodily remains calling out, "Face death and you will know how to live."

*

After I summoned the demons, I believed my journey with the bone-become-trumpet had ended, that the gift it had given me could not be surpassed—a heart stirred up in compassion for the suffering of others. But the ritual was not complete. I was a heap of bones, but not yet charred. I had not burned away my pride at having moved from terror and grief and anger to love. I had not yet realized I had nothing to give away, because I was nothing. My spirit had not yet been hollowed out.

Several years passed. The bone-become-trumpet lived happily on the shelf beside the shofar, untouched but now a welcome companion. The darkened cavities at the top of the ball joint, twinned eternal eyes, no longer threatened me as I passed by. Then my father died, followed a year later by my mother. At her funeral, my sister and I were ushered to a back row. In his eulogy, the minister, who had met with us the day before and greeted us as we entered the chapel, announced that our mother was survived by three sons, each of whom he named. Our names, our lives had been erased. Our three brothers refused to acknowledge us also, declining to shake our hands or speak to us when we approached them, a habit they have practiced faithfully for seventeen years.

Within days of the funeral, we found out our mother had disinherited my sister, me, and our families, having deemed that we, her two daughters, had "predeceased her." My sister remembered our mother sexually abusing her and suffered a harrowing breakdown. One of our nephews committed suicide. My teenage daughter became defiant and courted danger after danger, making me fear I would lose her too. I wanted to die, to end the suffering and the terror of living in constant fear of being blindsided by fresh traumas. Then my husband of twenty-one years left, without warning, and a year later we were divorced. By that time, 2009, I was living once again in a wild place, a place of violence and anguish, a haunt of demons.

In separating our property, I sorted through all the ritual objects that had graced our family Shabbats and holidays and simchas. I packed up the ritual objects my husband had brought to our Jewish family, a kiddush cup from his grandparents, his grandfather's tallit, an ancient and pearl-inlaid siddur or prayer book, and a lace head covering his grandmother had worn when lighting Shabbat candles. I loved these ritual items. I had used and cared for them for decades. But they belonged to him and his family and they needed to return to their home, so I gave them back, though with an ache in my heart that lasts until this day.

I came at last to the bone. The bone I had feared and loved. The bone that had lived with me for twenty-three years and taught me hard truths. I needed its help again now. Cast out from my family of origin, exiled from the family I had created, I no longer knew how to live. Living seemed a kind of death. I put my lips to the narrow end, desperate to blow it, to blast away all the evil and anguish of the recent years. I knew that would backfire, that I would instead be facing down the demons of my own heart once again, and I wasn't sure the encounter would end well this time.

What then to do with my strange companion? Cradling the young woman's thighbone over my heart, I felt its sorrow and loneliness. It had lived in exile too long: first from its homeland, Tibet; then from its people, the Tibetans, and the refugee community in Nepal. None of her people to know her, look on her with love and gratitude, delight in her. None of her people to pick her up, caress her, comfort her, speak to her in her mother tongue, use her for the purpose for which she had been born and made and set apart as sacred. Without that, her life was a kind of death. When I realized that, I could hardly bear that she should live another day in exile. I needed to return her home.

I called the Sakya Monastery of Tibetan Buddhism in Seattle, explained that I had a very old thighbone trumpet I wanted to return to the community. The man on the phone set up an appointment for me with the resident lama. "He's very close to the Dalai Lama," he said.

During the week before our meeting, I kept the bone near me. Though I knew it had to return home, I was loath to give it up. I loved that bone. Before I could let it go, I needed something more from it, like Jacob refusing to let the angel he was wrestling go without a blessing. But what?

I dug out *Magic and Mystery in Tibet* and located the description of the *chöd* ritual that had terrified me so long ago. I read through the scene of bloody dismemberment and mastication. I read again the exhilarating prayer of offering the celebrant chants while being devoured.

> *I give my flesh to the hungry, my blood to the thirsty, my skin to clothe those who are naked, my bones as fuel to those who suffer from cold. I give my happiness to the unhappy ones. I give my breath to bring back the dying to life.*
> *Shame on me if I shrink from giving my self!*[5]

This is where I had stopped reading on the flight home from Nepal, too shaken to read further, not capable of imagining there could be more to the ritual. But the drama was far from over, and this time I read to the end.

Once the dismembered and bloody celebrant is being devoured by the destructive forces, feeding them with her being, she must imagine that she is but a heap of charred bones left behind, a sacrifice for the sake of others. Then comes the final act: she must renounce her sacrifice itself, realize it is an illusion created by her pride, and that she has nothing to renounce, that *"[s]he has nothing to give away, because [s]he is nothing."* The heap of bones she has been reduced to symbolizes the destruction of her phantom "I." Once she relinquishes the elation she experienced at her sacrifice, having offered up her whole self, spirit as well as body, the sacrifice is complete and the ritual done.

I had not given up my whole self, spirit as well as body. I had not slain my ego. I was proud of sacrificing my need to be right, my hurt, my fury for compassion for my mother. I thought myself noble for not hating her. I was proud of the sacrifices I had made to nurture a marriage over twenty-one years. I assumed he owed me gratitude and faithfulness until death. I was proud of the sacrifices I had made to create a loving and joyful family of my own. I believed the reward for my investment of time and effort and care was a loving and sheltering family that would always be mine, that would never change.

To save my bruised and battered self, I was clinging to illusions.

My sacrifices did not exist, because there was no I. I was nothing. I had nothing to give, nothing to lose but my pinprick self that clung to illusions. I was nothing. I was emptiness. There was my freedom. There was the way to make a joyful sound: to be hollowed out.

*

At the monastery I was ushered into the lama immediately. I sat down across from him in his study, the bone on my lap. He was a slight man, no taller or heavier than I, and of indeterminate age. He sat still, waiting for me to speak. Shaking, I told him where I had bought the trumpet, how long I had had it, and that I wanted to return it. Three minutes. No more. Yet in that brief telling I felt my self inflating, stealthily, like a robber entering a house where the owners are sleeping. *Look at this noble gesture I am making*, it whispered, *what I am giving up, this beautiful possession for the good of your community, my precious bone.*

The lama listened, smiling and nodding. He knew what I was up to. He knew the thighbone trumpet had never been mine. That it would take me the rest of my life to complete the ritual, to relinquish my sacrifices—if I ever did. That I would have to face death clear-eyed again and again so I would know how to live. And he knew I would see that soon enough.

He did not question me. He did not judge me. He listened, his face opening to me. I don't recall him saying anything.

Suddenly, we both stood up and I handed him the *kanglang*. He accepted it graciously, smiled, and nodded again. I bowed and left him in his study holding the trumpet. As I approached the exit at the far end of a wide corridor, I heard his robes swishing toward the opposite end. I opened the door. Sunlight streamed in. Behind me, the sound of the trumpet rang out. Full. Clear. Joyous. And in the silence that followed, I heard the lama laugh.

His laugh woke me up more than the blast of the trumpet. His lightness stirred my heart, rang in my bones. His delight, like that of a child, tickled me. He was not warning evil spirits away.

He was not calling demons to him. He was rejoicing in a friend returning home, ready for whatever work she was called to do.

And then I was out in the sun, the lama's mirth a fragrance around me, my earnestness cracked by his laughter, my ego slain yet again, returning home, to an emptied and emptying self, a self hollowed out to make a joyful sound, ready for whatever work I was called to do.

"We seven billion human beings—emotionally, mentally, physically—are the same," the Dalai Lama says. "Everyone wants a joyful life."[6]

From time to time I miss my friend. But I remember her in joy.

Chapter 5

The Liminal Work of Sacred Clowns

In the 1980s, I was invited to attend a private week-long Sundance on Rosebud Reservation, in South Dakota. During the ceremony, I was captivated by the *Heyoka*, often referred to as a trickster or clown, though neither word does justice to the role such a figure plays in Lakota and Dakota life. While the other dancers were dressed in ceremonial clothes and jewelry, the *Heyoka* wore a skirt made of burlap, a yellow Happy Face scarf folded at his waist, and a Mickey Mouse pendant over his bare chest. When the dancers circled to the east, he moved west, backwards. When they danced toward the sacred tree, he backed away. He smoked cigarettes and gulped overflowing ladles of water in front of the fasting dancers. He mimicked the medicine man with his buffalo robe and horns. One evening, when the dancers were eating their one meal of the day around the fire pits, I asked him how he had come to be a *Heyoka*. He'd had a vision of lightning and thunder beings when he was younger, he said. It was not a role one chose; it chose you.

Not long after this, on a cross-country flight I happened to sit next to a man wearing a black suit with a clergy collar. He had a clowning ministry, he told me. It was an ancient tradition, nothing new-fangled. In the medieval church, when Mass was celebrated during Feast of Fools, a clown or clowns would pop out from a small door near the altar and run around creating chaos, swearing, making obscene gestures, singing bawdy songs, eating disgusting foods, and mimicking the priest and congregation. I was intrigued. Before meeting these two men, I hadn't ever considered the role of humor in sacred ceremonies or a designated role for turning solemnity on its head. But soon these intriguing exposures to sacred clowning faded.

Decades later, visiting the Poeh Museum and Cultural Center outside Santa Fe, I came across a sculpture by Roxanne Swentzell from Santa Clara Pueblo titled *Koshare*.

Koshare, by Roxanne Swentzell

Koshare is one of the five sacred clowns of the Pueblo nation. The exhibit identified him as "brother from the sky world who uses humor to teach us the ways in which to conduct ourselves so we may journey life in beauty." Again I was captivated. This time I wanted to explore this figure. Was this a liminal figure? Did the role he played have anything to do with liminality?

A *Koshare* exists outside normal categories, often the sign of a liminal figure. This figure is often androgynous or of ambiguous sexuality. He is not of this world, yet his task is to create or restore order in the community in this world. His corn husk horns and wild actions suggest the chaos he brings to rules and "the natural order of things," yet his goal is to teach people how to live in harmony. His black and white stripes suggest social conventions, yet his actions flaunt taboos, piety, and morals. He is, as Paul Radin describes this figure as he appears in Winnebago culture in *The Trickster: A Study in American Indian Mythology,*" an ambiguous creator and destroyer."[1]

More than simply an ambiguous or paradoxical figure, however, the *Koshare*, like the *Heyoka* and the medieval Catholic clown (and others), strikes me as a liminal figure or a figure with a liminal role. In *Trickster Makes This World: Mischief, Myth, and Art*, Lewis Hyde describes the trickster as a "boundary-crosser" who "confuse[s] distinctions," a "god of the threshold,"[2] who, Paul Mattick writes in his review of Hyde's book, violates "principles of social and natural order, playfully disrupting normal life and then re-establishing it on a new basis."[3] In an interview on her work, which includes many *Koshare* sculptures, Swentzell tells how *Koshares* invite people to become aware of what actions they must take to be in harmony with the community. They "reflect something people need to see about themselves…. Like when someone is greedy: instead of shouting, the clown will sit in front of his house, and act like a greedy individual, collecting rocks….That is what I try to do in my work."[4]

Koshares slip between, between genders, between insider and outsider status, between worlds, between sacred and profane, between chaos and order, between play and the solemn work of keeping a community healthy. Their role is unique. They do not preach or harangue. They use their bodies—gestures and actions, not words— to teach with humor. They walk around practically naked. They beg for food. They boast about their shameful acts. They mimic those in authority. No doubt about it: sacred clowns make people laugh. To provide relief from despair and trauma is one of their tasks as a liminal figure. But theirs is also *serious play* that invites the community to read *between the lines* of their playful gesturing so they can see the lives of individuals and the community in a different way, question what they are doing or what is happening. By disrupting the order of the everyday and the order of sacred ceremonies, they create an opening, a space that is neither conventional order nor absolute chaos in which people can see the world they've grown so accustomed to, both sacred and profane, anew.

If a sacred clown is not a prophet wielding the power of visions and words, neither is she or he a mediator like priests or saints are sometimes said to be. To bring two alienated parties together, mediators seek to actively reconcile them through deeper bonding or understanding. Sacred clowns *deliberately disrupt* the world, the way thunder and lightning crack a calm sky, in order to bring greater harmony in the community. We often talk about liminal times or spaces opening up when our lives have been disrupted by circumstances like disease or social or political trauma. It is the work of a sacred clown to intentionally disturb the community's life in order to open up a liminal space for healing or transformation. Neither saint nor sinner, a sacred clown playfully transgresses ritual protocols and social mores to restore balance, wholeness, holiness to a community. In this sense they might be seen as holy sinners, though in a far different sense than we usually think of holy sinners in the Western tradition. The ongoing work of these sacred clowns in harmonizing their communities in the present is a far cry from that of once-in-a millennium figures like the antinomians Sabbatai Zevi and Jacob Frank, self-proclaimed messiahs who performed "strange acts" that flouted religious law as a way to bring about redemption, a new age of the spirit, and instead left chaos in their wake.

Save for the near-extinct Christian clown, the examples I've bumped into and reflected upon come from indigenous cultures, in which the sacred permeates all of life and where there is no separate secular realm. And having a designated role or time for overturning a tradition's laws and rituals works only in a cohesive community that follows clear rules for behavior. Which makes me wonder: Is there a role in the spiritual lives of people in non-indigenous communities for such a figure? In communities that are not bonded together by a clearly defined set of shared practices and morals? What would that look like?

We all need to not take ourselves too seriously in our spiritual lives, weighed down as we are by earnestness or carried away by our own piety or enlightenment. The community-wide celebrations of Mardi Gras and Purim provide this playful perspective for Christians and Jews respectively, but only once a year, in attenuated form, and with no designated liminal figure. We cannot appropriate figures such as the *Koshare* or *Heyoka* (or tricksters like Raven for the Haida and other Pacific Northwest tribes, Coyote for the Hopi and other tribes, or High John de Conquer in African-American communities).

But what can we learn from these communities that understand the need for a liminal figure playing a liminal role in creating and recreating harmony in our faith communities? Artists *may* fill this role in faith communities, as they do in the wider world, as Hyde suggests, saying that "it is mostly in the practice of art that I turn to in hopes of finding where this disruptive imagination survives among us."[5] But I'm not convinced. I think we need something more in faith communities, a figure with a unique role. Sacred clowns. Can we find a way to bring holy disruption to our prayer and rituals, laughter to our community tensions? Laughter is essential to the sacred life. And disruption, upset, reversal, and surprise are often the way the sacred invites us to transform. This is the work of a sacred clown, to remind us that disruption of our habitual ways is not to be feared but welcomed; and to invite us to laugh, at our institutions and mores, our traditions and rituals, ourselves, our foibles, our propensity for losing our way in the world, our predicament as liminal beings.

Chapter 6

A Gathering of Different Lights: Invitation to Enter the Between

One year during Lent, I attended a Novena service, part of an ancient tradition of praying for grace for nine successive days, at the Chapel of St. Ignatius on the campus of Seattle University. "But you're a Jew!" a friend said. "Why would you do that?"

"All journeys," says Martin Buber, "have secret destinations of which the traveler is unaware."[1] This proved true for me that day. I thought I knew why I was going to a Catholic service—my intentions were clear—but an unexpected encounter during the Eucharist showed me otherwise.

Intention #1. To hear my longtime friend Victoria deliver the homily. Victoria, a Catholic laywoman with a PhD in systematic theology, has been active in ministry since 1979, serving as a pastoral life director, caring for several congregations over the years. Her velvet revolution tactics include faithfully guiding congregations, delivering homilies, and steadfastly explaining to the authorities and their spies why canon law does not prohibit her from delivering the homily at services. She's a stealth reformer—never screaming, never condemning, just quietly going about the business of her Lord, as a woman. She makes a way out of no way. She's also a person who lives a life of deep prayer and theological reflection. She's one of my heroes, and hearing a homily from her is always soul-stirring and soul-soothing.

Intention #2. To dwell in the beauty of the Chapel of St. Ignatius, where I often go to sit in silence. The chapel was designed by architect Steven Holl as "A Gathering of Different Lights." Vessels of light, windows of solid color fields—white, green, red, yellow, blue, orange, and purple—create an ever-changing kaleidoscope as the sun moves across the sky, as if God were saying, "This too is beautiful. And this." Standing to the right of the altar, on the same level as the congregation, is a larger-than-life Carrera marble sculpture of Mary created by Steven

Heilmer called *Gratia Plena*, Full of Grace. From a golden bowl
held over her head, milk cascades down to her feet. A mother
nourishing her children, abundantly. Above the altar, a corpus
from the Austrian Alps hangs on a newly-carved cross of Alaskan
cedar, stark suffering on a tree of life. It's easy to pray in this place
of constantly moving light and darkness, consolation and
desolation.

Intention #3. To pray. I *daven* (pray) at home in the
morning, and with other Jews in synagogues, at Shabbat and
holiday dinners, and at *shiva minyans* in houses of mourning. But
there are times when I need a different kind of prayer, prayer
without words, a cry of the heart, and often that comes more
easily when I am hidden in a sea of strangers.

With these intentions I walked to the chapel at the
appointed hour. The pews were overflowing, but I squeezed into
the last row on the left. I chose a back seat to respect the Christians
who were there "legitimately" and to respect the boundary of my
faith. As a person of faith, I was not a spectator, true, but I could
not be a full participant either. Some Jews won't step foot inside a
church, for religious and historical reasons. I honor that decision,
but as a Calvinist-turned-Jew who once taught in a Christian
seminary and preached in Christian churches, I enter churches
more as a fellow traveler than an outsider. For me, churches are
both home and the house of a stranger.

Victoria's homily was moving, but all memory of it was
eclipsed by what happened next. After a priest consecrated the
bread and the wine for the Eucharist, two priests and Victoria
stationed themselves before the congregation to offer the host and
the cup to all who came forward. As everyone shifted in their
seats, preparing to file out of their pews and line up to receive the
body and blood, I settled into my seat. I was content to be present
without partaking, to appreciate their sacred ritual without
desiring it for myself, to engage in parallel play of faiths—I would
pray while they prayed, each of us according to our lights. But
then, after one of the priests had issued the invitation for all to
come and receive the body and blood, he added words I had
never heard before, in any church or gathering. "All are

welcome," he said. "If you wish to come to receive a blessing from one of us, instead of the Eucharist, place your hand over your heart when you approach."

These words pierced my heart. I, too, could participate in this sacred ritual? As myself, as a Jew? Without subterfuge? With integrity—mine and theirs? I was welcome, as I was. There was no theological or moral need to keep my distance from this community intentionally praying to receive special grace. I could be apart and yet a part, *distincto non divise* as the Chalcedonian formula has it: distinct but not divided. A way had been prepared for me to participate, a space between had been opened for me to enter, a liminal space.

Perhaps, as Victoria told me later, this was old ritual hat for her and her people, but for me it was a shock. A brilliant shock. Yes, I knew immediately, I wanted, I needed to be blessed, and by a woman, *this* woman, a friend who knew and loved me, a friend I knew and loved, a friend with whom I had shared consolations and desolations, a person whose devotion to God anchored her life. I stood up and joined the line snaking toward Victoria, who was standing near Mary Overflowing with Milk. As I approached her, I placed my hand over my heart, then stood, trembling, as she smiled and blessed me. With what words? I do not remember. I do not need to. For as she spoke, her eyes meeting mine, my heart spilled over with tears of sorrow, tears of gratitude, tears of joy. What the language of words would hide, the poet Hayim Bialik writes, may yet be revealed, for "'there are yet to the Lord' languages without words: song, tears, and laughter," languages that "rise up from the void."[2]

A gathering of different lights. A gesture of welcome. An act of grace. An invitation to meeting, to presence. Here in such living moments, moments of surprise that outstrip our intentions, is the heart of interfaith or multifaith, words far too abstract and tepid to evoke the simple fact of people traveling different paths toward the One encountering one another along the way. "The You encounters me by grace," Buber says in *I and Thou*, "it cannot be found by seeking." We can, though, and must "go forth" toward grace and await its presence, each of us in our way. Our

paths are the radii of a circle, all intersecting the One. "Extended,"
Buber says, "the lines of relationships intersect in the eternal
You."[3] The way the colored rays of light in the Chapel of St.
Ignatius, extended, intersect in the sun.

   Rabbis, ministers, priests, and imams convening to discuss
their traditions' rituals and ideas can be helpful. Communities and
individuals inviting others to share in Passover, Christmas, or Eid
celebrations is lovely. But we need more. We need to make room
in our traditions for others without sacrificing our identity or
disrespecting theirs. We need to make room in our practice for
others to be fully present, not as spectators, not as honorary
members, but as fellow travelers who are welcome. As the
gathered St. Ignatius community did that day by welcoming all to
receive blessing, each in our own way. Simple. Profound. A
gathering of different lights. Full of grace.

Chapter 7

Feeding the Spirit: Dwelling in the Space Between Religious Traditions

Ritual is breath to me, breath and water, food and fire, home and wonder. The way humans move their bodies together in time—in intentional sequences of actions, to sanctify time and space and nourish the spirit—defines my way of being in the world. Growing up in an immigrant Evangelical community, I was formed, marrow and bone, by communal and individual sacred rituals, and I developed a need for the self-transcending power of shared gesturing toward the sacred that has persisted through decades of change. Now, as a Jew, I live in a quite different world, but one that is also rich in sacred rituals, ancient and modern, shared and creatively adapted across centuries and cultures—repeated practices that hallow the everyday world.

Though sacred ritual is often neglected or devalued today, the power of ritual to invoke presence, deepen meaning, strengthen bonds, and sustain individuals, families, communities, and peoples seems to me a wonderous thing, as does the variety of rituals people perform. My first taste of difference came at age seven when I spied on the Irish Catholic family that lived next door, the only non-Dutch Calvinists I knew in our community. They didn't read the Bible and pray at the table after dinner as we did; they prayed with beads and crossed themselves before images hung on walls. We lit candles only on Christmas Eve and birthdays; a candle burned on their kitchen counter most weekdays. They rode their bikes on Sundays; we weren't allowed to. These differences captivated me, seeding a lifelong curiosity about religious and spiritual practices other than my own.

Despite this need for ritual in my life, my awe at its power, and my deep and abiding wonder at the varieties of religious experience and the creativity of ritual, when presented with an opportunity to participate in a ritual of another's tradition or community, I'm often bewildered. I fumble around, flummoxed, not knowing what to do. Step aside? Stand back? Stick a toe in? Jump in? Dive deep and start swimming? I'm also hindered, I must confess, by a lingering fear born of shame. Will I be caught out as one who doesn't belong and be shamed or thrown out, the way I saw those who broke the church's rules barred from Communion, publicly humiliated, or excommunicated when I was growing up? Will I do it wrong? Will I embarrass myself? Will I offend someone?

Like many of my generation, born in the Western world during or just after WWII, I was never schooled in the sacred art of navigating the boundaries of religious communities and practices. Our world was one of absolutes and certainties we were born into, not competing religious claims among which we could choose. The rituals of my childhood and adolescence, such as The Lord's Supper and Baptism, were firmly closed to outsiders, even other Protestants, and we insiders were strictly forbidden to participate in the rituals of others. Participating in a Catholic mass or a Quaker meeting, or even attending a service in a Catholic or Pentecostal church, was dangerous: It put one's standing in the community and one's eternal salvation at risk. There was no need to question whether one would participate or not, no room to reflect on how one might participate.

But now that we find ourselves in a world offering more and more opportunities to encounter religious and spiritual practices unfamiliar to us, reflecting on how to navigate the boundaries of ritual has become necessary, even urgent. We need to ask how we as individuals might participate in unfamiliar sacred settings, and how communities draw the lines of participation for those who belong and those who do not. When we don't pause to ask these questions, we risk overstepping boundaries—or holding back, and missing opportunities to deepen our experience. I felt this urgency most recently as I fumbled my way through two Buddhist rituals in Laos.

I went to Louangphrabang as many do, hoping to feed my spirit. It is a holy city. Founded 1,200 years ago, it rests in a valley at the foot of a mountain range spanning northwest Laos and northern Thailand, where the Mekong and Nam Khan rivers meet, a narrow finger of land formed by a sacred confluence, blessing flowing on three sides. In 1359 C.E., to help spread Theraveda Buddhism, the Khmer king gave the ruler of the northern Lao kingdom a 32-inch bronze and gold leaf Buddha standing with his palms facing outward, making the mudra, or sign, of dispelling fear. This image, the Phra Bang, known as Delicate Buddha or Buddha Image, resides on the grounds of the royal palace in Louangphrabang and gives the city its name: Royal Buddha Image. More than 30 *wats*, temples or monasteries, both old and new, small and large, humble and gilded, anchor the city's streets. One, Wat Chomsi, sits atop a sacred hill, Mount Phou Si, overlooking the rivers embracing the city and the mountains cradling the valley. The monks who live in the wats hang out their saffron laundry for all to see, and chant with giant drums and gongs in open pavilions for all to hear. Every morning at dawn hundreds of them form a line at one end of the peninsula's main street, Sisavangvong Road, and walk single file up one side of the street and down the other, processing along sidewalks crammed with tourists and locals waiting to drop food into their begging bowls.

By chance, I arrived in Louangphrabang in October during Boun Lai Heua Fai, the annual Festival of Light or Fire Boat Festival that marks the end of Vassa, a three-month retreat, and monsoon season. Colorful bamboo and waxed-paper boats, some more than 50 feet long, were displayed on the sidewalk outside every *wat* and shop in town. Each creation was more enchanting than the last, all carrying cargo of delicately fashioned temples, stupas, thrones, dharma wheels, stars, lanterns, flags, bodhi trees, and lotuses. The larger boats were shaped like phoenixes, dragons, fish, and *nagas*, the serpent-like creatures some believe live in the depths of the Mekong, once named Nam Nyai Ngu Luang, Great River of the Giant Serpent. These dry-docked boats were waiting for the evening of the full moon, when their candles and lanterns would be set alight and families and groups from the city and its 58 surrounding villages, many in their tribal dress, as varied and colorful as the floats, would parade them, drumming and singing, from Wat Mai, down Sisavangvong Road, to the tip of the peninsula. There they would wait in the courtyard of the largest *wat*, Wat Xieng Thong, for their turn to descend the steps to the Mekong carrying their boat on their shoulders, lower it into the water, guide it to the strong current, and release it, burning, down the river.

The night of the launching, after watching the glowing boats glide down the temple steps, I walked along the bank of the Mekong among the partying crowds, enthralled by the burning boats trailing fire through black water as fireworks colored the moonlit sky. The mood was ecstatic. The almost unbearable beauty of a chain of vessels carried along by a flowing river, being consumed by flames as they traveled, seemed to lift everyone's spirits. It was a vision of life, in all its glorious and heart-rending ephemerality, a wonder so arresting I had to keep stopping to still my heart as I followed the procession down the river. It was a vision of the gorgeous mystery of our existence, the holy, the *mysterium tremendum et fascinans* of Rudolf Otto. Many of the smaller boats were quickly devoured by fire, or they sputtered into dark skeletons that drifted toward shore. The large boats glowed as they sailed, moving slowly, gracefully, turning this direction and that on their journey, or heading straight down the middle, all moving farther and farther from the place they began.

At the far end of Sisavangvong Road, I followed a group of revelers down the bank to a floating dock, where, one by one, people were releasing circular platforms of banana leaves decorated with flowers, betel nuts, incense, and a lighted candle, pushing them out as far as they could toward the middle of the river so the current would carry them, burning with hope and promise, as far down the river of blessing, The Mother of All Things, as possible before returning them to shore. I was holding my own float, crowned with saffron marigolds, given to me by my guesthouse host. Earlier that day, I had asked several people about the meaning of the ritual. Like most traditional rituals, it opened to diverse meanings. "It's an offering to the *nagas*, the spirits of the river," my host explained. "Some older people still make this offering daily, bringing fruit, leaves, flowers, rice, *lao* [whisky distilled from sticky rice]." "It's a prayer for the new year," a woman said, "to send bad luck away from one and bring good luck to one." Two teenagers told me, "You make a wish for the new year, and hope for the best."

The silence of the scene—no cheering or reveling here—and the care with which each person approached the river and released their vessel pulled me forward. Fear of intruding upon or violating the sacred space of another, a familiar hesitancy, held me back. This time, I did not let it stop me. I lit my candle and joined the line. When my turn came, I stepped onto the dock, submerged with the weight of too many bodies, splashed to the end, bent down, and let my offering go. It felt like the ritual of *tashlich* on Rosh Hashanah, when we Jews cast bread upon living water as a sign of casting off our sins of the past year and recommitting ourselves to living lives of justice and lovingkindness in the new year. What good fortune, I thought, to witness such a celebration of light and renewal, and to take part in it, in my own way, alongside so many others, all of us engaging in parallel play of the spirit. Watching the river push my float back to shore, where it joined many others caught in the mud and trash, most with their light extinguished, troubled me only a moment, before a still, joyful gratitude returned.

The next morning, I got up early to walk back to Sisavangvong Road to witness the feeding of the monks. Still floating on the unexpected joy of the drama of the lights and ritual of release, and, eager for more, I sat down in the first empty place I saw, across from the post office, near Wat Mai, where the parade had begun the evening before and where monks began their procession. I didn't want to miss a moment of this experience. Before I could settle, a woman thrust a shallow basket of rice and several small, individually wrapped candy bars and other commercial sugary snacks to me, gesturing how much it cost. Confused and surprised at the amount, I shook my head no, but she set the basket at my feet and insisted. *Okay*, I thought, *fair enough, the price of admission. She needs to earn a living. I don't want to be an ugly tourist.* I paid her.

As the monks passed me, striding with firm intent more than solemnly processing, I scrambled to put a rice ball or candy bar in each monk's bowl or sack. In seconds my basket was empty. Immediately the woman swept away the empty basket and set a full one at my feet, asking the same price. I paid her. I was so busy keeping up with filling the monks' sacks and paying her that I barely saw the monks. Were most old, young? Well fed, malnourished? Solemn, serene? Were they blessing people as they passed? To me, spinning like a Tasmanian devil caught in a capitalist nightmare, they were an orange blur. When the vendor set a fifth basket before me, I stood up and walked away.

Frustrated, I walked the length of Sisavangvong Road, following the route of the fire boat procession, toward Wat Xieng Thong, where the boats had been launched. As I approached the *wat*, I noticed fewer tourists and more local women lining the road. The women sat on chairs or stools, huge pots of home-cooked rice standing beside them. As each monk passed, the woman would place a small ball of rice in his sack, lowering her head in reverence. The monks bowed in return, in gratitude and blessing. Several monks had their own ritual with the women. As a woman dropped rice balls into a monk's sack, he dropped into her waiting basket a few of the sugary snacks they had collected from tourists. They were emptying their begging bowls of junk food to make room to receive more rice as they continued down the other side of the road, completing the ritual circle of feeding. What the women did with the snacks, I don't know. Give them to their children? Give or sell them to the women selling food baskets to tourists by the post office? Eat one or two? But whatever the outcome, their wordless trading stayed with me, a rich, compassionate exchange between monastic life and lay life, communal life and individual lives, women and men, rice and gratitude, reverence and blessing, need and nourishment, matter and spirit. It seemed as great a wonder as boats flaming down the river of life.

After the monks had completed their circuit and the crowd began dispersing, I ran into two Canadian travelers I had trekked with a week before in the mountainous jungle north of Louangphrabang, near Nong Kiaw. They had been provided with balls of rice by their guesthouse and had enjoyed feeding the monks. "There's a stand near Wat Xieng Thong that sells rice," they told me. "You could have bought some there. Better luck next time." For a moment I felt dejected, wishing I had come prepared with rice, as they had, instead of blundering in, so eager to be experience an exotic event, I had almost missed that beautiful ordinary moment between the women and the monks; so eager to have a rare "spiritual" experience, I had almost missed being present to the spirit of this exchange. Would it have been better, I wondered, to have participated as my fellow trekkers had? Was theirs the "right way" for non-Buddhists? But if I had done as they did, sat where they sat, I might have missed the exchange between the women and the monks. What then? Should I have stood by and observed the action rather than taking part in it? How, I wondered, does one participate in the rituals of others without becoming a spiritual tourist or falling into spiritual consumerism?

Spiritual tourism or consumerism, what might be called terminal spiritualism, in which spiritual practices are no longer cultivated as a means for discovering and realizing meaningful goals but pursued as ends in themselves, has been one of my biggest worries in life—perhaps because I have experienced and witnessed that the spiritual life in its many life-giving forms can be an inestimable treasure and I do not like to see it devalued in any way. I worry that in our search for meaningful experiences, as we seek out new traditions and practices to find what may fit, our longing may lead us astray. Eager to feed our spirits, we're tempted to devour spiritual experiences rather than enjoy them. Instead of cultivating wonder at the diversity and beauty of the world and deepening our experience of it, we may act, unintentionally, as if every experience is ours for the taking. We may even pursue and amass exotic spiritual experiences the way we pursue and amass designer goods and status symbols. Urged on by good intentions (*Truth is universal, All paths lead to the One*), we may rush in, seize upon, and appropriate practices that appeal to us in others' traditions, without stopping to wonder at their beauty, their wisdom, their glorious difference; without asking, What does this ritual mean to this community? How does it feed their spirits? What can it mean for me? How can it mean for me? Can I participate in this ritual with respect and depth and enjoyment? How?

The questions raised by my experiences of sending a fire offering down the Mekong and feeding the monks in Louangphrabang are ones I've been living for years. But only after fumbling my way as a non-Buddhist through these two Buddhist rituals back-to-back did I begin to wonder in earnest how to walk in beauty in a world blooming with so many colors of the spirit. How could we think about ritual, communities, individual identities, and boundaries so that we could learn to participate more gracefully and graciously? For me, the path led from an impoverished notion of participation to one that embraces and encourages discernment and diversity.

Participation is not a binary concept. Most communities are not hermetically sealed; they're porous. The question is not, To participate or not? Are you inside or out? The question is, How does one participate respectfully and meaningfully in a ritual belonging to and observed by another? Not asking these questions leads to misunderstandings, disrespect, hurt feelings, violation.

When I was a lay leader in a small synagogue in the South, a non-Jew visited our Shabbat services for several weeks, each time charging onto the bimah, insisting he open the ark with the Torah scrolls. I explained to him each time that this was an action only members of our community could perform, and he, a Christian, one actively proselytizing us in our lobby each week, arguing that we didn't understand the prophesied true Messiah, was welcome to join us in prayer from the pews, but not to participate in opening the ark. Rejection clouded his face. He argued. Got angry. Left. I knew some of what he felt. Before I converted to Judaism, during Shabbat services one morning, I wore a large traditional *tallit* I had just purchased, excited to pray in it. Afterward, the rabbi complimented the beauty of my *tallit*, acknowledged my intention, studies, and observance of the commandments, and gently told me to wait to wear it until after I had lived longer as a Jew and formally joined the community. After the shame and rejection wore off, I saw how my enthusiasm, my need to belong, my failure to think communally instead of individually, my presumption had led me to crash the boundary of this community I had grown to love. I am still grateful to this rabbi for his kindness in teaching me respect for a community's boundaries, patience, and humility, and for showing me that there are many ways to participate in and be present to another's rituals, including being a spiritual "participant observer."

"Participant observation" is the research technique used by anthropologists and sociologists in which a researcher is accepted into a culture or community that is not theirs to deepen their understanding of that community's structures, relationships, and values. Participant observers are not objective observers who stand outside the community. Neither are they subjective observers, standing inside as members of the community. They are in but not of the community or culture they are studying, with both sides of the relationship, the researcher and the community, committed to the health of that relationship. This approach was popularized by Bronisław Malinowski, Margaret Mead, Franz Boas, Zora Neale Hurston, and others in the last century, and though it has undergone criticism and revision, it is still in use. Today, five ways of being a participant observer are recognized: non-participation, passive participation, moderate participation, active participation, and complete participation. Each can be an appropriate and meaningful choice for someone contemplating participating in a ritual or tradition that is not theirs. Each is a way to give oneself time and space to pay attention to the world in the way they choose.

One can choose not to participate in a ritual, that is, not to be present during a ritual. Many people today make the choice not to attend or to walk away from a ritual, for many different reasons—because they had no religious upbringing and have no desire to engage in religious practices of any kind; because, though born into a religious community, they have chosen to leave all religious practice behind, finding ritual practices irrelevant, empty, hypocritical, restrictive, oppressive, or abusive; because, as members of a specific religious tradition they have decided or agreed not to participate in the practices of other traditions; or because, despite being curious, they may be put off by what they consider the distastefulness, violence, immorality, or danger of a practice, such as speaking in tongues, exorcism, or snake handling. Though eager to discover and embrace the variety of contemporary women's spirituality, I have chosen not to participate in certain feminist Goddess rituals, and I have walked away from a healing and empowering ceremony led by witches and warlocks. Though clearly meaningful to others, these were not traditions and practices I felt I could participate in wholeheartedly, even passively, as an observer.

Choosing to be a passive participant, a bystander witnessing a ritual, is a choice I have made many times in my life. This is how, decades ago, I participated in a Catholic charismatic prayer meeting where people spoke in tongues, in a blood-drenched sacrifice to the Hindu Goddess Kali in a valley in the mountains of Nepal, in the worship of the *Kumari Devi*, the living goddess Durga, in Kathmandu, and in the celebration of Kwanzaa in the Lowcountry of South Carolina. I could have chosen to participate this way during the feeding of the monks in Louangphrabang, too, as many tourists do. By standing to the side and paying attention to what was happening from the very beginning, I might have seen and understood much more about what it means for lay people to feed Buddhist monks. That distance might have given me room to absorb different aspects of the experience than I did and reflect on them. But I also might have missed the interaction with the vendors and the reverence passing between the monks and women.

Many other times in my life I have chosen to be a moderate participant observer. As a moderate participant, one takes part in a ritual, but behind a clear boundary set by the community, neither fully outside nor fully inside, between. I experienced this when attending a private weeklong Sundance on Rosebud Reservation in the 1980s. Non-Native Americans were welcome to participate, not by entering the sacred circle, but by standing inside the arbor surrounding the circle, and moving and praying in support of the dancers inside the inner circle. This wise welcome-stand-there-and-not-here is what my rabbi reminded me of when he welcomed me to pray among the congregation in the pews but requested I not wear a *tallit* or ascend the bimah and offer a blessing before the ark before I had become a Jew. This is perhaps how the two Canadian travelers had fed the monks. They had been invited, by the town, the monks, and the host of their guesthouse. They had come prepared with the appropriate food. And they sat among other tourists, not among the women near the wat. This, I hope, is the way I participated in the Fire Boat Festival. I had been invited. I did not join the parade or touch a boat. I stood behind the people crowding the wat steps. I waited until the line diminished to set my float in the Mekong. I did not assume I understood what they were doing, and I entered out of my experience, reaching toward theirs.

Yet another way to experience a ritual is to choose to be an active participant in another's tradition, or a "fellow traveler" to use Harvey Cox's lovely words. In *The Future of Faith*, Cox writes that once he "realized that Christianity is not a creed and that faith is more a matter of embodiment than of axioms," a way of life built on trust more than a set of beliefs, he "began to look at people I met in a new way." He realized, as a Christian, he had "an unusual opportunity to participate as a 'fellow traveler' in the liturgies and holidays" of his Jewish wife's traditions.[1] Not a Jew, he would not, for example, ascend the *bimah* and open the ark. He would not be the one to make *kiddush*, sanctify the wine, on Shabbat evening or lead the Passover Seder, but he could pray and sing and dance and eat and converse with the community. A fellow traveler inhabits a closer *between* than a moderate participant, walks a concentric circle closer to the heart of a community, but a clear and transparent boundary remains. Inhabiting that *between* space, so close yet not completely inside, enables one to pay attention in yet another way, to both sides of the encounter. As Cox says, being a fellow traveler enabled him to

learn things he "had never known about [his wife's] faith" and
things he "had never realized about his own."

   The year I studied Jewish traditions and lived in and with
a Jewish community, I was a fellow traveler. I could have
remained a fellow traveler. Instead, after much prayer and
reflection, I chose to become a "complete participant," a full
member of the community: I converted. Complete participation is
a choice for those who convert to or otherwise join a new
community and those who are born into religious or spiritual
communities. As the sociologist Peter L. Berger argues in *The
Heretical Imperative: Contemporary Possibilities of Religious
Affirmation*, we're all heretics today, for the Greek word *herein*
means "to choose."[2] After the Enlightenment, religion can no
longer be taken for granted as an inheritance. We must all choose
if we will or will not be people of faith, how we will participate in
the traditions and rituals of our own chosen faith, and how we
will participate in the faith practices of others.

   Each of these ways to participate in the rituals and
spiritual traditions of others can deepen our understanding of
another's faith, traditions, and rituals and give rise to meaningful
experiences. Each one can be a respectful choice. The point is to
choose, after discerning which kind of participation the
circumstances and one's own identity and commitments call for
and allow. Not by rushing headlong in a race to consume new
information or amass new experiences to feed our insatiable
spiritual egos; not by giving in to feelings of rejection or exclusion
when we are welcomed and asked to stand there and not here; not
by insisting on a universalism in which all rituals and traditions
are homogenized or distilled to a bland essence palatable to all, in
which their life-forming, life-giving taste is stripped away. But by
taking the time to discern—in patience, humility, respect, and
humor—how to participate, in this ritual, at this moment. Not by
eschewing all spiritual practice or by being gluttons of the spirit,
but by choosing when, how, and with what we will feed our
spirits. By nourishing our spirits with wonder at the myriad
creative ways human beings gesture toward the sacred. And by
having compassion on our bewildered selves, bumbling our way

through a world blooming and buzzing with opportunities to experience the sacred, fumbling toward love and stumbling toward light.

Built Ritual Environments

Chapter 8

Ever Becoming—Never Being: Dwelling in the *Sukkah**

Ufros aleinu sukkat shlomecha.
> Spread over us the shelter of your peace.

This poetic line anchors one of the Jewish evening prayers. It comes after the *Sh'ma*, the prayer affirming the oneness of God, in the middle of a blessing that begins "Help us, Our God, to lie down in peace, and raise us up, Our King, to life," and ends with "You guard us and deliver us." A blessing that acknowledges that when we sleep, we exist in a liminal state, somewhere between waking life and death.   A place where our spirits wander, untethered from everyday physical and mental awareness, habits, and images. A time when we are vulnerable, in need of shelter. Recited after sundown, in a darkening world, on the cusp of surrendering control, it is a prayer to calm anxious hearts.

In our waking lives, too, we are wandering, we are vulnerable, in need of shelter. For we are liminal creatures, neither necessary nor impossible. We exist, but contingently. We did not come into being by necessity, and we will cease being—at least in the form we are now.

> *Our days are like grass; like wildflowers, we bloom and die.*[1]

We are sojourning here, wandering in a world we seem ill-equipped to inhabit yet continually labor to make our home. Frail creatures, highly susceptible to onslaughts of weather, climate, human beings and other animals, disease, accidents, chance, injury and death by countless means, we become anxious. To protect ourselves, guard and deliver ourselves, we hammer out armor or

---

*The white spaces in this essay evoke the openings in the roof of the *sukkah*.

grow carapaces—thick, heavy, rigid, impermeable—and climb inside. Faith. Fantasies. Theologies. Ideologies.   Habits. Goals.   Destinations.
Personae. Relationships. Communities. Houses. All shelters to prevent exposure, guard against threats, woundings, dying. Shelters we depend on to live and thrive. Shelters we shut ourselves inside, closed off from the world. Shelters we turn into prisons and lock ourselves inside. Narrow places. Structures that hold us tight, comfort us, keep us from remembering we are wandering   in a wilderness, beset by dangers, realizing how unstable our lives, how precarious our existence.

During the holiday of *Sukkot*, the Feast of Booths or Festival of Tabernacles, Jews are commanded to dwell in *sukkot* (plural of *sukkah*) or temporary huts for seven says (in Israel) or eight days (in the diaspora) every fall, starting the fifteenth of Tishri.[2] Eating, sleeping, praying, studying, and socializing in the sukkah is a way to reenact the forty years the Hebrews wandered, in the wilderness, between *Mitzrayim* and *Yisrael*, The Narrow Place   and the Promised Land, between slavery and freedom, neither here nor there, a place they did not know, where they were exposed to dangers, in the environment and in themselves, they had never encountered   before—ineluctably,   inescapably,   irredeemably vulnerable.

The translations of *sukkah*—booth, tabernacle, wilderness shelter, thatched hut, canopy, tent, temporary dwelling—do not capture the experience of dwelling in this short-lived, porous structure. The name *sukkah* derives from s'*chach*, the word for the roof material, which must be vegetation, organic material, that has been separated from the ground, like palm fronds, pine boughs, wisteria vines, reeds, or bamboo stalks.   The s'*chach* must be arranged so that there is more shade than light and one can see the sun, moon, and stars when looking up.

The roof does not represent a limit, but rather an invitation to go beyond.
One must go beyond oneself.[3]

In a poetics of space, it is not only the roof of the *sukkah* that extends an invitation. The *sukkah* has three walls, which means it is open on one side, with no door to close or lock. It is open not only to the changing weather and atmosphere—rain and hail, sleet and snow, heat and humidity—but also to guests, both invited and uninvited: squirrels, racoons, birds, and insects who feed on the harvest fruits and vegetables that decorate the sukkah; friends, family, and *ushpizin* or spirits of the ancestors who are welcomed as "exalted guests"; angels, curious strangers,   or any being who wanders by. A *sukkah* opens to all being, is welcoming of whatever may come—like Abraham and Sarah's tent, a testament to hospitality, an invitation to others.

The manner of living on earth, just like that of living in space or the body, reveals as much about the spirit of a man   as it does his ideas of behavior.[4]

To dwell in a *sukkah* is to go beyond oneself, to open to the world, to others, to risk vulnerability, embrace uncertainty. "A house," the phenomenologist Gaston Bachelard writes in *The Poetics of Space*, "constitutes a body of images that give mankind proofs or illusions of stability."   The house is a refuge, with "powers of protection against the forces that besiege it." The house acquires the physical and moral energy of a human body and becomes "an instrument with which to confront the cosmos."[5] When we leave our house to dwell in a *sukkah*, we shatter our illusions of shelter, refuge, protection, and stability; we risk opening, openness, hospitality, connection, and instability.   Bachelard quotes Phillip Diolé, the psychologist and "ontologist of underseas human life," who, after diving deep in the sea, explored deserts, reflecting that, "When we change landscapes, we don't just change our position, our place, we change our psyche."[6] Our bodies orient us in the world, establish our attitude, ready us for action. The spaces we dwell teach our bodies, ourselves, how to live. They transform us, body, mind, and spirit.

A *sukkah* is an anti-house, an anti-refuge, an anti-shelter.

When we dwell in a *sukkah*, we emerge from our carapace, we step out of our armor, to experience being as becoming, in all its frailness, instability, vulnerability. "Ever becoming, never being" was the motto of Joseph Conrad, that lover of the sea, a body of water in constant motion, an eternal mystery. This is why the holiday of Sukkot is also called *The Season of Our Joy*—not only because it celebrates the movement from slavery to freedom during the Exodus, and the fruits of the harvest,   but because it invites us to open ourselves to what is not us, to what is and to what is not yet, to break free from our hardened way of being, from our stance of confrontation, and greet the cosmos, greet living, with open arms and to set aside comfort and safety to experience the joy of living as ever becoming, never being.

[*The sukkah*] *pays respect to living, and living precariously.*[7]

A sukkah is not meant to last. It must be built anew each year, with *s'chach* that has been freshly separated from the earth, still green with life, yet dying. A *sukkah* embodies impermanence, celebrates it. It is an invitation to openness, to connection, to becoming. It is an antidote to our natural drift toward closing ourselves off. It guards against the calcification of our being.

I take refuge in You from myself. There is no
shelter or safehold from You but in You.[8]

What gives one the courage to leave the sturdy shelters we erect for ourselves and dwell in a *sukkah*? Radical trust in the Oneness of being and loyalty to the Beloved Community in which all are "free, free at last," in the words of Martin Luther King. Faith, some call it. "Innumerable are the ills which beset human life and present death in as many different forms," writes John Calvin, before cataloguing diseases, heat and cold, familiar objects, sharp tools, drowning, falling from a horse, roofs caving in, savage beasts, snakes in high-walled gardens of delight, houses burning down, fields subject to hail, mildew, drought, and other injuries; poison, treachery, and robbery at home and abroad.   "Amid these perils," he concludes, "must not man be very miserable, as one who, more dead than alive, with difficulty draws an anxious and feeble breath, just as if a drawn sword were constantly suspended over his neck?" What is the cure for this fear and anxiety caused by living under the dominion of chance?   Trust in divine providence. "He shall cover thee with his feathers, and under his wings shalt thou trust."[9]

> *The [true] place of every creature is [total] incapacity,*
> *standing in true humility before the door of Exalted Glory,*
> *without any ability to grasp this Treasure.*[10]

Dwelling in a sukkah, we become sojourners, we humbly embrace being on the way. We remember how fleeting and frail our existence is—as individuals, as peoples, as species—and gather the gifts of our lives, harvest our joys, celebrate life impermanent, life abundant. We eat, sleep, pray, study, and socialize in porous structures with no hard limits, no unyielding foundation, no impermeable boundary between outside and inside, in a space that is neither house nor wilderness, a space between,   a liminal space where we leave behind our old ways, old habits, old haunts and open to the world, to others, go beyond ourselves in radical trust and experience that wholeness of being that is ever becoming, shalom. We discover the joy in being ever becoming, always on the way.

> *To find God means to find the way without end.*[11]

The *sukkah* of shalom, of ever journeying toward the One, toward wholeness, is open to all—Jews, Christians, Muslims, Hindus, Buddhists, Sikhs, Jains, Baha'is, Sufis, atheists, agnostics, everyone, whichever community one belongs to, however one identifies oneself. All we have to do is step inside. When the season between burgeoning life and impending death comes around each year; whenever it is autumn in our hearts;   when our days are troubled and our hearts lost in a wilderness of fear and anxiety, threatened on all sides; when we're in danger of hardening our being, closing against the world, let us answer the call to create a *sukkah*—whether literal or metaphorical—and dwell within it, to live under the *sukkah* of shalom, a peace in which fear and anxiety retreat, a wholeness, a Oneness, that invites us to go beyond ourselves, that opens us to the other, to the joy of living precariously in a world we share with others, all of us ever becoming.

Ufros aleinu sukkat shlomecha.
                                    Spread over us the *sukkah* of your shalom.

Chapter 9

By the River of 1000 *Lingas*

> *In the same river we both step and do not step, we are*
> *and are not.*
> —Heraclitus[1]

Living in a secular age, on earth carved up into sovereign nations, we're in the habit of thinking of rivers as dividing. Rivers lie *between*. Rivers *cut through* the dry land and separate the two banks, which do not touch. Rivers serve as natural or physical boundaries or dividing lines between peoples and countries. Twenty-three percent of the world's internal boundaries and seventeen percent of its state and province boundaries are defined by rivers. In Western minds, the mythic River Styx is seen as dividing as well. It separates the living from the dead with a sobering finality; once you cross over there is no turning back. Seen horizontally in this way, from a perspective of a fragmented and flattened earth, the cosmos stripped of its sacred dimension, rivers divide. But seen vertically, or in depth, with an eye to the sacred dimension of life and the unity of the cosmos, rivers unite. They join heaven and earth. According to one Hindu myth, the god Vishnu opened a hole in the firmament of heaven and released from his lotus feet a stream called the Vishnupadi, which flowed across the Milky Way to the moon and then into the Ganges.

I experienced this sacred unifying power of rivers on a side trip from the Angkor Wat temple complex in Siem Reap, Cambodia, to what is widely known as the River of a Thousand *Lingas*, though the remote site's formal name is Kbal Spean, or Bridge Head. In spite of its provocative name, not many people make the trek to this river whose banks and bed are carved with images sacred to Hindus. The site is not easily accessible, an hour's tuk-tuk ride outside Siem Reap, up in the Kulen Hills, at the end of a mile-long hike through jungle. And it's not nearly as grand as the temples that dominate the landscape in the valley below, rising from the earth like behemoths, declaring the transcendence of human beings over "nature," the triumph of spirit over matter. But it was exactly this modest, overlooked character of the site that made it impossible for me to resist visiting it, as well as its promise of a mingling of nature and spirit, a living, lifegiving correspondence between human beings and the earth.

I was not disappointed.

Starting at a waterfall splashing beside the trail, the ancient carvings come into view. The river's sandstone banks reveal sculpted images of the gods Shiva and Uma, Vishnu and Lakshmi, Brahma resting on a lotus, Rama and Hanuman, the bull Nandi, and the serpent Ananta-Shesha. Carved into the river's bed are thousands of *lingas*, cylindrical pillars representing Shiva as absolute reality, formless and timeless, but which are more often taken to be symbols of the phallus or generative power of Shiva. These *lingas*—all worn down to a nub—are artfully joined with *yonis*, horizontal, lipped discs representing the goddess Shakti, and commonly understood as her womb or as the gateway of all birth.

Hardly among the earth's most impressive or even Southeast Asia's longest rivers (that honor belongs to the Mekong River at 2,703 miles), The River of a Thousand *Lingas* is a short, narrow, shallow portion of one of Cambodia's many smaller rivers, the Strung Sreng. Yet as I meandered along those 492 feet of a river no bigger than a stream, traveling uphill and down, crossing from bank to bank wherever possible, watching and listening to the water rushing, eddying, flowing, and falling over scenes of creation, gods and goddesses, and the life-giving powers of male and female, at once revealing and concealing startlingly beautiful works of art, I was overcome by the vital spiritual force of this humble river. That force I can describe only as oneness, a witness to and affirmation of the unity of the cosmos, an intentional, unceasing bringing together of aspects of reality that may appear separate or far apart: female and male, human beings and gods, heaven and earth, human beings and the earth. If what can be seen in Cambodia's magnificent temples is the power of human beings to assert themselves, proclaim their unique place in the world, this river bore witness to a different power, the power of human beings to reunite, to rebind, re-*ligio*, what seems divided in the cosmos, and so invoke harmony. As Heraclitus, that student of rivers, said, "That which is in opposition is in concert, and from things that differ comes the most beautiful harmony."[2]

What I knew of the history of this stirring site contributed to this sense of the power of religion to bring together or rebind differing aspects of existence for the good of all. The sculptures of the gods and goddesses are said to date from the ninth century C.E. Some speculate that they were added to sanctify the water flowing from The River of the Sky or the Milky Way, where Vishnu and Lakhsmi lie on Ananta-Shesha, King of All *Nagas*, down to the valley to bless and fructify it. The *lingas* and *yonis* are said to have been carved by hermits between the eleventh and twelfth centuries C.E., to create a path of power for the Khmer kings. By joining *lingas* and *yonis*, these artists of the sacred were calling our attention to the life-giving union of male and female regenerative powers and the indivisibility of the heavenly and earthly kingdoms, thereby undergirding the power and authority of the earthly rulers. They were also affirming the unity of the microcosm and macrocosm, the divine process of creation and regeneration that continually recreates the cosmos. The continuous flow of water running over the gods and goddesses, the *lingas* and the *yonis*, perpetually binds the cosmos together, from above to below, below to above, bathing all in blessing.

The wonder of this to me was that this was a work of sacred art embedded in nature, a creative collaboration that cannot be accurately called either natural or human-made. To create this river, human beings, one small part of the earth, had worked *with* the earth itself. And they had worked together in this way not only to mark the inseparability of human beings and nature, but also to bear witness to the depth and oneness of reality, to bind up our continually fragmenting world, and to invoke a flow of blessing to sanctify life here below. Carved both by nature and human beings over centuries, the river babbling downhill through the jungle was a moving prayer inviting us into the flow of Oneness, the Whole of reality, the sacrality of all.

That sacred communing is how it felt to me as I stood on the river's banks listening and watching as the waters of the earth flowed over images created by human hands. The feeling of flow and oneness reminded me of the feeling I had had decades before when I came upon a string of tattered Buddhist prayer flags blowing in the wind high atop a mountain in Nepal, small pieces of cloth anchored by rocks and continuously moving, sending blessings to all beings. Like those colorful flags, these sculptures in the river, being worn away every moment by the water flowing over them, were the living embodiment of impermanence, a reminder of the Oneness of existence, the sacredness of life, and a prayer for its continuation even as it is perishing. That's when I began to think of the River of a Thousand *Lingas* as The River of Prayer.

Which shocked me.

For many today, prayer is a meaningless term, fusty at best. For others it is a simple, indisputable truth: talking to one's God or gods. For me, prayer had become a question I no longer had an answer for. Though I'd been schooled well enough in formal and spontaneous, private and communal prayer, and the classic forms of prayer—petitionary, confessional, intercessory, thanksgiving, praise, and contemplative—in Christian, Jewish, and Sufi communities, I was constantly perplexed and often embarrassed by the words *pray*, *prayers*, and *prayer*. The words themselves have indeed had become for me precarious, though not in the original etymological meaning—from the Latin *precarius*, obtained by entreaty, from *precari*, to ask, beg, entreat, pray—but in its modern sense, not securely held, or dangerously likely to collapse.

Following the third-century Christian Neoplatonist Origen of Alexandria, I'd long ago given up petitionary prayer, beseeching a personal all-powerful God to fill my personal needs and desires, no matter how puny or noble. I'd lost the habit of confessional prayer as well, bringing my failings before the face of a merciful judge hoping for mercy, forgiveness, renewal, transformation. Instead, I'd come to see spirituality as many mystics do, as a never-ending dance with the One, The Unnamable, The Ineffable, "The Seeker Who is Sought, The Lover Who Is Beloved," as Ibn 'Arabî says.[3] And prayer had become for me a language of lovers, a never-ending song that was constantly changing—from silence to roaring to praise to thanksgiving to complaints, petitions, protests, pleadings, weeping, laughter, longing, cries of despair, shouts of joy, confidings, confessings, murmurings, babblings, whispers, ecstasies—joining Lover and Beloved in a sacred in-between ever re-creating itself, ever fresh and freshening. Searching for ways to understand and articulate my urgent, raw, ever-changing experiences of communing with the One, I adopted one of Martin Buber's ways of talking about prayer, paying attention, or being present to, presence, the sacred that is always with us in our everyday life but that we rarely take notice of unless we are shocked into awareness by beauty or trauma, or we are invited by sacred ritual or architecture to look again, to look deeper.

Yet as I sat down in wonder by this rushing River of Prayer, by the waters coursing through a path carved in the earth by nature and human beings in concert, these ideas and words about prayer I'd wrested from my life sounded static, stillborn, too incorporeal, too personal, too individual, too *small* to convey the awe of experiencing this earthen, transpersonal, transhistorical, transspecies, trans-being river of prayer moving before me, its presence spilling over its banks and filling the surrounding woods with its noisy work of calling us to attend to Oneness. For prayer is the meeting between the One and human beings.

This was *living* prayer—one long *linga* burbling, splashing, gurgling, and roaring through the riverbed *yoni*; spraying, misting, rippling, dripping, deepening, shallowing, bending, and snaking as it sculpted the earth; shining, stippling, shadowing, obscuring, and unveiling with the seasons and each moment, a moving riot of sound and sight and spirit. "All movement is through love," says Ibn 'Arabî.[4] This prayer was a river of love.

This was prayer made of earth, truly *corporeal* prayer. Not praying with one's own body, bowing or swaying, kneeling or prostrating. Not praying *for* the earth, as if we were or ever could be separate from it. Not weeping for the earth and the violence we have wrought upon it. But earthy prayer, prayer rising out of earth. Praying as part of the earth, in our shared earthen skin, as humus-creatures, humans praying with Earth, joining our voice with the Earth's. Prayer that is a testament to the fact that "we live in the flesh of the world," as Maurice Merleau-Ponty says.[5]

This was *communal* prayer, *communing* prayer, a prayer unifying the cosmos, stirring blessing for all being, joining all in one glorious, ever-moving whole, one sacred, ever-transforming, ever-freshening in-between, one fluent present, marrying earth and heaven, visible and invisible, body and spirit, human beings and all of nature, individuals and communities, male and female, emptiness and fullness, hidden and revealed, past and future, worlds upon worlds.

This was truly *praying without ceasing*, an invitation to enter the flow of the water instead of remaining secure on one bank or the other, one world or the other, a call to live in *correspondence* or *in-between-ness*, as the anthropologist Tim Ingold expresses it in his book *Correspondences*. We remain divided, he argues, because we interact rather than correspond. Standing apart, and sure in our identity, we interact with others without changing ourselves. "If, today, our world is in crisis, it is because we have forgotten how to correspond." In order to "understand the world as one that we can inhabit both now and for the foreseeable future," we need a

> shift from interaction to *correspondence*. This shift...entails a fundamental reorientation, from the between-ness of beings and things to their *in-between-ness*. Think of a river and its banks. We might speak of the relation of one bank to the other....But the banks are perpetually forming and re-forming as the river waters sweep by. These waters flow in-between the banks....To say of beings and things that

they are in-between is to align our awareness with the
waters; to correspond with them is to join this awareness
with the flow.[6]

For Ingold, turning our attention from the divided banks with
their bridges to the waters flowing through is a condition of
sustainable living in the twenty-first century, something the
sacred artists who carved the River of a Thousand *Lingas* knew
and broadcast to the world with their carvings more than a
millennium ago.

Now when the sterility of social interactions and endless
transactions of late capitalism isolate us and wear us down; now
when we despair over our flattened, divided world; now when we
long for harmony, oneness, communion of all being; now when
I'm uncomfortable hearing someone say, "I'll pray for you"; now
when I'm revolted by ostentatious public prayers that serve the
speaker only; now when I struggle to pray; now when I'm certain
I will never understand what it means to say, "I pray," I return to
that deafening riot of a river. I sit down by its waters and follow
its movements, the play of light on surfaces and depths. I bathe in
its song beyond words. I enter that vast in-between-ness where all
may commune—all being, including the unseen, the unheard; the
whole of the earth, including humankind; all time, including
eternity; the whole cosmos from above to below and below to
above—and rest.

Chapter 10

On Sam Mountain

At the peak—932 feet above the Mekong floodplain—beyond the holy caves and the Cham, Buddhist, Hindu, and Mother-Goddess temples that litter the twisting pilgrim road, a mother and father are teaching their young son how to pray. They buy a dull brown tennis ball of a bird from an old woman trolling the site with a cage woven of twigs. Standing before a simple ancestor shrine, the father cups the bird in his hands as the mother's hands show how to receive the offering, close around it, shelter it softly—just so—then release. In the boy's hands, the bird flutters. He startles, laughs, then turns solemn, steadies his gaze, and begins to chant. His teachers watch, transfixed, as his hands float up, open, and the bird flies free, higher and higher above the green, green weave of rice paddies stretching across peoples and borders far below.

While other tourists photograph the vistas or drink beer under rough palm thatching, I buy a bird.

"Careful! Disease!" a woman calls.

"Can't free every prisoner!" a man chirps.

I, a child schooled in prayers and purity, a woman bent on escape yet at home in cages, know this well. But in my hands, a tiny body quivers. Heart beating. Feathers fluffing. Feet scratching. Warmth spreading.

In my skin, I am learning to hold life, without suffocating, without squandering—just so. With my body, I'm discovering how to fly free, how to trace an unseen path of meeting, how to join heaven and earth.

Chapter 11

Between the Dead and the Living

Every Tuesday morning, my six-month-old grandson and I pray with the dead. We stroll to a nearby cemetery to wander its roads, nodding to other COVID-walkers we occasionally pass, smiling through our masks at our shared secret, this eye of calm amidst storming uncertainty. We walk slowly through the quiet, under murmuring cedars and maples, through throngs of gravestones humble and lavish, beyond the Russian and Greek Orthodox crosses, over the footbridge into a Japanese section, past fields of smooth white arches marking those claimed by war after war— "The Arlington of the West"—pausing only to listen to water bubbling from three staggered granite columns, or the generous spirit calling from the embrace of the curved stone bench serving as its headstone, *Come rest with me awhile*.

When we arrive at the small Sephardic cemetery, cordoned off by a simple chain strung between posts, we stop. It's the burial place of Jewish communities that fled Spain for Rhodes and Turkey during the 1492 expulsion, and Rhodes, Turkey, and other countries during the Holocaust. As I push the stroller over the curb onto the grass separating the graves from the road, I smile at Ruben Zev and say, "Let's visit our people." He knows our ritual. He knows that when we stop, I lift him into my arms and we begin to roam, swaying and singing, a breeze kissing our cheeks like the breath of the Shekinah, the Divine Presence Dwelling Among Us. The moment I begin chanting the prayer for the dead, *El Malei Rachamim*, God Full of Mercy, he turns to me with eyes that have yet to declare a color, his face beaming, every cell of his body rising to meet me, then nestles closer, and we travel that way together, around the perimeter, along the intersecting paths, through the names—Sara, Abraham, Boulisa, Nessim, Rica, Marco, Luba, Isaia, Palombha, Israel, Alegre, Ruben, Infant, A Pure Soul. As I chant in Hebrew, my heart sings its own translation, *Womb of Mercy, grant rest and wholeness to these souls, carry them on the wings of the Shekinah . . . Please, Breath of the All-*

Merciful, shelter them under the shadow of your wings, bind them up in the bond of life.

It was not my mind or my will, not tradition or theology, piety or sentiment that guided me here, to this place, this practice; it was my body. Scouting for an off-street walking route one cloudy morning, we stumbled first on the expansive, tree-studded city of souls and then on this neighborhood of tightly packed stones engraved with Hebrew letters, Torah scrolls, menorahs, and stars of David, some adorned with oval medallions harboring the face of the person, some crowned with a sculpted lamb. Answering a call only it could hear, my body turned aside, pushed the stroller into the crowded cemetery, lifted Ruben close, and began walking through the stones, singing the plaintive melody.

Once again my body proved a wise master to me, its disciple. Once again my body showed me the way to being present, to paying attention—the only definition of prayer or meditation that makes sense to me. From that first moment we wandered among the stones together, his vulnerable body against mine, vibrating to the deep tones of the prayer, it was clear that we were here not to pray for the dead but to pray with them. We were here not to save their souls or lessen their punishment or ensure their eternal rest. The dead can do more for the living than the living for the dead. But transactions have no place here. Here there is only presence. Here—amid traffic roaring down Aurora to the west and Meridian to the east, humming along streets to the north and south—Ruben and I enter an oasis of being, an eternal present. They're here with us, these dead, as we, the living, are with them. All of us bound up in the bond of life. Held close in a weave of holy presence, we commune with one another. "But the living are wrong/to make distinctions that are too absolute," Rilke says in *Duino Elegies*. "Angels (they say) often can't tell whether/they move among the living or the dead."[1]

Perhaps it's the hypnotic melody of the prayer, or Ruben's innocence, that allows me, no stranger to absolute distinctions and no angel, this glimpse of moving through presence that knows no sharp divisions. As we wander, singing, love for these strangers, whoever they were, whatever they did, whoever they are, whatever they may be, floods me, spilling over into a love in which Lover and Beloved are one, and love flows to me and Ruben from them and from us to them and back again, all of us caught up in a peace that passes understanding, alive in wholeness, shalom. When I sing *amein*, may it be so, I can almost hear their voices answering, *amein v'amein*. To seal our bond and show my thanks, I find an older grave with no signs of recent visitation and place a rock on it, a sign of constancy in a world that is constantly shifting, and read the name engraved there out loud. When Ruben starts toddling and talking, I will teach him to say *amein* with me and listen for the answering voices. I will show him how to place a rock on a grave and say the name like a prayer, to say in his heart, with his body, We are here with you. You are not forgotten. Not one of you.

Searching for a person whose name we have not yet spoken, or heading back to the stroller once we've completed our ritual, we often pass two body-sized flat stones lying in puzzle pieces, the only trace left of an encampment here two years ago, when this cemetery and its sister across the street, *Bikur Holim*, became a gathering place for people with nowhere else to live. Some got high, shot up, had sex on the gravestones, sold sex. Sleeping bags, tents, and RVs siphoning water and electricity crowded the dead. Stones were defaced and broken, the grounds fouled with trash, needles, human feces. Local Jewish communities protested, but when the city of Seattle did nothing, they cleaned the site and repaired the damage, then sued for the cost. Where are those sojourners living now? How? Under what names? Who will remember them? What mercy is theirs in this life? What justice? Who will be present with them? Meet them in love? Sing wholeness with them?

If not us, who? If not in this moment, this life, when?

Ruben Zev's world expands every day: twelve inches to his mother's face, several feet to his father's arms, across the room

to his white-haired *savta*, up to waving branches, the sky. I pray
his world will open wider and wider until it extends to the end of
time and the ends of the earth—and beyond. He may not
remember us praying with the dead. But I hope he'll carry deep
within the wisdom of the body, the rhythms and melodies of our
people, the touch of love, the joyful taste of presence and the
wonder of communing, the fragrance of mercy, the gift of moving
through the world without making distinctions that are too
absolute, a reverence for the earth and all its inhabitants: the dead,
the dying, the living, the camped and the decamped, the lost and
the found, all of us strangers sojourning here on earth, this world
of endless change and uncertainty, this holy between, all in need
of compassion, all in need of communing, all in need of shelter,
we the vulnerable.

Chapter 12

On the Way to the Woods, a Detour

The labyrinth at Whidbey Institute on Whidbey Island, Washington

I'm wary of labyrinths. Too trendy. Too arty. Too glib. Too one-size-fits-all spirit dressing. Protestant, Catholic, Jew, Muslim, Buddhist, Sufi, New Ager, Pagan, seeker, atheist, meditator, mystic, addict, recovering addict, hospital patient, nature enthusiast, experience collector, curiosity hound—come one, come all, the empty center beckons, waiting for you to fill it with meaning, a Rorschach test for the feet.

*

The way to the woods from my cabin leads past a labyrinth tucked in a forest meadow on the edge of the Chinook land at Whidbey Institute on Whidbey Island. Passing by, I can see why this labyrinth is a popular destination. It's modeled on the famous thirteenth-century labyrinth inside Chartres Cathedral, eleven circuits divided into quadrants and surrounded by an outer ring.

But this incarnation, neither ancient nor storied, offers what
Chartres does not, spaciousness and the beauty of unadorned
nature. At 86 feet in diameter, it's far roomier, and more
physically challenging, than its 42-foot French cousin. The single
path that curves toward the grass and earthen center is defined by
fist-sized, rough-cut, gray-green granite rocks and filled with
fragrant cedar chips. And the whole is limned by the glorious
greens and reds of the Pacific Northwest woods—alders, birches,
Douglas firs, true firs, madronas, hemlocks, spruces, pines, and
cedars rising above an understory of salal, ferns, mosses, nettles,
huckleberry, osoberry, oceanspray, and red-osier dogwood. It's
beautiful. I'll give it that. A shining jewel in a rare setting. But I'm
not one for jewels. I'm on my way to hike in the lush forest
beyond, explore the web of trails spanning 100 acres. Just passing
by this lovely plot.

*

I don't like labyrinths. I like wild, they're tame. I like wilderness,
they're domesticated—like hiking trails in the Swiss mountains,
meticulously groomed by government crews who arrive the
second a tree falls, as soon as the snow stops, or immediately after
a hay wagon turns over, to groom the landscape and clear the
way. Labyrinths are so civilized, even outdoor labyrinths like the
one I'm walking past—nature with the stench of humanity all
over it. No, that's not for me. That does not soothe my soul. The
deep woods, the company of ancients, trees hundreds of years
old, never felled or pruned by human hands—that's where I'm
headed. Just a few strides away, a narrow, overgrown footpath
leads into the old growth forest. Almost there.

*

Passing the entrance to the labyrinth, I hesitate. Two large slate
stepping stones mark the path inward. They're polygons,
irregular shapes, but like the curved and scalloped moonstones in
the temples of Angkor Wat, they mark the passage from the
profane world to the sacred, a liminal space that gives you time to
arrive, ready your heart, purify your spirit, before stepping inside

a place of holiness. They're an invitation to leave the ordinary world and enter sacred time. I step onto the outermost stone and pause, both feet turning toward the entrance.

*

I hate labyrinths. I want to wander in the forest. I want to bushwhack or ramble along a wilderness trail, not trod a narrow path to nowhere. I want to roam free, not twist and turn at the behest of another. I want to struggle to find my own way, not walk lock-step in the footsteps of others. I want to move into the unknown, not retrace my steps back to the place where I began. What do I want with a mapped circuit, however intricate and beautiful and wide, one way in, the same way out?

*

My right foot moves to the innermost slate stepping stone. The left joins it. At the edge of this stone, on the boundary of the stepping stones and the labyrinth, two waist-high piles of rocks flank the path. Cairns, chortens, way markers left by a stream of pilgrims. The last threshold.

*

What's the risk? It'll take only minutes to complete the circuits—in and out probably half a mile, two-thirds at most. An easy walk. I'll be back on my way into the woods in no time, trekking, adventuring, and if boredom or impatience overcome me before I've completed the designed circuit, I'll jump the granite barriers and head straight for the ungroomed green, where one can be alone and listen to the silence, without the expectations, the demands, the constraints, the stifling patterns of others. Where the self can breathe free of enclosures, no limit to bump up against.

*

I step inside the labyrinth, past the two stone guardians, and walk fast, purposefully following the laid-out path, turning sharply here, clipping a corner there, back and forth, this way and that, again and again, eager to be done with the circuits and on my way. My eyes fix on the ground, following the lines of rocks, so I will not misstep but keep walking steadfastly, all the way to the end. The sooner I complete this task, the sooner I'll be reveling in the expansiveness of the woods.

Careful to stay on the path, not stumble on a rock or kick one out of place, I step around broken branches, spruce cones, trim olive-brown slugs, and mottled yellow-and-black banana slugs. On one of the outer circuits, spruce branches hang low over the path. I duck under them, and the needles scrape the back of my neck. My steps slow. My breaths deepen and lengthen. Soon I'm lost in the walking, my thoughts wandering freely as my body flows along the path, my heart flying here and there, my spirit roaming. I am light, at rest. There are no choices to make here. No forking paths. No alternate routes. No side loops to other vistas. No escape routes, like the roads they build for logging trucks that lose their brakes on the way down the mountain, gaining speed, losing control. No dead ends. Here there is one path. One path only. The way in is the way out. All has been laid out. Everything has been determined. All that is required of me is to walk, to be on the way, the way laid out before me, the way laid out for me, laid out by someone else. A path laid out by another—yet walking it I am free. Freed. Relieved of the burden of fear—Will I meet a bear or bobcat or a man on the trail? Relieved of the burden of anxiety—Will dark fall before I find my way back? Will I get lost? Relieved of the burden of choice—Shall I take the lower or the upper loop? Hike into the mountains or along the river? Stay on the trail, or step off? All I must do—all that is required of me—is follow the path laid out before me. One path to the center, the same path out to where I began. The only choice—given over and over, with each new turning, a new invitation: to surrender to it.

The givenness of the world. The invitation to surrender and be free. A secret of being always on the way.

A secret of liminality—to be drawn off your intended path, pulled away from your desired destination, to find yourself in a place you would rather not go, graced by what cannot be found by seeking.

A secret of creativity—the way the form of a sonnet or sestina leads the poet to new meaning, unexpected beauty.

A secret of love—the way you bind yourself to another to find yourself free, tasting a freedom you hadn't imagined before.

A secret of determinism and freedom, the way we choose within the limits passed on to us, by our species, our genes, our cultures, our families. We are free, but not absolutely. We are not gods. We are determined, but not absolutely. We are not puppets or automatons. We're playing chess with the universe, says William James. The board is lined. The pieces placed. We know the rules. We make our moves. We play long or we play short. We play wise or we play foolish. We play awake or we play sleeping. We play angry or we play laughing. We play fair, or we try to cheat. But we play. And, the chess master always wins. Rabbi Akiva says it this way: "Everything is foreseen, and free will is given to everyone."

No answers here. No adoration of paradox. Only gifts.
The gift of the labyrinth—a bounded path created by another, an invitation to enter and walk in freedom, to hold being determined and being free together, for a moment, in one's body, in one's self.

Resting in the gift, I walked the labyrinth in the forest meadow to the center and out again, returning to the entrance. As I passed between the stone guardians and stepped onto the first slate stone leading back into the ordinary world, I paused. What choice was mine now?

Wandering in the woods, the pleasures of that freedom, could wait for another day.

Chapter 13

Stepping into the Between

The labyrinth at the Whidbey Institute on Whidbey Island, Washington

The Way In

At the entrance to a labyrinth, flanked between two low cairns guarding the threshold, I hesitate. Why am I here?

I'm new to labyrinths and know only this: they're not mazes. In labyrinths there are no intricate branchings, false veerings, or dead ends. One can't get lost in a labyrinth. There's only one path: the path in to the center, when reversed, is the path out to the circumference. And that path is clearly circumscribed; every walker must follow it—no detours, no alternative routes, no exceptions.

The labyrinth spread before me is magnificent. On a blanket of shredded red cedar, fist-sized green-granite rocks demarcate the circuitous path, forming a pattern modeled after the labyrinth inside Chartres Cathedral. But this labyrinth is twice the diameter of the French original—an expansive 86 feet across—

and it's tucked in a forest meadow on Whidbey Island,
surrounded by soaring western red cedars, western hemlocks,
Douglas firs, ponderosa pines, white pines, Pacific yews, Sitka
spruces, red alders, bigleaf maples, and madronas. In rhythm with
the wind, the trees sough and squeak, giving off a faint briny scent
of the ocean nearby. All around, in a green weave of huckleberry,
osoberry, red-osier dogwood, nettles, salal, and ferns, small gray-
brown birds flit in and out, rustling leaves and chirruping. Who
wouldn't want to walk this path?

Still I hesitate. I'm not here for an answer. My heart is too
ragged to offer up a question to carry with me as I walk. I'm not
here to pray. My spirit is too weary, too taut. Wordsworth's words
pound in my blood:

> *The world is too much with us; late and soon,*
> *Getting and spending, we lay waste our powers.*

Silence and solitude are what I crave, an emptiness I can fall into
and rest.

Whenever I lose my way, when the clamor of meeting
obligations, resisting distractions, handling trivialities, and
chasing desire deadens my heart; when I'm desperate to revive
my languishing spirit—father dying, mother scheming, brothers
betraying, friendships unraveling, vocation vanishing, another
marriage souring, dread resurrecting—I retreat into solitude and
silence, seeking an emptiness in which to find my way again. I
pray, meditate, sit by rushing water, hike into the mountains,
dance. Walking a labyrinth might carry me there as well,
especially this labyrinth in the woods, whose center, a grassy
circle round a rock-ringed circle of dirt, lies directly ahead of me,
its promise of emptiness unexpectedly close.

Life is the flight of the Alone to the Alone, says the mystic
Plotinus.

I am here to fly.

I step through the cairns onto the path laid out before me. Stirred by my feet, the red-gold cedar releases its fragrance, welcoming me.

On the third step, jagged rocks block the way forward. It's tempting to step over the barrier and walk straight into the center, just a few feet away. Two easy strides would take me there. But the restorative emptiness I'm after can't be rushed or forced; years of trying have taught me that much. Obeying the granite markers, I turn away from the center.

A few steps farther on, a pine branch the size of my forearm litters the path. I pick it up, vow to pack it out, keep the path pure. Leave no trace behind. *That means you, too,* I say, looking up at the trees and laughing. I'm already lighter, happy to be on my way, each step carrying me closer to my destination.

The path winds and winds, again and again, doubling back on itself, now leading me closer to the center, now taking me farther from it. Back and forth I walk. Round and round. How long now to the center? How many more turnings?

I hurry on, gathering more broken-off limbs along the way, pine and fir and spruce, the leavings of a windstorm. They mar the path, they hinder, they grate.

The path ahead stretches into a long, flowing curve along the perimeter, no obstacles in sight. I pick up the pace, but before I can settle into a rhythm, a blockade of rocks interrupts my stride, and I stumble, almost dropping my bundled greens. Regaining my balance, I walk on, more slowly now, wary of barriers appearing out of nowhere, sudden turnings, sharp corners, my eyes fixed on the path directly beneath my feet. More fallen branches. One bough is three feet long. As I stoop to collect it, my unwieldly bundle escapes my grasp and scatters across the path. Balancing on my haunches, I gather the severed limbs, cradling the long bough against my body with my left arm and carefully layering the smaller branches onto it. Back on the way, I continue gathering tree scraps, lost in my task. I want the path cleared, the way to emptiness empty.

Suddenly the goal of my journey opens before me. Three steps will take me inside the grass-bordered, rock-enclosed earthen circle at the center of the labyrinth.

The Center

The center is a trash heap. A dump. A mess of detritus from others' journeys, others' lives. Junk left behind. Hideous. The beauty of granite and cedar, grass and dirt, silence and solitude trashed by human leavings. A dented golf ball propped up high, dead center. Bottle caps. Sea shells. A red die with three white dots showing. Quarters, dimes, pennies, foreign coins. Decomposing pine cones. Aluminum ring pulls from pop-top cans. Long fingers of crystal quartz. A barnacle-encrusted beach stone. A steel bolt. A pink-orange, big-bellied plastic laughing Buddha, tipped on its side. Feathers everywhere—some still downy and sleek, others scraggly, almost bare.

Crowded. Deafening. Noisome. Fouled.

My spirit can't breathe.

Life is the flight of the Alone to the Alone.

Where have I flown?

I kneel for a closer look at the garbage strewn in the dirt. A blue plastic button from a man's dress shirt. A black-and-white metal button proclaiming "The Stevedores." A crumpled business card. Scraps of paper with typed and handwritten notes, the letters blurred by rain and dew. A lime-green silicone finger puppet, a monster with bared teeth and eight long tentacles popping out of its head, each one ending in a bulbous eye. A tiny wooden heart painted black. A sand dollar broken open, emptied: its mouth, with its five teeth, the five white doves of the spirit, gone.

The rock nearest me is etched with slime. The trail leads from the grass where I'm kneeling, up the rough granite, over the top, and down to the dirt and debris. Even the slugs have left their trace, marked the path with their existence, their presence. Is this what it means to exist? Is this the goal? Our deepest desire? To leave one's mark? To announce I, I!, was here! I walked the path. I made the journey. To insist on ourselves, force ourselves on the world? Litter it with our selves?

I've brought nothing to mark my journey, left no trace on the trail. Nevertheless, I have arrived at the center. Haven't I?

I have arrived. *That's* the barrier: I have arrived. How can I be alone with the Alone, dwell in emptiness, when I have not emptied myself, when I am here clinging to my judgments, my needs, my desires—all the lovely white doves of my spirit I cherish above all else? I want to be the only one here—all others intruders, trespassers. I believe my ascetic ways to be the mark of spiritual maturity; signs and markers are for those less schooled in wisdom. I demand that my sensibilities banish all others—no plastic, no kitsch, no blemishes, no flaws.

It is not those who have traveled here before me who are fouling the center; it is I, my jealous, demanding ego, my constricted self. Intent on clearing a way for my soul, purifying the path to emptiness for myself alone, I have shrunk my spirit. My heart has become tiny, hard, black—no room for the world, no room for others. I have forgotten to love. To love like the host of unnamed, unsung seekers whose hearts, in the flight of the Alone to the Alone, were opened to a world of love, expansive love, a love that forgets self and remembers the One, a love that carries one beyond the self to its encompassing, a love that embraces all beings, trees, rocks, slugs, other selves, the whole of creation, a community of being.

You are the center-point of the sphere and its encompassing, says Ibn 'Arabî. Without the encompassing, there is no center. The way in is the way out. The flight of the Alone to the Alone leads out to the world.

This is why I came: to lose myself in the One, empty myself of all the lovely white doves of my spirit, so I am free to love.

I look again into the littered center, the signs left in the dirt. These leavings are not refuse; they are pledges, thanksgiving offerings, confessions, sacrifices, tokens of love, cries of the heart.

I'll stop drinking. I will never gamble again. I'll quit smoking. I'll go to rehab. I won't chase after money anymore. I'll give up porn. I renounce false gods. I'll stop demeaning myself. I will tell the truth. Thank you for healing me. I dedicate my talent to You. I sacrifice my ambition to follow the vocation You have called me to. I lay my hardened, black heart in your merciful arms. I lay down the burden of myself. Thank You for saving my life. I sacrifice my pride, my piety, my purity, my righteousness to Your truth. Take my innocence, my jealousy, my rage, my anxieties, my desires, my grief, my song, my doubt, my certainty, my indifference, my fear, my faithlessness, the slime of my existence. My trammeled heart—Yours. All I have, all I am—Yours. Thank You. I love You.

As the chorus of voices grows louder, I hear its invitation. I take a branch from my bundle and lean it against the outside of the rocky border. Then, one by one, I lay down the remaining broken pieces I have collected, overlapping them, weaving them into a lush, unbroken wreath round the hallowing center.

Who knows what those who walk this labyrinth after me will make of this wreath of scraps? Soon it will turn brown and brittle, and someone will clear it away. Yet I leave it here, the trace of my journey—a confession of pride, my ungenerous heart, my diva spirit; a thanksgiving offering for the signs others left behind, pointing the way to true emptiness; a pledge to keep opening my spirit to love; a token of love; a cry of the heart, I once was lost but now am found.

This is why I came: to join the chorus.

The Way Out

Empty-handed, I begin the walk outward, from the center-point to its encompassing. The path out is the same as the path in. It is the walker who is not the same.

A slug has joined the path. Mud-brown. Glistening. Smooth upper body, lower body crenellated. It holds still, wary of the presence looming over it. I bend toward it. It senses my breath and retracts its feelers and head, making itself small, waiting for the danger to pass. Peace be with you, I say. To the slug? To myself? To the companions who have walked this path before me and who will walk it after me, the ones who leave traces and the ones who enter and leave empty-handed?

The path winds outward, passing under the low-hanging branches of a fir. I walk under them, upright, not stooping. Dew-moist needles brush the crown of my head, as if blessing me. Three times the path winds under these boughs, three times they caress me. On my last approach, I raise my lips to kiss them.

Walking on, I look out, beyond the outer circuits, toward the forest, the lush green circle of ancient trees and burgeoning life encompassing the labyrinth. As I turn and turn, following the path, the landscape changes. To the South, cabins, stacked wood, and a sanctuary built of hand-hewn cedar. To the West, a path leading into old-growth forest. To the North, a path leading into wetlands, meadows, farmland. To the East, the entrance, soon to be the exit, and just beyond it, a mound of granite rocks, set aside to repair the path. South, West, North, East. A never-ending round of wonders widening to a boundless embrace of Being.

Suddenly the exit is before me, the place where I entered. Returned to a new beginning, to set out once more into the world. Standing between the cairns guarding the way out, "my heart new open'd," I pray never to stop traveling, in toward the center and out toward the encompassing—to be always on the way to love.

Chapter 14

Standing on Moonstones: The Art of Dwelling Between

Moonstones at an entrance to Bakong, a Khmer temple in Cambodia

Moonstones, *sandakada pahanas*, are granite or sandstone steps found at the doorway of a temple or at the foot of the steps leading up to a temple. When they first appeared, during the reign of the Anuradhapura Kingdom in Sri Lanka in 377 B.C.E, they were placed only in Buddhist temples and they shared a standard design: a semi-circular or half-moon stone slab elaborately carved—a half lotus in the center ringed by concentric bands of flowers, swans, a foliage pattern called *liyawel*, a procession of elephants, bulls, lions, and horses, and flames—each a symbol of the spiritual path. But as kingdoms and regions changed, so did the moonstones. The bull and lion carvings disappeared under the influence of South Indian Hinduism in the eleventh century C.E., and after the fourteenth century the shape of the moonstones shifted to a triangle or full circle or oval, and the carvings became simpler and followed no set pattern.

Often said to be unique to Sinhalese architecture, moonstones are also found in the early (late ninth century C.E). large mountain temples of the Khmer Empire in Cambodia. The later (twelfth century C.E.), more famous Khmer temples, including Angkor Wat, Bayon, Angkor Thom, and Ta Prohm, do not include this architectural feature. After visiting these later temples and being suitably impressed by their scale, grandeur, and bas reliefs, I traveled thirteen kilometers east of Siem Reap to Hariharalaya, an early capital of the Khmer Empire, to visit the three more ancient temples in the Roluos group: Preah Ko, Bakong, and Lolei. I stopped first at Preah Ko, and it was there I first encountered moonstones, at the bottom of the stairs leading up to the main outer entrance.

Though I didn't yet know to call them *moonstones*, the first time I stepped onto those stone slabs, I sensed their uncanny difference immediately. There was no mistaking them for the path leading to the temple or the bottom steps of the staircase leading into the temple. These were not utilitarian, block-cut steps, but smooth expanses sculpted with curves to resemble a half lotus petal and bordered with an eroded line of tiny seeds or beads inside an intricate chain of what looked like foliage or script perhaps. I felt these stones, softened by countless seasons and feet, welcoming me. I felt their broad expansiveness holding me, their curves embracing me, inviting me to linger there, the way well-designed architectural spaces affect one's body, prompting and shaping the experience one has.

To my surprise, I accepted the moonstones' invitation. I did not rush past them, up, up, up into the temple, treating them like so many stepping stones to speed me to my destination. Without understanding why, I stood still on the top moonstone, my feet centered in a blank surface, framed only by a curved border of beads and foliage tracing the shape of a lotus petal. Later I read that when the temples in Roluos were built, the official religions of the Khmer Empire were Mahayana Buddhism and Hinduism, perhaps explaining why no bulls or other sacred animals were carved on these moonstones, to be trampled underfoot. I also read that in Buddhism the lotus symbolizes primordial purity, cosmic renewal, expansion of the soul, and detachment, and the foliage or *liyawel* edging symbolizes the tangle of worldly desire.

But as I stood on those stones, I wasn't thinking of symbols and meanings. My whole being was being altered, shaped, by the space those stones created. It was a physical experience. I felt in my body, with my body, the power of standing there, there on those smooth, worn, heavy stones that were neither temple stairs nor path into the world. There. Not on the ground but inches above it. Not on the first step up into the temple but inches below it. There, floating on a stone cloud between the interior of the temple, the sacred, and the world outside, the profane. Between. A place of power. Between. A place of trembling. Between. The place where one metaphorically takes off one's shoes before stepping on holy ground, the place where one puts on her shoes again before returning to the everyday world. I was standing on a threshold, *limen*, between two worlds, between the interior of the temple and all that lay outside, between the sacred and the profane, between the spirit and the body, between the already and the not yet, tingling with the power of between, a space charged with the promise and the danger of moving between worlds.

Stirred up by the moonstones at Preah Ko, I eagerly sought them at the two other Roluos temples I visited that day, Bakong and Lolei. Each time I stepped onto the massive yet delicate stones, I was caught up in the experience of standing on the threshold between worlds, dwelling in the transformative space those stones created. Shaped by those stones, I began to know the wisdom of liminality. Before climbing the stairs into the temple, I lingered on that threshold, grateful for their gift of place, of time, to dwell in that space between, before crossing over into another way of being. One doesn't leap into the sacred, one doesn't intrude upon it or storm it: one prepares to enter it—heart, mind, spirit, and body—with fear and trembling. As I made my way out of the temple back into the world, I lingered again. When one has dwelt for a time, a moment, in a realm set apart, one does not throw oneself back into everyday existence willy-nilly: one reenters slowly, mindful of where one has been and where one is going, and the perils of crossing over.

Moonstones at the main entrance to Preah Ko in Cambodia

These stones laid down by ancient Khmer architects were a threshold, a place of crossing over for human beings, human bodies. They were no Jacob's ladder, no staircase from one world to another for angels, messengers, beings of pure spirit, to ascend and descend, carrying their divine announcements and delivering their aid. And I was glad for that. I'm suspicious of ladders, spiritual hierarchies of any kind, and the body-spirit dichotomies they are built upon. Mount this ladder, climb these rungs, scale this mountain, as if one ascends to a loftier, more spiritual plane of existence in a linear fashion, step by step moving higher, ever higher, inexorably, away from this earthly existence. These moonstones were no ladder for spirits; they were a liminal space for bodies, offering a place in which to shape-shift, undergo a transformation, more like the pillow on which Jacob lay his head to dream, to dwell for a time in that space between waking and sleeping. For the spiritual life, this task of becoming fully human, body and spirit, is not one of climbing out of one world into another, but of continually moving back and forth between a more spiritual and a more bodily way of being in this our one world, between experiencing the world inside the temple and experiencing that same world outside the temple, between the sacred and the profane.

Crossing over from the sacred to the everyday, changing from one state of being to another, is dangerous. Moonstones demarcate the boundaries of life inside the temple and life outside the temple while connecting the two, creating a physical place where a person, body-mind-spirit, can safely pass from one way of being in the world to another and back again, a place for ordinary human beings (not shamans and people undergoing initiation or other special rites) to undergo a transformation of being. Physical places are often designated as liminal spaces by religious traditions: natural places such as springs, caves, shores, rivers, marshes, calderas, and mountain passes, but also human spaces such as crossroads and bridges. The moonstones the architects of the early Khmer temple complexes incorporated into their design are humanly created liminal spaces. I left Cambodia grateful to have experienced, in my body, with my body, because of my body, the wisdom of these architects and the power of the transformative spaces they created out of stone.

Caught Between Worlds

It was only later, after months of frustration with my writing, that I began to understand why those stones had captivated me. I was stuck, caught between worlds, and I had been for decades. The stones taught me how to move.

Like many others, nonwriters as well as writers, I had accepted that the religious world and the secular world were two separate, permanent habitations, two mutually exclusive communities and worlds, two irreconcilable ways to live one's life, and that one had to choose between them. And many do. Many religious people choose to live their lives entirely inside the temple, within the borders of a religious tradition, never venturing outside. And many who are not religious choose to live their lives entirely outside the temple, in a world disenchanted, never entering the temple, or visiting only as tourists or art historians.

But—thanks to temperament, character, providence, fate— I could not choose between them. I longed to belong somewhere, but I couldn't make myself fit wholly within one world or the other; there was always some rebellious flesh squeezing out beyond the boundary. So I ran back and forth, back and forth— now toward the visible world and the glories of the body, now toward the invisible world and the glories of the spirit—like Hagar running between the hills Safa and Marwah in search of water for her son Ishmael. If only I could find what I thirsted for and stop running, like Hagar, who after seven circuits found the salvation she was seeking for her child, when an angel kicked the ground with his heel and water came rushing out, creating the well she called ZamZam.

For a time, I hoped that writing fiction would save me. I believe in the miracle we call art, in the power of words to reveal hidden possibilities, call us to attention, create openings for the mind to slip through, transform the self, animate lifeless lumps of clay.

But I wasn't prepared for a vocation as a creative writer. As a theologian, I had lived and taught, preached and published from inside communities of faith. Fluent in the languages of Christianity and Judaism, I tried to make the words and images inherited from those traditions come alive in the contemporary world and speak afresh, especially to women's experiences. My work was pouring old wine into new wineskins. Becoming a writer, however, meant stepping outside the church and synagogue, into the wider world, where the familiar words and images I had drawn on were not recognized or understood or, if understood, rejected. If I wanted to be heard, I had to learn to speak the common language of the secular world in a voice that sang, a voice that stirred up fresh meaning from the *more*, that inexhaustible well of meaning that lies beyond the limits set by reason and tradition. Instead of pouring old wine into new wineskins, I would have to turn water into wine. But isn't that what artists do? Take the ordinary stuff of the world and transform it into a delicious, intoxicating draught?

I set to work. Standing outside the temple, in the everyday world shared by religious and nonreligious people, using ordinary words, I tried to bear witness to the sacred, point toward an abiding *more*, the mystery and complexity that surround and sustain and enliven our mundane existence, and an otherness that breaks through our ordinary reality. But I kept missing the mark, and I found myself once again in that troubling between, this time between unchurched people and militant secularists on one side, and people of faith, religious conservatives, and fundamentalists on the other. To those in the secular world, my words sounded too religious—arcane, puzzling, or foolish. As one reader of my novel *Woman of Salt* told me: "I just skipped past all that talk about God; I wanted to know what happened to Ruth!" To those in the religious world, my words sounded too secular—empty, misguided, or blasphemous. "You've lost your faith," several readers wrote me after that same novel came out. I wasn't turning water into wine; I was mixing water and wine, polluting one and diluting the other. Instead of creating a bridge carrying meaning from one world into the other, my words fell into the void between.

Finding myself still trapped between, in no one's land, drove me mad. I wondered if I should retreat, say, I'm not religious, I'm spiritual, meaning: I'm deep, I accept the reality of things reason can't explain, but I'm also free thinking. No dogma for me, no outdated concepts or images or rituals, no shackles of tradition. I considered following the path of aesthetic contemplation laid out by Fernando Pessoa in the early twentieth century in *The Book of Disquiet*, his response to being "born in a time when the majority of young people had lost faith in God for the same reason their elders had had it—without knowing why." Most of his peers "chose Humanity to replace God," but because Pessoa was "the sort of person who is always on the fringe of what he belongs to, seeing not only the multitude he's part of but also the wide-open spaces around it," he "didn't give up God as completely as they did" and he "never accepted Humanity." How then did he live? He "kept a distance from things."[1]

But these ways were not for me. I couldn't step away from the choice any more than I could choose between writing literary novels destined to be labelled "fiction" or religious novels that would be shelved as Christian or Jewish fiction. As a writer in love with God and in love with the world, enthralled by the Bible and by novels, spellbound by sacred ritual and by the quotidian, pulled toward spirit and toward body, I was unable to shake off either obsession. More than this, I was unwilling to choose between truth pointed to by religions and religious experiences and truth pointed to by literature, science, philosophy—all the traditions of human inquiry.

I knew my predicament wasn't unique, that other "nonsecular" writers were struggling to find a voice fitted to the urgency of our day. Imitating Bernard Malamud or Cynthia Ozick, Flannery O'Connor or John Updike, writers who had successfully found a voice and a language that bridged the two worlds, wasn't an option, for the world to which their art responded no longer existed. What then? What are creative writers in the 21st century who are also people of faith to do? What are writers living during the Fourth Industrial Revolution and in a global world, a post-Einsteinian universe, and a new geological era called the Anthropocene, who also experience God, the anguish of sin and evil, the liberating power of repentance and forgiveness, the transformative power of sacred texts and rituals, and the holiness of this world, to do?

The problem for those of us writers who are neither fish nor fowl comes down to this: We have no ready-at-hand words to explore this between where we live. We can't naively use words like God, faith, prayer, sin, original sin, evil, repentance, grace, covenant, redemption, or resurrection. To secular people, people with no experience of religion or spirituality, or who eschew them and choose to live within the limits of reason alone, these words are too strange; they're part of an antiquated worldview or a private language game they don't understand. "What does grace mean?" people ask. Or, "What's baptism?" "No one believes in miracles anymore," they say. Or "People aren't sinful, they just don't know any better." When we use these words, our secular friends and neighbors often shake their heads in bemusement, or they may pity us for our addiction to the opiate of the masses, or laugh at our delusions, or smile in contempt at our primitive ways. To the non-religious, we who live between often look and sound like fools.

To religious people, these same words are too familiar. Many religious people— those currently religious as well as those who were raised religious but left their tradition behind—are quick to assume they know not only what words like these mean but what they should mean. When we betwixt-and-between writers use these words, our more conservative religious friends and neighbors often object or try to set us straight. They believe we've emptied these words of their true meaning and filled them with vapid truths from the God-forsaking secular world, or lies that contradict the Bible and orthodox theology. To our formerly religious friends and neighbors, the self-identified "recovering" Catholics or Mormons or Pentecostals, these words often trigger the trauma they experienced growing up in their traditions. Because of this volatility, I long ago stopped telling people I was a theologian or grew up religious. Fundamentalists went after me like a dog with a bone, trying to save my soul. Disaffected Christians and Jews blasted me with a litany of the hypocrisy, abuses, and absurdities of the traditions they had left. To current or formerly religious people, we who live between often sound like traitors to tradition, heretics.

How to speak then? With what words, in what voice? We who are not defending the faith, translating religious terms for the nonreligious. We who are not reforming faith for our generation or reinterpreting familiar stories for the religious, following Paul Ricœur's hermeneutics of a second naiveté. But we who inhabit the space between the secular and religious worlds, those of us who long for a tongue to "sustain the weary with a word," for ears that "listen as those who are taught" (Isaiah 50:4). Are we left with silence, a silence that gnaws at one's liver, throws the heart out of rhythm?

Moonstones at the Lolei temple in Cambodia

Standing on Moonstones: The Vocation of a Writer?

Stepping onto moonstones in Cambodia opened a new way for me, a way beyond choosing to speak the language of one world or the other, and a way out of silence. One can also choose, those stones taught me, to spend one's life crossing back and forth between two ways of being in the world, between the sacred and the profane.

The sociologist Emile Durkheim's basic distinction between the sacred and the profane in *The Elementary Forms of the Religious Life* is helpful here. For Durkheim, the sacred transcends everyday existence; it is extra-ordinary and thus potentially dangerous, awe-inspiring, fear-inducing. The sacred refers to things set apart by a community, things made strange, including persons, rites, duties, texts, places, buildings, animals, trees, objects, words—anything can be marked as sacred. The profane refers to ordinary existence; it includes everything—persons, places, practices, objects, texts—that is regarded with an everyday attitude of commonness, utility, and familiarity. The sacred and the profane are distinct, not separate: the significance of the sacred lies not in itself, in any inherent quality of a person, place, or thing that has been intentionally set apart, but in its distinction from the profane.[2] Objects or persons or places designated as sacred may become profane, and vice versa. This is why religious communities consecrate a building as sacred space when it is to be used for prayer and worship, and they deconsecrate the space when the building is sold to be turned into condos or to be used by another religious community.

Nothing is inherently sacred or profane. Nothing. Everything and anything in our world becomes sacred or profane by shifting our relation to it. I think of it this way: sacred and profane refer to two ways of being in the world. The world is one, but we experience it in two different ways, if we are able and willing, now as ordinary, now as outside the boundaries of the ordinary. As light is both wave and particle—not one or the other; as the human being is both body and mind—not two separate substances that need to be artificially joined by a pineal gland, so human existence is both sacred and profane. Standing on moonstones, I understood that the sacred and the profane aren't two separate worlds; they are two ways of being in one world. Standing on moonstones turned my frustration at being caught between worlds into gratitude for the gift of dwelling between.

Though some see the world as divided and choose to live in the world seen from one point of view only, the religious or the secular, others experience the world as one and move back and forth between experiencing that world now as sacred, now as profane. That's the situation of many people of faith today, creative writers and other artists included. We're continually moving back and forth between the sacred and the profane. We don't stand with religious people inside the temple or with the unchurched and secularists outside. We enter the temple to experience the strange truth there and try with our writing to make those strange truths familiar to those standing outside, to reveal the shared human experience hidden inside the strangeness. We also step outside the temple to experience the familiar truth there and try with our writing to make those familiar truths of our common, everyday existence strange, to cast a loving gaze on them until they shine with the infinite and give off a fragrance of the beyond, that which is more than we can say or grasp and that troubles our souls. We're continually crossing over from one to the other, making the familiar strange and the strange familiar, turning water into delicious wine and wine into the water of life. That is our task as writers, as artists: to transform, not translate, to illumine, not define.

If there is a secret to this life between, with its constant crossings, it's not just accumulating better writing techniques (though those certainly help), but learning to dwell in the between. Entering or leaving, we linger on the threshold, listening for the truth that is not found inside the temple or outside the temple, a truth that does not belong to the sacred or to the profane, a truth that lies between. Perhaps that is our calling, to dwell between, to be "threshold people," in the words of anthropologist Victor Turner[3]—not only those of us caught between the religious and the non-religious worlds, but all writers. "Not to belong anywhere, to be displaced, is not a bad thing for a writer," says Ariel Dorfman. "If you can deal with it. If it doesn't destroy you."[4] Dwelling between—dangerous, yes; but not a curse. A gift.

Threshold people are urgently needed now, for we're living in a liminal period, a time of transition, of uncertainty, doubt, and disorientation. We may even be entering what the philosopher Karl Jaspers named an "axial age" or "pivotal age," "an in-between period between two structured world-views," in which radically new ways of thinking emerge, shaping future religions and philosophies of an entire civilization, such as occurred between the ninth and third centuries B.C.E. in Persia, India, China, and the Greco-Roman world with the birth of Buddhism, Confucianism, Taoism, and Platonism.[5] During such times, Arnaldo Momigliano explains, "[n]ew models of reality either mystically or prophetically or rationally apprehended, are propounded as criticism of, and alternative to, the prevailing models."[6]

We may now be in such an age of criticism and alternatives, when we need writers and other artists imaginatively to apprehend new models that will help us navigate our turbulent present and carry us into the future. That is the power of art, to be an act of exploration not conclusion, a journey into the unknown not a mapped destination, to dwell in the between. The temples, synagogues, cathedrals, churches, and mosques we have built and worshipped in for centuries are emptying and crumbling, and the everyday world that we have known and loved is disappearing, dying, species by species, galaxy by galaxy. All we have known and depended on is disintegrating, all structures dissolving, all certainties called into question. For a new vision and integration of our world to arise, we need people who withdraw from the world to ask radical questions, imagine new structures, create new spaces for us to be shaped by—out of words as well as paint and stones and ideas. We need writers, artists, and thinkers who speak not to people inside the temple only or to people outside the temple only, but to all people in search of new meaning, new words, new voices to guide us beyond this polarized and disorienting age to a radically transformed world. We need writers, artists, and thinkers devoted to the art of dwelling between, people continually crossing over between the sacred and the profane to find words, hear voices, see visions that do not yet exist. We need threshold people. We need people standing on moonstones.

Moonstones at an entrance to Bakong temple in Cambodia

Chapter 15

Playing in the Between: The Power of Ritual in Art

> *At the beginning of God's creating*
> *of the heavens and the earth,*
> *when the earth was wild and waste,*
> *darkness over the face of Ocean,*
> *rushing-spirit of God hovering over the face of the waters—*
> *God said: Let there be light! And there was light.*
> Genesis 1:1-3[1]

Embodiment has long been central to the way I think. Though my mind has been disciplined by analytical thought, I remain, at bottom, a kinetic learner. I think with my body. We all do, of course, as we must, given we're earth creatures and not angels. But for me, the physicality of thinking, a moving body-mind, is vital. When my body is engaged, I know more deeply, think more creatively. It's often my body, not my mind, that leads me into new ways of thinking, new ways of acting, new ways of being. What has facilitated that attitude for me has always been ritual, which engages and moves the whole person, body, mind, and spirit. That's why I began my academic career studying the history of religions, concentrating on the work of Mircea Eliade and Victor Turner, and phenomenology. And why, though I trained as a theologian and later became a creative writer, ritual and embodiment still ground my work. It's only recently, however, that I've begun to understand how liminality plays into my work as a creative writer. What I want to explore is the nexus of embodiment, ritual, liminality, and creativity that I experience as a working artist.

I have found two of the metaphors for liminality that I mention in the Introduction and develop in Chapters 14 and 18 especially helpful in understanding liminality in relation to imagination and creativity: *barzakh* and twilight creation. The metaphor of *barzakh* is borrowed from the medieval philosopher-

mystic Ibn 'Arabî. For Ibn 'Arabî, the *barzakh* is an isthmus
between Reality itself, or the Absolute Mystery, and the sensory
realm of our everyday world. He calls this isthmus the
mundus imaginal, the imaginal world, a world of images where the
material takes form and form materializes. In this liminal space,
this between of imagination, the images that arise are dynamic
and polyvalent. They are not identical with the material object
they represent, nor are they a substitute for the non-material
reality they point to. Instead, while maintaining the distinction
between the material and non-material realms, these images unite
the two worlds in such a way that they vibrate with new meaning.
These images in the realm of the between are true, just as the
reflection of oneself in a mirror is true, but they are properly
understood only when we acknowledge that their meaning is not
literal but figurative, only when we receive them as true images
that nevertheless speak "as though" or "as if."[2] This true "as-if-
ness" is one key to liminality as it occurs in art.

   The other metaphor comes a Yemenite *midrash* on creation.
Between that which is necessary to exist and that which is
impossible, the *midrash* teaches, there exists the realm of the
possible, the twilight creation. In the twilight, ten things were
created: "the mouth of the earth, the mouth of the ass, the mouth
of the well, the rainbow, the manna, the staff, the *shamir* (a
mysterious worm that wrote on metal and was used in
divination), the writing, the writing instrument, and the tablets."[3]
I was so taken by this imaginative rabbinic commentary that I
wrote a novel inspired by it, my own *midrash* on Exodus and the
wonder-working prophet-poet Miriam, her generation's keeper of
the well. In that novel, the mouth of the well opens a space
between the ordinary world and the possibility of new life, a
womb of the possible that enables Hagar, Yosepha, and Miriam to
envision a way out of no way. And the way into that womb for
these women is ritual—drumming, singing, chanting, poetry,
dancing. The body leads the way.

   Like the mouth of the well, all the twilight creations are
openings—so many mouths!—that belong to the isthmus between

worlds. Each is an opening where the Creator and the earth creature meet, on different ground than the ground of what is necessary or what is impossible. They meet in the time and space of the possible, like hard seed planted in soft ground. And from their meeting, new life is created. A way out of no way is born. From the womb of the possible, through these openings, all the wonders of our world are brought forth.

Four of the ten twilight creations—the *shamir* (a mysterious worm that wrote on metal and was used in divination), the writing, the writing instrument, and the tablets—have to do with writing. This focus no doubt reflects the rabbis' trust in the power of the word to call things into existence, to create: "God said: Let there be light! And there was light." (Genesis 1:3) These four also speak to the mystery and miracle of the art of writing, the creation of that which is not necessary but possible. For the act of writing, like the *shamir*, is mysterious; it can reveal what lies beyond ordinary perception. The act of writing is an opening to new ways of perceiving for the writer, just as the writing, that which is written, is for the reader. As Edmond Jabès writes in his novel *The Book of Questions*, "The writer steps aside for the work, and the word depends on the reader."[4]

The instrument of writing, too, is mysterious, for who can tell whether it is the hand of God, divine inspiration, or the hand of Moses, the writer's imagination and skill in working with her materials—or both—leaving traces on the page? And what are tablets, written on clay with a divine finger and *given* to a messenger, if not like the completed story or essay, brimming with a surplus of beauty and meaning, that the writer barely recognizes as the work of their own hands? Many writers have experienced reading their own work and thinking, *I wrote that?* Writing brings forth wonders. And it does this by creating in the twilight, standing on the isthmus of the true "as if," working in the realm of the possible.

Linking artists with the "as though" or "as if" and "the realm of the possible" may summon up John Keats's famous concept of "negative capability" in art. Discussing artistic achievement in a letter to George and Tom Keats in 1817, Keats described "negative capability as when man is capable of being in uncertainties, Mysteries, doubts, without any irritable reaching after fact & reason."[5] The concept of negative capability has been stimulating for many artists, with good reason.

But for me, the images of isthmus and twilight point more adequately to my experience of creative writing. And they do so without setting up an antagonism or mutual exclusion between art and reason. Knowing in art is not *against* fact and reason, the realm of the necessary. Nor is the intention of most artists to storm the realm of the impossible and conquer it. No dualistic thinking, no adversarial relationship is needed for us to distinguish between these different ways of engaging the world. All it takes is stepping into a moment or a space between, to step onto ground that is neither the hard ground of fact nor the groundlessness of unbounded fantasy but the soft, fertile field of the possible, to discover what seeds will sprout and grow. One need only enter the between that is neither the often-blinding day of rationality nor the opaque night of irrationality, but the twilight in which that which is possible can appear.[6] Writing, whether fiction or creative nonfiction or nonfiction, is not expressing a pre-conceived idea or image. It is not a straight line speeding to a mapped destination. It is entering and exploring the unknown, which includes doubts and mysteries, but also much, much more: questions, an endless path, wordlessness, silence. As Reb Denté, one of Jabès's characters, teaches:

> Writing means going on a journey, at the end
> of which you will not be the same,
> at the bottom of the page filled.[7]

The question then is, How does one enter that between, the field of the possible between what exists and what does not yet exist, between what we know and what we can't know, the realm of the unknown yet imaginable, the world of imagination, that active liminal space of the true "as if"? The body leads the way.

For me, as for many artists, it is ritual, an intentional sequence of bodily actions, that opens us up to or helps us enter the field of the imagination, that faint, half-seen, half-heard, inchoate space or moment where the world of forms we know softens and gives rise to new forms. It's when we intentionally enter that liminal space, step onto that isthmus with its soft fertile ground, enter the twilight of the possible, move into the imaginal world or presence, that we can more easily envision and create new forms, images, structures, events, and ways of being that can transform ourselves and our world.

The Role of Ritual in Creativity

Ritual gives rise to creativity. Far from being simply a mindless, repeatable sequence of events, the enemy, as it were, of novelty and originality, ritual, as an embodied thinking activity that that enacts meaning, entails freedom of the mind.

Pitting ritual, which works on our unconscious physical awareness, against freedom of the mind, is yet one more vestige of the dualism plaguing art. In a phenomenology of the flesh such as Merleau-Ponty's, there is no contrast between these two; for both physical and mental actions are often performed out of habit, and those performed out of a conscious choice are interactions of brains, world, bodies, and other bodies. The mind, he says, is "the other side of the body," and we have no idea of a mind that would not be doubled with a body.[8] The writer Clarice Lispector echoes this honoring of the body in all we do in "Fair Tidings for a Child": "In everything, in everything your body will be an asset. Our body is ever at our side. It is the one thing which stays with us to the end."[9]

The interplay of ritual enactment and freedom of the mind is apparent in the ever-changing rituals of many traditions. Ongoing practice of a ritual not only enacts meaning, it also, as an embodied thinking activity, invites more thinking, new meanings, additions, alterations. Consider, for example, the home-based rituals of Judaism, which are adapted by Jews in every culture, every household, to their own needs and temperaments. Lighting candles to usher in Shabbat, for example, may be done by one person or several in a household, by a woman or a man, with a brief traditional or nontraditional blessing, or with the addition of silence, song, or poetry. Likewise, no two Passover seders are the same. Though Jews in Afghanistan, Morocco, Iraq, Egypt, Israel, and the United States all follow the same *seder* or order, each culture and household includes different kinetic traditions that enhance the blessings and readings. Afghani Jews beat one another with green onions to re-enact out the affliction suffered by their enslaved ancestors. Moroccan Jews walk around carrying matzoh on their shoulders to re-enact the Hebrews leaving Egypt with their unleavened bread. After the exile in Babylon, some Jews began opening the door at the beginning of the seder during *ha lachma*, the bread of affliction, inviting all who are hungry to come and eat, a practice some households still follow today. Some North American Jews set aside a piece of symbolic *matzoh* after it has been broken as a pledge to all those still suffering that they will resist oppression. In my household, we re-enact crossing the Red Sea on dry ground by singing and dancing through two walls of undulating blue fabric.

All these examples of individuals and communities changing a set order or structure to enact fresh meaning reveal the flexibility of ritual and the creativity of ritualizers within a tradition. Like jazz saxophonist John Coltrane riffing on "My Favorite Things," or pianist Thelonius Monk improvising on the hymn "Abide with Me," they take an inherited form and play with it to create something new.

Ritual as an embodied thinking activity makes room for creativity not only in religious practices but also in the artist's life. It is the intentional repetition of a sequence of bodily motions that enables many artists to enter that isthmus or twilight, to stand in that place or moment dividing yet connecting that which is and that which is not—that blurred space with no hard lines of separation—and to give ourselves over to imagination and use its power to find new ways of thinking, acting, feeling, sensing, being in the world. As I argue in Chapters 16 and 18, ritual helps us break out of habits of thinking and doing, similar to the way art and philosophy do, as described by the philosopher Alva Noë.[10] While Noë speaks of art "interrupting" habit, Arthur Koestler, in his classic study of creativity in biology and culture, *The Act of Creation* (1964), speaks of creativity "defeating" habit.

> Habits are the indispensable core of stability and ordered behaviour; they also have a tendency to become mechanized and to reduce man to the status of a conditioned automaton. The creative act, by connecting previously unrelated dimensions of experience, enables him to attain to a higher level of mental evolution. It is an act of liberation—the defeat of habit by originality.[11]

Noë's language of "interruption" is preferable to Koestler's "defeat," for both habit *and* creativity are vital for human flourishing, as both thinkers acknowledge. Homeostasis and change exist in ongoing relation in all life. Habit gives rise to creativity and creativity gives rise to new habits. Both are necessary.

Though neither Noë nor Koestler speaks of ritual as a way to lead one to investigate habit or nurture creativity, to step back from our ordinary ways of thinking and doing in order to open space for creative acts, many artists are familiar with this power of ritual.[12] It's common for artists to talk about rituals of preparation for practicing their art.[13] Writers are often asked about their creative "habits" by interviewers and fans or aspiring writers, a question I find moving, because it suggests a longing to find a key to unlock one's own creativity. "Do you use a special pen or pencil when you write?" they ask. "Do you listen to music? Do you follow a certain routine?"

In *The Creative Habit*, dancer and choreographer Twyla Tharpe describes ritual as an "automatic decisive pattern of

behavior" to help overcome those first steps into creativity, which
are difficult because of our fears, doubts, and distractions. Because
it's automatic, "you don't think, you don't will, you don't decide,
you just 'step into it,'" she says. "Moving inside" the routine
"gives you no choice but to do something; It's Pavlovian: follow
the routine, get a creative payoff." Like Beethoven's morning walk
and scribbles "limbered up his mind and transported him into his
version of a trance during the walk."[14] Note Tharp's physical
language, the language of motion—not unusual for a dancer and
choreographer but also germane to ritual. More than anything,
rituals of preparation "arm us with confidence and self-reliance,"
she says, as they did for primitive people, who appeased the
universe with rituals out of fear, to gain control.[15]

It's not only for negative reasons—to silence distractions,
overcome fears or blocks, or appease the gods or our own
demons—that artists practice rituals. Artists' rituals are not
primitive acts. They're not superstition. They are intentional acts
we perform to cross a threshold from ordinary reality to a space
where the imagined world is joined with the real. Engaging in a
familiar ritual helps us step onto the isthmus, into the twilight, the
field of the possible, that creative space where the real and
imagined worlds are distinct from each other yet connected.
That's where I have to step into as a writer, that space between
what has gone before and what might be, between what has
happened and what might happen, what exists and what does not
yet exist. I can't write well if I am not in that space. This is as true
when I write creative nonfiction as when I write fiction.

An essay is not a logical argument; it is a trial, an attempt,
a foray, a line of thought moving around an image or word or
feeling or hunch. Whether I'm writing a story, novel, or essay, I
want—I need—to access what is beyond my reasoning,
underneath ordinary logic, outside linear thinking. I want to let go
of planning, what is necessary, banish limiting beliefs, what is
impossible. I want to lose control, not gain control as Tharp says,

though the paradox is that by losing control one finds one's footing in the field of the imagination. I want my relationship to space and time—all ordinary reality, all that is profane—to be altered, as it often is when I perform Jewish rituals like lighting Shabbat candles at sunset on Friday, when I am buzzing from the six days of the week, and when feeling peace and gratitude and joy wash over me.

Every artist has their own way of stepping onto the isthmus, into the twilight, and entering that plasticity of mind, openness to seeing and hearing and experiencing and imagining new things. Susan Sontag didn't answer the phone (a habit I swear by). Alice Munro walked three miles. Toni Morrison got up before dawn, made coffee, and watched the light come up. Haruki Murakami gets up at dawn and runs. "The repetition itself becomes the important thing," he says. "It's a form of mesmerism. I mesmerize myself to reach a deeper state of mind."[16] Tharpe goes to the gym every morning. She moves out of her apartment, into a taxi, out of the taxi, into the gym, in the gym, out of the gym, into a taxi, out of the taxi, into her apartment, crossing threshold after threshold.

Marcel Proust wrote in bed. So did Edith Sitwell, George Orwell, Mark Twain, Marcel Proust, Colette, and many others. Wordsworth wrote in bed *in the dark*. Many writers today follow this practice. This practice is significant, for the bed can function for an artist as a kind of built ritual environment that invites liminality and creativity. To be in bed is to signal one's detachment from the everyday world. To lie in bed is to inhabit a space between sleeping and waking, a kind of intentional twilight consciousness or dream state. To write in bed is to let go of fixed goals and open oneself to where imagination leads.

To prepare myself for the hard work of writing (I know I'm truly writing when I sweat), I often sit still and follow my breath, then pray or meditate—I move my spirit, or, more accurately, I feel my spirit moving, rushing-spirit brooding over the face of deep, dark, moving waters of what is possible but is not yet born. "Brooding," one possible translation of the verb (*merachephet*) in verse 2 of Genesis 1, seems an apt metaphor for this practice, for it suggests a *body* hovering over the possibility of new embodied life, a reminder that creating, that moment between chaos ("wild and waste") and the appearance of light, is a *physical* act. Creating is not the work of a preexisting disembodied form or thought in search of a body to house it, but an embodied thinking activity.

To help me brood, I also move my body, I do yoga or take a walk outside. Or I practice blind or free drawing, engage my hand and my brain in a different way. When I begin a story or essay, I write by hand on unlined paper, with a soft pencil, alone at my scarred cherry dining table—not my computer desk. I work in solitude. Silence. No music. I step onto the page, and I wait. I listen. Sometimes there's an image or question or voice or structure on the edge of my hearing, my consciousness, that I want to explore. Often I sit with nothing. I stay still. And I wait. Wait until a voice or image or rhythm or word arises.

When I'm in the middle of working on something, using my bed as a ritual environment becomes part of my practice. When I wake up, I lie still with my eyes closed and let my mind roam in the fertile ground between full-consciousness and sleep. In this state, when my usual thinking habits are not in play, a new approach to whatever it was that stumped or eluded me on the page the day before will pop into my mind. Or I'll hear a word I used in my last draft and know it's not quite right, and better ones start auditioning for the part. Or something I didn't know was missing from the narrative appears suddenly, something necessary that I need to add. All this work of revision happens without any conscious effort, because I am in bed, at play. Only when this twilight fades as day breaks in my mind do I open my eyes and leave the makeshift sanctuary of my bed.

When I'm working at my desk and I get stuck, I get moving. I do the dishes, sweep the floor, throw in a load of laundry, take a walk, and my moving limbs stir up my imagination. There's nothing special about these physical acts. But by engaging in them, I can often—not always, it's not guaranteed by any means—bump myself out of my habitual ways of perceiving and thinking and into that liminal state, a state of attention, a state of play, serious play, somewhere between consciousness and unconsciousness, where imagining flows (movement!) and something new emerges that I did not plan or anticipate, something that surprises me. And when it comes to editing, I work by ear. I stand in the middle of the room and read the words aloud, listening for the sounds, the rhythms, the meaning beyond and beneath the words on the page. The body leads the way.

It's not only ritual preparation for writing and ritual strategies for unblocking writing that involve the body. The process of writing itself is a bodily experience, whether one is dragging a pencil or pen across paper, pressing one's fingers against a keyboard, or tapping a screen. This physicality is significant, for it is the relation between a maker and their materials, a between that the anthropologist Tim Ingold calls "correspondence," that is key to understanding making as a unique *embodied thinking activity*. For Ingold, physical materials such as clay, metal, stone, wood, ink, paint, and paper are not inert vehicles for expressing ideas; they are *active* in the process of creation and *necessary* to that process. All making is, in this sense, a bodily experience. He argues that though Baudelaire (and many other artists, myself included) may speak of a "frenzy of creation" that sweeps the artist forward, "the materials perpetually hold them back."[17] This feeling of being held back is true of my experience of writing. The *resistance* of the materials—sounds, rhythms, words—to the vision or imagination guiding the work and propelling me forward is not only unavoidable, it is fruitful. This is why when I'm asked about my writing, I often say, *I think with the words and sounds and rhythms, I think on the page*, or *I have to get back to the page to find out where I'm going.*

The resistance of the materials to the maker's imagination, Ingold argues, creates a dynamic *between*. "It seems that composer, performer, architect, writer, draughtsman, and painter alike are continually *caught between* the anticipatory reach of imaginative foresight and the tensile or frictional drag of material abrasion, whether of pen on paper, bow on string, or brush on canvas." Given that artists experience this fraught between, "[t]he trick, then, is to be able to hold the foresight that that pierces the distance like an arrow in check *with* the close-up, even myopic engagement that is necessary for working with materials."[18]

To be caught between materials and imagination is not a negative or frustrating experience; it is generative. For that between, though tense, is fraught with promise. In that between, the artist is drawn to correspond with their materials rather than simply interact with them or dominate them with a predetermined idea, and it is out of that lively correspondence that new creations arise.

Working *between* materials and imagination, holding foresight or imagination or vision *with* the close-up engagement with materials, the artist finds herself in a liminal space, a space much like philosopher Alva Noë's third state of metainstability in perception. In a state of metainstability, one does not merge two distinct perceptions, or focus on one or the other in sequence. One is aware of both simultaneously, as distinct yet related. (See Chapter 18) This experience of two different yet concurrent modes of perception describes the working state of an artist well. In the visionary or actively creating space, the artist does not merge with her materials or her imagination. He does not flip back and forth between them. Instead, the two operate simultaneously: The "designerly process of making is one whose close-up engagements are guided by foresight," and "the skill of artists is their practised ability to keep their distance whilst in the thick of the labours of proximity."[19] This is why, as Ingold points out (and many artists, including myself, can confirm), writers often can't remember what they are writing about and painters can't see what they are painting. They are working in a third space, between imagination and materials. Only when the essay or novel or painting is finished do they have an Aha! Moment. *So that's what this is!*

The experience of being caught between materials and vision or imagination that occurs in the act of writing or any kind of making is reminiscent of what happens in liminal experiences in ritual, when there is a break from or distancing from the profane way of relating to the world in order to draw close to something beyond that may give rise to something new. Ritual practices can lead or ease an artist into a liminal space at the beginning of projects. They can also help artists inhabit that space or state between imagination or vision and their materials as they work. And they can help them reset when they find themselves *over*thinking a story or novel, trying to control an outcome instead of letting their imagination guide them through the sounds and rhythms of the words to a place they could not predict.

Playing in the Between: A Writer's Vocation

It's no accident that the word play has surfaced several times in this chapter. Playing is central to the work of the writer or artist, and to the nexus of embodiment, ritual, liminality, and imagination we have been exploring throughout these essays. Victor Turner recognized this connection in his later work, when he began focusing on ritual as cultural performance and the "human seriousness of play."[20] After many years of practicing ritual and writing, separately and together, I have come to see the importance of play as well, in ritual and in art. For me, the work of writing is play. When writing, I disengage my mind from practicality, usefulness, all thoughts of output or product, goals or definite ends. I set off on an adventure with words to see where we'll end up. I become an explorer in search of new discoveries. I enjoy the ride, even when "nothing happens," even when I'm tearing my hair out because I can't get down on paper what lies just behind my hearing. Why? Because I'm at play. At play, even the hardest challenges leave one feeling energized rather than depleted.

When I teach writing, in addition to analyzing the
elements of craft with students and pressing them to work harder
than they ever have, I always encourage them to play. I want them
to have fun, to leave behind their expectations and untether their
minds from ordinary logic and causality to see their way, to hear
their way, sense their way, feel their way into something new—
and enjoy doing it.

First published almost 90 years ago, Johan Huizinga's
classic study, *Homo Ludens: A Study of the Play Element in Culture*,
is still fruitful for thinking about ritual, liminality, and creative
work in relation to play. Huizinga's non-dualistic view of play,
ritual, art, and the relation among them underpins many of these
essays. He argues eloquently and compellingly for the ubiquity of
play, its significance in culture, its unique role as a form of
embodied *thinking*, and its affinity with ritual, and its role in
poiesis.[21]

Even in its simplest forms on the animal level, he claims,
play is not reducible to "a mere physiological phenomenon or a
psychological reflex"; it is enacted meaning. "[I]n acknowledging
play you acknowledge mind, for whatever else play is, it is not
matter."[22]

> In play there is something 'at play,' which transcends the
> immediate needs of life and imparts meaning to the action.
> All play means something. If we call the active principle
> that makes up the essence of play, 'instinct', we explain
> nothing; if we call it 'mind' or 'will' we say too much.
> However we may regard it, the very fact that play has a
> meaning implies a non-materialistic quality in the nature
> of the thing itself.[23]

Though it enacts meaning, play lies outside the reasonableness of
practical life; it has nothing to do "with necessity or utility, duty
or truth." And, like Keat's negative capability, it is "supra-
logical."[24]

Echoing Emile Durkheim's notion of ritual as a break with the rhythm of ordinary life, Huizinga says, "We find play present everywhere as a well-defined quality of action which is different from 'ordinary' life."[25] In play, as in ritual, we step out of our workaday relation to the world. Though he refers to "archaic ritual" as "sacred play," he emphasizes that "[t]he ritual act, or an important part of it, will always remain within the play category, but in this seeming subordination the recognition of its holiness is not lost."[26]

Like ritual, *poiesis*—understood broadly as creating, the process of bringing something into existence through imaginative, artistic, or intellectual effort—proceeds "within the play-ground of the mind." It too occurs in "a world of its own…, [where] things have a very different physiognomy from the one they wear in 'ordinary life' and are bound by ties other than those of logic and causality."[27] Like ritual, *poiesis* is "born in and as play—sacred play," which, even "in its sanctity [verges] on gay abandon, mirth and jollity."[28]

I experience ritual and creative writing in this way: "as born in and as play—sacred play." Play because they occur beyond the bounds of logic, causality, and practicality and lead to fun that resists all explanation; sacred in the sense that they take place in a fertile or holy between, a liminal space in which one experiences a world beyond the everyday that transforms one's relationship to that world. (see Chapter 18).

As liminal creatures, body-mind-spirits, we're all constantly moving back and forth between different ways of being in the world, different powers of engaging the world, different ways of being present—between body and mind, word and idea, image and perception, imagination and materials, heart and mind, sacred and profane. We move in both directions, any direction, all directions, each in our own way, in our own rhythm. If we're lucky, we pause in the space or moment between and look around, listen; in the movement of the outward becoming inward and the inward becoming outward, we discover something new. But for me, it is most often the body that leads the way—into

thought, into prayer, into the twilight of the possible, the isthmus
between the seen and the unseen, the in-between, the imaginal
world, where I become neither a truth-teller nor a liar when I say,
"I saw and heard this form; I did not see and hear this form." It is
the space, the moment, where I become a creative writer listening
for a voice singing true, a voice between a shout and a whisper.
Failing again and again to hear. Failing again and again to capture
what I hear on the page. But trying.

> On the matter of spiritual realization mankind does not
> cease to err,
> For God's secret is poised between the shout and
> the whisper.[29]

Chapter 16

Strange Tools: Fiction as Holy Possibility

"How to bear happiness?" That's the question a character identified only as "Number 81 in line" asks of DMV Clerk Number 7 in the closing story of Kevin McIlvoy's posthumous collection, *Is It So?*. Clerk Number 7 refers the matter to Clerk Number 9, who promptly leads the questioner upstairs, through "narrower and narrow flights and past numberless corridors," until they reach the Office of the Clerk of Happiness, who sits at a desk petting and licking the questioner's "tongue-shaped paper proof of number" before pressing it onto a spindle. This entire set of events takes place in the boldfaced title of the story. The clerk's answer appears in roman font as the story itself, which reads, in its entirety:

> Number 81, what you thought is not true not true
> not true not true not true: you thought
> that your beloved could annihilate you or would if
> you created a space in you no larger than an alms
> bowl, and asked, "What is the sin in us living in joy
> together?"
>
> How to go?
>
> Go the way you came.
>
> Next, please.[1]

What to make of this story, cryptic yet marvelously evocative? The long, bolded black title, made heavier by its large type, almost eclipses the story. Or perhaps it magnifies the story's clarity and light by contrast. And yet the answer is no less perplexing than the question. Is the clerk one of Kafka's maddening bureaucrats? A wise guide? God? All three? Is this a dream? A parable? Is it a

short story at all? All that's certain is that we've entered strange
territory.

"Art starts when things get strange."

So writes philosopher and cognitive scientist Alva Noë
in *Strange Tools: Art and Human Nature*.[2] For me, Noë's striking
claim illuminates the stories in *Is It So?* and also the work of
Clarice Lispector, who shares McIlvoy's gift for strangeness. A
beloved Brazilian writer of novels, novellas, and short stories,
Clarice (Chaya) Lispector came to Brazil in 1921 as an infant with
her family, Jewish refugees from the pogroms in Ukraine. For
years she wrote weekly columns for the *Jornal do Brasil* called
crônicas, a form that straddles fiction and nonfiction. Kevin "Mc"
(pronounced "Mac") McIlvoy, who died in September of 2022,
also wrote across genres and forms: novels, novellas, short stories,
and poetry. A beloved teacher, he was raised in Illinois in a family
who first attended a Polish Catholic church (his mother's family
emigrated from Lithuania) and later an Irish Catholic one. This
formed him, he said, in different kinds of mysticism.

Both writers have been called experimental, offbeat, or
volatilely strange. To describe their work, critics reach for words
like absurdist, surreal, and irreal. But what if, instead of
measuring them against "reality," we look at their work as a form
of inquiry into our ways of perceiving reality and the way we tell
stories? What if we receive their stories as opportunities to deepen
our understanding of ourselves, or what Noë calls "strange
tools"?

What makes a work of art a strange tool? For Noë, such a
work is "useless": it is no help in getting things done; it yields no
information or explanation. And yet we make such works to think
with. They help us find our way around in a world where we
often "get lost in the complex patterns of organization that make
up our lives." In other words, "the true work of art is
philosophical."[3] Like philosophy, art is a *practice*, a method of
research aimed at "illuminating the ways we find ourselves
organized, and so, also, the ways we might reorganize

ourselves."[4] Like philosophy, art interrupts and subverts our conventional ideas and activities, creating space for transformation.

Take the art of storytelling. Just as philosophers are preoccupied with our habitual ways of thinking, Noë writes, so "literary artists take all the ways we find we must express ourselves, or write down our stories, or articulate our lives, and they make that their problem. They try to invent new ways of writing…. Writing, so familiar, so dominant, so hegemonic, is made strange."[5] If a story results, it invites us to wonder what we could see *in* or *with* that story.

If narrative, the meaningful sequencing of images, is the habitual human form of storytelling, as Antonio Damasio argues in *The Strange Order of Things,*[6] McIlvoy and Lispector challenge us to investigate our familiar ways of organizing narratives and imagine other possibilities. They invent playful new forms that invite us to look again at the profound mystery of human being, perception, and expression.

Consider the strange forms their stories take. McIlvoy's "glimpses, glyphs, and found novels" (as the book's subtitle calls them) are brief, spare, full of gaps, silence, absences, and leaps of logic. They are more like resonant ruins than complete structures, as McIlvoy once suggested to an interviewer. One glimpse, "Passerby," walks the reader step by step through each extra's appearance in Gene Kelly's famous dance in "Singin' in the Rain," each one waiting for their "moment in the lights," even if it's only a few seconds and no one notices how they matter to the whole. In another, "Cake all day," we overhear a man and woman in a senior care center who talk only about cake ("Cake was convincing evidence that God existed: The Baker") as they look out on the world together, but who are underneath the words, and through the words, deeply present to one another, "alert in the listening." The glyphs offer snippets of conversations, notes sharpied on hatboxes or windshields, responses to confederate statues being removed—a chorus of voices singing of complex lives. The found novels are all tiny clusters of words found in a public library: stenciled on the ceiling, stamped on a book spine, and written over a urinal ("**The appearance of the Deep Blue Sealant rising up through the drain holes indicates the need for** [illegible]"[7]).

Lispector's stories are no less strange.[8] Some swirl around metaphysical questions: origins and identity in "The Egg and the Chicken," imagination and the existence of God in "Forgiving God," creation in "Brasília" ("We are all deformed by our adaptation to the freedom of God"), and the mystery of being in "Dry Sketch of Horses" ("The beasts never abandoned their secret life that goes on in the dark"). In "Report on the Thing," a dizzying rumination on time, the narrator says: "This is a report. Sveglia [a clock] does not allow short stories or novellas no matter what. It only permits transmissions. It hardly allows me to call this a report. I call it a report on the mystery."[9] In "The Fifth Story," the narrator compresses five "true" ways to tell a story of killing cockroaches (one of Lispector's recurring images, a nod to Kafka) into a few pages. Eschewing linear flow, these stories move more like eddies that whirl up riches from the depths. Almost all are vertiginous, disorienting.

None of these stories has a familiar narrative arrangement or arc—whether Aristotle's beginning-middle-end, Freytag's dramatic pyramid, Joyce's epiphany, Chekov's lyric, or a contemporary collage arrangement. They're hard to parse, destabilizing the reader, who often wonders, *Who's speaking? What's the context? What's happening? What?* They're not after explanations, logical coherence, or tidied-up completeness. Instead, they make us wonder: What is a story? And, if form is meaning, if meaning emerges from *the way* a story is told, what do these strange forms suggest?

For one thing, both these writers felt themselves pressed against the ungraspability of the mystery in which we live and move and have our being, and both nevertheless used the tools they had—words, syntax, narrative—to point us to that mystery, saying, *Look closer, look underneath, look beyond.* Their stories reach toward what is just out of reach; they exist at the limits of language, toward what Lispector calls in *Discovering the World* "a more delicate and difficult reality, less visible to the naked eye."[10]

For we are aware, she says in her dedication in *The Hour of the Star*, of the existence of many things we have never seen, like the atom's structure, which is "none the less real" in spite of its invisibility.[11] One of her narrators puts it this way: "Beyond the ear there is a sound, at the far end of sight a view, at the tips of the fingers an object—that's where I'm going."[12] Both writers are in search of words and forms that can faithfully enact that "beyond." Lispector's characters call this unreachable mystery "the breath of life," "pure movement," "the mystery of the nature of beings," "the secret life that goes on in the dark," or "extreme presentness." McIlvoy's characters call it "this underworld aliveness" or "the most-all-ness" of a thing, which art can never reach because it is able to rise only to a "thing's almostness."[13]

Because these stories are inquiries, invitations to wonder at the mystery just beyond our reach, their language, word by word, sentence by sentence, is as fresh and alive as their forms, though often difficult to comprehend on first reading. They draw us in even as they baffle us. Both writers are music lovers and compose as much by sound as sense. Both invent words. Both disrupt syntax. Yet it's hard to read either's work without sensing how they glory in the possibilities of language, even as they mark its inadequacy. This is one reason their work is at once mournful and ludic.

Though both writers challenge readers' expectations, neither is difficult for the sake of being difficult. Neither is out to confound or trick the reader. Nor do they aim to call attention to their own cleverness. Nor are they concerned with "building beauty," for, as the narrator of Lispector's "Brasília" says, "that would be easy." Instead, their art is about erecting "inexplicable astonishment. Creation is not a new comprehension, it is a new mystery."[14] In accepting their invitation to be destabilized and disoriented, we may find ourselves in this new mystery, created anew. Not surprisingly, Lispector and McIlvoy each enflesh the mystery of being in their own way.

A strong temptation in reading McIlvoy's *Is It So?* is to reduce these stories to something graspable, whether to recurring themes (death, aging, memory, suffering, sin, joy), the narrator's

arc, flashes of Buddhism, or vestigial Catholicism. These elements
are all present, but to dwell on them would be to betray the
disturbance the collection causes. The table of contents itself
warns against imposing order, for though the stories are grouped
there according to form—as glyphs, glimpses, and found novels—
in the book, they appear in a different order. Already our
expectation of how collected stories are organized is exposed and
called into question.

The opening stories focus on appearance and its relation to
the elusive deeper reality of things, on the almost impossible task
of seeing what is there in things, in nature, in persons. In
"Wineglass," the graying narrator and his wife "more generously
imagined each other in readiness for further erasure." In "A
wish," the narrator notes the difficulty of drawing a wineglass. If
he draws it wrong, from memory, the base seems to slide off the
table. If he draws it "almost right, an unnatural disturbance" in
the wallpaper pattern results. But if he could draw it rightly and
wrongly at once, he could "stop drawing what appears before
me" and draw "what reappears." The undertone of these stories
echoes Noë's account of his conversation with an artist about the
science of visual perception. When Noë spoke of the "tiny
distorted upside-down images in the eyes" and marveled at how
we see so much on the basis of so little, the artist responded with a
question similar to the one McIlvoy seems to ask in these opening
stories: "Why are we so blind, why do we see so little, when there
is so much around us to see?"[15]

Lispector's stories also invite us to wonder at the "more"
of our existence, though for her that often means plunging us
deep inside the passions and anxieties of her characters, whose
interior worlds roam wider, burn hotter, and run more wildly
than those of McIlvoy's characters. Joy, love, and mystical ecstasy
form an ostinato bassline in her work, whereas in McIlvoy's they
sound more like grace notes. Yet, like McIlvoy, Lispector calls our
attention to what is not being seen or can't quite be seen, to what
goes on in the dark, the powerful undercurrents of people's lives,
the unique mystery of each human being. Blindness, literal and
metaphorical, winds through her stories. In "The Smallest Woman

in the World," a series of characters from different walks of life observe a pregnant eighteen-inch-tall woman from Africa—each of them paying attention only to something that fits neatly inside their own experience. These seeings-not-seeing cascade toward the woman, "the rare thing herself," and her own experience of herself, as herself. Contrary to the ways she is perceived, she is "laughing, warm, warm...delighting in life." Similarly, in "Happy Birthday," a family gathered for an eighty-nine-year-old grandmother's birthday party sees only what she appears to be, not who she is: a woman who knows that life is short and "death is her mystery." In "The Egg and the Chicken," Lispector questions the act of seeing itself: "In the morning in the kitchen on the table I see the egg," the story opens. "I look at the egg with a single gaze. Immediately I perceive that one cannot be seeing an egg."[16] That observation launches the narrator into brooding on surfaces, what is obvious and what is hidden beneath, the elusive thing a person is hungry for: soul, sacrifice, metamorphosis, the mystery of selfhood.

The stories in *Is It So?* raise a question that disturbs the book's own narrator: Even when we pay attention, when we make an effort to see the world in all its vivid colors and shapes, what about the unifying transparency that surrounds the world? Can we draw or write the whole that embraces us all? In "A difficulty," which takes the form of an enigmatic conversation between the narrator and his wife, the wife offhandedly remarks that drawing a goldfish is "a difficulty." Not so for the narrator. "I get goldfish, really get them," he says. "I can be them, draw them—still, and moving." For him, it's the clear plastic bag that is "the problem." That transparent surround, the whole in which the fish swims, frustrates "drawing magic." Likewise, he can draw mouths and other parts of the human body, but the nose, which "holds it all together," eludes him.

The next story, "If a small ocean," echoes this. Speaking of Fra Bartolomeo's Magdalen, the narrator says he "gets" drapery; he can "be drapery." What eludes him is "gesture and form." The magic of art, whether drawing, music, birding, or writing, threads through the stories in *Is It So?* But it is always coupled with a plaintive acknowledgment that the narrator is never able to draw, write, or compose as he wishes. There is something more that frustrates his skill as an artist. Art is for him "an unsolvable crisis of beauty."[17]

Lispector too is keenly aware of the inability of art to capture the wildness of being, the mystery of existence. The wife in "The Imitation of the Rose" muses that "extreme beauty made her uncomfortable." In "Boy in Pen and Ink," the narrator confesses, "I don't know how to sketch the boy. I know it's impossible to sketch him in charcoal, for even pen and ink bleed on the paper beyond the incredibly fine line of extreme presentness in which he lives. One day we'll domesticate him into a human, and then we can sketch him."[18] In "Inaugural Address," a group of artists creates a line "guaranteed to be eternal," a "metallic line that does not run the same risk as the line of flesh." They sacrifice for this work of art, even though they know that it does not and cannot understand them, that it will "find them strange and be ashamed of [them]. And that living is a suicide mission."[19] Art investigates the mysteries of human living, love, sacrifice, and being, but it cannot "get" us.

As McIlvoy's collection moves forward, yet another question emerges. In "Blue Squill," the story that gives us the collection's title, the narrator's sister, "adept at using biblical jargon," puts to him a stark choice, one reminiscent of Moses's directive to Israel in Deuteronomy, "Choose you this day, life or death." She asks him to choose between two sentences that correspond to two ways of being: "Why is it so?" or "It is so."[20] One could read this from a Christian point of view, as a choice between skepticism and faith, or from a Buddhist perspective, as a choice between resistance to reality (which causes suffering), and acceptance of it. Neither reading does justice to this narrator, who sidesteps the choice, offering a third way. He asks his sister, "Is it so?"

What are we to make of this third way? In rejecting the "why" and turning the statement into a question, this narrator reveals that he is not out to make sense out of the human condition, to order the chaos of life, or to show the mystery of grace in action. He is unlike Flannery O'Connor or Raymond Carver. Neither does he seek to dispassionately affirm impermanence, nor to enlighten us with Zen koans. And though there's plenty of absurdity in these stories (in a style more akin to Beckett than Kafka), they don't seem aimed at exposing the cracks in our carefully organized bureaucratic world. The narrator of "Blue Squill"—like McIlvoy, I would argue—is after something different.

The epigraph of his collection, from Tzvetan Todorov's *The Fantastic*, yields a clue: "The fantastic is that hesitation experienced by a person who knows the laws of nature, confronting an apparently supernatural event." Between nature, with its regular laws, and supernature, which appears to break those laws, there is…hesitation. The moment in which a person grounded in reality experiences something seemingly beyond reality is a liminal moment, a moment not of certainty or doubt, faith or skepticism, but of inquiry and wonder. The realm of the fantastic is the realm of the between, the possible, the imagination. It is the territory of the strange. "Is it so?" means "Come into the strange with me and look around."

Near the end of "Blue Squill," the narrator recounts how as a ten-year-old he taught his baby sister to walk. If he gave her a tennis ball, "she would stand, start walking, holding it slightly before her, gazing self-hypnotically at the yellow sphere." Then this: "Her walking with her magic friend: those days gave me such laughing-out-loud joy. At all points when I remember that period in her life and ours, greater joy arrives, and it has broken open more room in me for welcoming the magic hour and the magic object held forth as a projection of holy possibility in a world that has lost all sense of the sublime."[21] The fantastic, the realm of "Is it so?" is "holy possibility," the domain of art, which holds out to us magic objects we gaze into to experience new ways of moving through the world. Strange tools indeed.

A practicing Buddhist who was raised Catholic, McIlvoy uses words like "holy" circumspectly: *Mother of God, christs, miracle, mystery, saint, Jesus, church, the garden*. His characters sometimes find themselves in moments of deep, calm awareness untinged by guilt or sorrow—what some might call grace, others mindfulness—like his character Lagan in "Yew," who is recovering from an operation to restore his sight. As he walks through a graveyard, Lagan is picked up by a stray dog he names Yew, and together they walk "along the wall of the churchyard." Lagan never enters the church. He "can't walk the miles and miles of Time to meet the singers, to hear the whole hymn lifting them to another condition." But he finds peace and healing in the vicinity, letting the church's "mercy-light" warm him, in the company of his own miracle of connection. "You're a miracle," he tells Yew.[22]

No conventional religion or spirituality here. No soul storms or mystic ecstasies. Yet McIlvoy's writing is spiritual and mystical, as he himself notes. "Eventually," he said in an interview, "you have to face what [Julio Cortázar] calls the metaphysical phase in which you have to confront the fact that your thinking was simple-minded; you have to recognize that what you have done with language reflects spiritual mysteries and mystical experiences."[23] Like Lispector, McIlvoy seeks to write a "more delicate and difficult reality" that cannot be represented in conventional narrative with ordinary language. He too wants to point to the elusive whole, the unseen connections that bind us all together, human to human, human to animal, human to nature, all of us to an emptiness-cum-fullness, a silence full of sound.

Lispector's work presents much more immediately as spiritual and mystical. She, a Jew living in a Catholic country, uses religious language freely, most of it drawn from Christianity: *God, forgiveness, grace, sin, Christ, the cross, communion, miracle, mystery, angels, annunciation, Jesus, the garden.* She embraces ecstasy, which as she says in *A Breath of Life* means "losing the illusory multiplicity of worldly things and starting to feel everything as a whole."[24] Many of her characters (frequently women) experience ecstatic "soul storms,"joyful or horrifying, that well up without warning amid their daily lives (often in kitchens or living rooms) and overwhelm them, physically, mentally, and emotionally. In "The Servant," the maid Eremita drinks "from some unknown fount," ancient and pure. She has found a trail in the forest where she has experiences "in a single glance, too fleeting to be anything but a mystery," of "wholeness of spirit," and for which she has no words.

Though Lispector's characters often find themselves suddenly overcome by something beyond nature, they don't know if their experiences are "mystical or mystifying." But the stories *are* mystical. Lispector is always seeking to write that "more delicate and difficult reality," always writing toward that whole beyond the multiplicity we get lost in. The epigraph she chose for her novella *Água Viva*, translated as *The Stream of Life*, from Michel Seuphor, makes this yearning explicit: "There ought to exist a kind of painting totally free of the dependence on the figure—on the object—which, like music, represents nothing at all, tells no story, and propounds no myth. Such painting limits itself to evoking the incommunicable realms of the spirit, where dream becomes thought, where trace becomes existence."[25]

Lispector and McIlvoy eschew conventional forms to offer us stories to think with. They're not interested in realism or linearity. Their vocation is, as Lispector says in one of her *crônicas*, to honor the silence, the emptiness, that enfolds and undergirds our existence: "Since one is obliged to write, let it be without obscuring the space between the lines of words."[26] Half a century apart, both writers revel in words because they want us to hear the silences, to see between the lines. By stripping down his stories, by opening so many gaps, McIlvoy calls our attention to what is not there, or perhaps to what we sense but cannot draw or write. He reveals that transparent bag the goldfish swims in, the building that once stood where a ruin now greets us, the vibrant person underneath the weary-worn shape standing before us. With her veerings and whirlings and eruptions, Lispector does the same. They both point to "holy possibility," saying, "Look! There's so much more to see."

"The general form of a work of art," Noë says, "is: *See me if you can!*... Every work of art challenges you to see it, or to get it."[27] Works of art are puzzling, and their magic often doesn't strike us on first encounter. McIlvoy's and Lispector's stories certainly bear this out. They may in fact be "all too complicated for a sufficient number of readers to relate to," as an editor tells "the author" in "Mollycrawlbottom," McIlvoy's rejection-letter-cum-story.[28] But for those who love ruins and eddies; who stand in awe before the mystery of the whole and human being; who don't want to remain lost in the complexity of our habits and conventional ideas; who choose inquiry over certainty, puzzlement over answers; who want to gaze into a story in order to walk toward holy possibility, toward the space between the lines, toward the sound at the tip of the ear; for those readers, these stories, these strange tools, will satisfy a deep hunger we may not even know we have.

Chapter 17

In a Crisis, Call in the Poets: The Need for Liminal Leaders

> *How much philosophers would learn if they would*
> *consent to read poets.*
> —Gaston Bachelard[1]

Though I came late to this realization, my intellectual faith journey has been a quest to join theology and art, ideas and imagination. My vocational shift from theology professor to creative writer, from making arguments to telling stories, is but one example of this. I'm convinced that to think well about the meaning of our lives we need art. I'm not talking about incorporating the arts as illustrations of already formed ideas or generating new images for inherited concepts, but the need for imagination and the creations of artists to open up new ways of thinking that our rational minds alone cannot grasp. Art and imagination are not an escape from or denial of reality. They don't correspond to an ideal set of invisible forms or imitate the reality we see. The imagination is not, Gaston Bachelard says, "the faculty for forming the images of reality; it is the faculty for forming images which go beyond reality, which sing reality…[I]t invents a new life, a new spirit; it opens eyes which hold new types of visions."[2]

The power of art and imagination lies in the ability to look so deeply and attentively at the world that we see through and beyond what is to what is possible. They are visionary. And in times of crisis, it is vision we need—not in place of common sense or hardheaded reasoning or creative action, but in addition to them. Vision is liminal. It is neither the old way nor the new, but a space between, a dynamic space inviting us to unform and reform so that we can transform.

One of my most moving encounters as a seminary professor was with a first-year Pentecostal student who came, deeply troubled, to my office and confessed he was losing his faith, the Bible and theology classes were unraveling all he held dear, and he could not think his way out of his distress. After we talked awhile, he shared a dream he had just had. Exploring that dream imagery together led him to embrace his crisis of faith as a liminal moment, which gave him the courage to stand firm in his present uncertainty, free from anxiety, trusting that he would find a way to faith transformed. And he did.

The power of vision to light a way forward when one's world has collapsed was confirmed for me recently by the philosopher Jonathan Lear's book *Radical Hope: Ethics in the Face of Cultural Devastation*. Lear grounds his reflections in the experience of the Crow chief Plenty Coups, who with his people faced the destruction of their culture, their world, and with it the loss of all meaning and all notions of how to live a good life. Many despaired. But Plenty Coups found a path of hope, the first step of which was acknowledging that the traditional way of life—a way of life in which there was no separation between sacred and profane—was over, and no one could change that. His words are poetry: "But when the buffalo went away the hearts of my people fell to the ground, and they could not lift them up again. After that, nothing happened. There was little singing anywhere."[3]

How, then, when all is lost and one doesn't know what to hope for or aim for and can't guess or plan for the future, does one live toward a lifegiving future? By visions. Plenty Coups remained faithful to three prophetic dreams he had had earlier in his life—not visions of the future but visions with rich imagery that gave him the strength and courage to avoid wishful thinking, optimism, nostalgia, and despair, and instead "respond to reality with radical hope, trusting that "we shall get the good back."[4] That was what was required, Lear says, a visionary who could see past disorientation to a transformed future that was not yet clear, in other words, a poet. The devastation called for "a new Crow poet: one who could take up the Crow past and—rather than use it for nostalgia or ersatz mimesis—project it into vibrant new ways for the Crow to live and to be." Lear understands poet here in the "broadest sense of a creative maker of meaningful space," adding that "the possibility for such a poet is precisely the possibility for the creation of a new field of possibilities."[5]

By "astonishing imagination" and fidelity to his visions, Lear says, Plenty Coups transformed "the destruction of a *telos* into a teleological suspension of the ethical" that enabled a new genuine way of life to emerge.[6] Similar transformations happened in the first century of the Common Era. When Jesus was martyred by the Romans, Christians re-imagined him risen in the body of Christ and giving rise to the spirit. Astonishing imagination. When the Romans destroyed the temple in Jerusalem, Jews re-imagined Judaism oriented around Torah, communal prayer, and deeds of lovingkindness as the new sacrifices. Astonishing imagination. Another way to say this might be: The best ones to lead the way in social and cultural crises are those who, instead of retreating to the security of the past, are willing to enter the liminal, the between, in all its sorrows and dangers, and out of that space envision a way forward that is transforms a culture and revivifies it.

A less dramatic example of how a poetic imagination can lead the way in times of radical discontinuity is the novel *Death Comes for the Archbishop* by Willa Cather. Part of the novel's genius is its sophisticated exploration of lived theologies in a time of cultural change and confrontation—from Christology, ecclesiology, missiology, redemption, celibacy, miracles, and Mariology, to strict theology—as it follows the wanderings of priests Jean Latour and Joseph Vaillant from Europe to Ohio to the New World and the United States of America's newly acquired southwest territory once owned by Spain and Mexico. The story circles round the question, How does one plant vines from the old world (European Christianity) in a new world, a seemingly barren wilderness that harbors a world and religion more ancient than that of Europe, Native American peoples with "their own Garden of Eden"? Some characters cling to the past; others abandon it, betray it, or play with it. Some dare to question the superiority of European traditions to Native American traditions, and to teach the priests that "their country is part of their religion" and their "gods dwell in the land just as the Christian God dwells in churches."

Father Latour and Father Joseph are the poets, creative makers of meaningful space, creative visionaries who engender hope and make a path to the new. Like Plenty Coups, they acknowledge that "everything passes" and one must respond to what is, stumbling toward what will be. Each in his own way, one by creative action and the other by creative reflection, suspends his belief about what should be done and how it should be done, and instead responds to the reality facing them—whether a twisted cruciform tree, a "Gothic" mesa, the voice of God in an ancient cave, a battered woman, a murderous priest, or a Navajo friend—in surprising ways. Bishop Latour's recognition that the European hierarchy had no idea of life in the New World enables him to open to new forms of his religion, exemplified in his choice of architectural style for the cathedral in Santa Fe. Observing the majesty of the southwest landscape and that the Indians move through it like "fish in water," he becomes aware that Europeans "master nature." So the cathedral he builds is not a Gothic structure dominating the landscape. It is one that harmonizes with the surrounding mountains, one "worthy of the landscape."[7] Astonishing imagination.

We live in a time of spiritual and religious upheaval as urgent, I believe, as the crises of the first century C.E. We cannot go back to the old ways, and we can't yet see a new flourishing life of faith. Nostalgia won't help, and it's not enough to be optimistic. We need the courage to look to the future of faith with radical hope. For this, theologians and philosophers are not enough, however creative they may be. We need poets, visionaries, generous-hearted people of imagination who clear a space between what is gone and what is yet to come, where we can open our imaginations to radically different possibilities, trusting that "we will get the good back." We need threshold people, people who are able to enter the fraught between, look around, and offer us a way forward. They may be poets in the broad sense, like Plenty Coups, creative makers of meaningful space. They may be novelists like Cather, or poets like Yehuda Amichai, Nelly Sachs, Joy Harjo, Naomi Shihab Nye, or Jericho Brown. Whoever they may be, let us consent to listen to them—and not despair.

A Dynamic Nexus

Chapter 18

The Body Leads the Way: Ritual, Liminality, and Imagination

> *What is now proved was once, only imagin'd.*
> —William Blake, *The Marriage of Heaven and Hell*

Ritual, or ritualizing, as I suggested in the Introduction, is a unique embodied thinking activity. It is an intentional sequence of acts or gestures or body movements, performed individually or in community, that enacts meaning by sanctifying space and time, carving out a moment from the endless flow of time and erecting a temporary shelter in the vast expanse of our world, a "holy between," a liminal time and space we can step into to cross over from the profane to the sacred and back.

This broad view of ritual and liminality as the body leading the way to transformation underlies all the previous essays in this book. In this chapter, I look more closely at the interplay of embodiment, ritual, liminality, and imagination that lies behind that understanding.

Embodiment: Ritual as a Way of Enacting Meaning

Ritual involves the whole being, our embodied selves, *in action, in motion*, whether we're lighting candles, receiving the Eucharist, performing *rakat*, Sundancing, walking a labyrinth, forest bathing, or sitting in prayer or meditation. This embodiment is one reason those who study ritual today choose to speak of *ritualizing* more than *ritual*, which often has a connotation of being static.[1] You can't read or speak ritual; you must *do* ritual. And that doing generates a surplus of meaning, which enables each individual to experience the same ritual anew at different times in their life and different individuals to each participate in their own way in a shared ritual. As the ancient *midrash* imagines, manna tasted different to each of the 600,000 Israelites, depending on their

unique situation and need: to young men like bread, to the elderly
like wafers made with honey, to babies like mother's milk, to the
sick like fine flour mingled with honey, and to those lacking faith
as bitter as linseed.[2]

Words recited over and over or shared with others—
sacred texts, prayers, liturgies, creeds—invite multiple meanings
too. The Kabbalists speak of "the seventy faces of Torah," which,
Gershom Scholem explains "simply represents the inexhaustible
totality and meaning of the divine word."[3] Words are miraculous.
They create worlds. And yet, even when they are used poetically
and not in common, ordinary usage, words are not enough. We,
embodied beings, earth creatures, require the receptivity, the
openness and movement, the unity and flow of gesture as well as
the distinctions and precision that words, naming, offer. As the
rushing-spirit hovering over the face of the waters flowed and
flows into "Let there be light!" so gesture and word go hand in
hand in the creation of meaning.

Meaning, as Maurice Merleau-Ponty emphasizes in
Phenomenology of Perception, is not a product of the mind, but a
creation of the body-mind. It arises from our interactions with the
world; meaning is embodied. "Truth does not 'inhabit' only 'the
inner man,' or more accurately, there is no inner man, man is in
the world, and only in the world does he know himself."[4] The
body, then, is not a thing or object bumping up against others or a
vehicle for expressing concepts, ideas, or experiences, but our way
of engaging the world. "My body appears to me as an *attitude*
directed toward a certain existing or possible task," he writes.
"And indeed its spatiality is not, like that of external objects or like
that of 'spatial sensation,' a spatiality of position, but a spatiality
of situation."[5] How our bodies are situated in the world, our
attitude, understood in this context as *readiness for acting*, is not
merely a physical sensation or an awareness of our location; it is
already a knowing.

Gesture, therefore, understood widely as bodily motions,
including speech acts or language, is not bodily movements that
express pre-conceived thoughts; gesture, by situating us in the
world, orienting our bodies in our environment, *enacts* meaning.

The gesture itself, whether linguistic or non-linguistic, brings meaning into existence. When confronted with an angry face or gesture, Merleau-Ponty explains, "the gesture doesn't make me think of anger, it is anger itself."[6] Gesture is fundamental to meaning. And, as Mark Johnson emphasizes in *The Aesthetics and Meaning of Thought*, "meaning is not dependent on language." There is meaning "beyond and beneath language," for example, in two people dancing slowly to soft music in low light.[7]

As besotted as I am with words, it is gesture, understood in the narrower sense, as non-linguistic bodily motions, that fascinates me. Perhaps because gesture evokes meaning beyond and beneath the sharp distinctions and control that words bring. Perhaps because gesture feels less distancing than words, closer to the immediacy of experiencing the differentiated yet unified whole that is our world. And perhaps because, like visual image gesture shares more directly in the physical world, the realm of bodies and movement, and allows for an even wider scope of interpretation and participation than words, offering greater inclusion with greater diversity.

Whether these felt comparisons are accurate or not, the creation of meaning through gesture intrigues me, and this creation of meaning through gesture comes down to ritual. Ritual actions *situate* us in our world, they *orient* us. In rituals we move our bodies as attitudes directed toward an existing or possible task. Ritual choreography—facing Jerusalem or Mecca when praying, circumambulating the Kaaba or a *stupa*, turning toward the four directions, or whirling like the planets—is designed to facilitate this orientation of the body, to evoke a certain attitude toward the task at hand.

Ritual spaces are designed to situate the body as well. The temple in Jerusalem opened to the east, with an outer court, sanctuary, and the holy of holies guiding bodies toward the ineffable even as they shielded them from it. Roman churches open to the west, the setting sun, the Day of Judgment that marks the end of temporal life and the beginning of eternal life. Gothic cathedrals lift the body toward the heavens. Many contemporary churches, with their vast, transparent windows, orient bodies outward, toward the natural world. The Sundance circle centers on a cottonwood tree, the *axis mundi* around which all action occurs, and dancers enter and exit from the east. The circle or wheel of a *stupa* rests on a square, with each side, north, south, east, and west, having its own gate, with its own meaning, that one can choose to enter. These choreographic and architectural directives or nudges are born of the wisdom that ritual enacts meaning and the body leads the way.

Much of why I was drawn to Judaism and converted when I was 40 was because it is purposefully embodied and action-oriented, gesture-affirming and ritual-rich. Jews may be known as a "people of the book," but we communicate faith and traditions through a treasury of shared rituals. Part of the genius of Jewish tradition is that it transforms everything into gesture or ritual. Laws are perforce enacted—wearing a *tallit* and *tefillin* for morning prayers, not wearing wool and linen together, cracking each egg carefully to see if it contains a blood spot, lighting Shabbat candles and sanctifying wine and bread every seventh day—every table an altar around which the kindom (*sic*) of priests gathers. The community's history and sacred narratives are also enacted, so that Jews in every generation, in whatever culture they find themselves, may experience them "as if they were there," as the Passover *haggadah* teaches. *Shabbat* practices *enact* the Creator resting on the seventh day and glorying in the goodness of creation. The *kashrut* practices and seder of Passover enact the Exodus from Egypt, the candles and latkes of Hanukkah enact the Maccabean revolt, and dwelling in *sukkahs* enacts the wandering in the desert.

The philosopher Marc-Alain Ouaknin calls Jewish ritual "gestural memory," or "the third way of transmitting myth," alongside oral and written transmission.[8] I don't interpret this phrasing as perpetuating a dualism in which myth and ritual, mind and body, are separate and mind takes precedence over body. Gestural memory does not express or represent or re-enact the meaning of an event or thought that has already happened, nor does it simply symbolize mythic reality: *It enacts fresh meaning for the doers.* The doing is not an aesthetic add-on or a dressed-up idea; it is essential to meaning. As Merleau-Ponty wrote, meaning is inseparable from the act. Rather than a re-presentation of what happened (whether in myth or history), it is a doing that is thinking. As many commentators, ancient and contemporary, have noted, Israel's response to the revelation of the Torah at Sinai, *naaseh v'nishma*, "we will do and we will hear" (Exodus 24:7), underscores this emphasis on action leading to understanding. The body leads the way.

Rituals, then, may be understood as intentional sequences of symbolic acts or gestures or body movements that enact meaning and create connections across time and space for those who perform them.

Dichotomies of myth and ritual, thought and action, belief and behavior underlie much ritual theory, as Catherine Bell has demonstrated in her extended critique of ritual theories that assume such bifurcation. Her view of ritualization as a strategic way of acting in specific social situations emphasizes ritualizing in a way that avoids these dichotomies, as does Ronald L. Grimes's emphasis on ritualizing as enactment.[9] In describing the activity of ritualizing, however, I prefer to borrow the phrase anthropologist Tim Ingold uses for the fundamental human activity of *making*. He calls making—in all its variations, from basket weaving to cathedral building to fashioning a hand axe—"a unique embodied thinking activity."[10] Ritualizing, too, is an activity of the mind, a unique embodied thinking activity.

As enacted meaning that arises from and with bodily movement, rituals open to an inexhaustible well of meanings, widely diverse yet shareable, that can ground and orient participants' lives, individually and communally. As enacted meaning, rituals situate our bodies in the world in an unfamiliar way, a way unlike our usual stance, and by doing so, open up a space or moment for participants to enter in which they can imagine, experience, and live into fresh meaning. This is an experience of a liminal moment or space. This capacity of ritual to interrupt or disrupt our usual way of moving through the world and open us to new ways of perceiving, being, and acting is one reason why participating in rituals can be so powerful.

Liminality: Ritual as a Way to Enter the Between

Sociologist Robert Bellah makes this astonishing observation in his summary of paleontology and neuroscience in *Religion in Human Evolution*: "Other apes lack two skills that are important for humans: the ability to throw accurately, undoubtedly helpful for hunting with weapons, and the ability to keep together in time, without which skillful dancing [and other sequences of novel postures] would be impossible."[11] Rituals are a kind of skillful dance we *homo sapiens* perform together. Other animals besides human beings ritualize, but certain kinds of sequenced actions are available only to human beings. Similar to the Paleolithic art found in the caves of Lascaux and Chauvet, ritual is found at the very beginning of history. Like art, which the philosopher R. G. Collingwood saw as "the primary and fundamental activity of the *mind*"[12] ritual, far from being "primitive" or "archaic," is fundamental to how we understand ourselves and act in the world. We, the dancing apes—the most liminal of apes?—move together in time, performing a specific set of symbolic gestures intended to transform our relation to ourselves and our world, out of which something new may arise.

Rituals, for Bellah, are summed up best by the anthropologist Clifford Geertz: rituals are not representations of religious events but religious *actions*, actions that create worlds; rituals create the world as imagined, which is joined to the world as lived, which in turn leads to the transformation of one's sense of reality. "In ritual, the world as lived and the world as imagined, fused under the agency of a single set of symbolic forms, turn out to be the same world, producing thus that idiosyncratic transformation in one's sense of reality," opening vistas and mysteries, *creating*, as George Santayana, says, *another world to live in*.[13]

This view of ritual as opening to another world was illuminated by the sociologist Emile Durkheim in *The Elementary Forms of the Religious Life*. In his descriptive analysis of dancing in tribal societies, Durkheim suggested how ritual and liminal experiences are linked.

> One can readily see how, when arrived at this state of exaltation, a man does not recognize himself any longer. Feeling himself dominated and carried away by some sort of external power which makes him think and act differently than in normal times, he naturally has the impression of being himself no longer. It seems to him that he has become a new being ... . And as at the same time all his companions feel themselves transformed in the same way ... everything is just as though he really were transported into a special world, entirely different from the one where he ordinarily lives, and into an environment filled with exceptionally
> intense forces that take hold of him and metamorphose him.[14]

As Bellah points out, this description of what happens during rituals makes it clear that, for Durkheim, ritual is disruptive and transformative; it is "a break with the rhythm of everyday life."[15] "[T]he world of ritual is quite different from the one 'where his daily life drags wearily along.' It is the world of the sacred in contrast to the profane everyday." In ritual events participants experience "collective effervescence," a state in which they experience "a different and deeper reality" and feel they are "transported into a special world," a feeling that disrupts their experience of the ordinary lived world and effects a transformation in their relation to the world.[16] Ritual does not represent or symbolize the sacred; in ritual the profane *becomes* sacred.

In his recent book, *The Power of the Sacred: An Alternative to the Narrative of Disenchantment*, Hans Joas points to two significant contributions of Durkheim that are still relevant to our understanding of ritual and the sacred: the *power* of ritual in human existence and the recognition that "sacredness" exists

outside religious institutions.[17] These are the two insights from
Durkheim that have guided my reflections on ritual from the time
I wrote my first essay on ritual and liminality (Chapter 1 on
dancing). I also agree with Joas that while Durkheim's distinction
between the sacred and the profane, the "quotidian and the
extraquotidian-ecstatic" is essential, we need to "develop a richer
phenomenology of such experiences of self-transcendence" than
he provided[18] and that his theory of ritual "requires a far more
radical revision of our ideas about human action."[19] This is the
direction in which the essays in this book moved as I explored
ritual and liminality through practicing ritual and participating in
rituals, alone or with others.

Taking cues (not systems) from Durkheim, Bellah, and
Turner, as well as contemporary anthropologists and
phenomenologists, I have pursued my own understanding of
ritual. Ritual, I have come to believe, is an intentional sequence of
symbolic actions that enacts meaning by joining the world as lived
and the world as imagined in such a way that it interrupts our
ordinary way of being in the world and bumps us into a liminal
space, a fertile betweenness.[20]

The word *liminal* comes from the Latin word *limen*,
threshold. When looked at primarily in the context of rites of
passage rituals, the liminal state is seen as a passage from one way
of being in a society to another; it is a temporary phase defined by
ambiguity, the moment *between* one's old way of being in a
structure and being reintegrated into that same structure with a
new role or status. Crossing a threshold is an apt metaphor for the
understanding of liminality in rites of passage, and it is also
fruitful for understanding liminality more broadly, as its ongoing
use in multiple disciplines confirms.[21]

The image of threshold may be helpful, for example, in
speaking of ritual as it is developed here, as an intentional series
of actions that enact meaning. This broad understanding of ritual
as creating a temporary fertile between, however, also invites
different metaphors for imagining a dynamic between that both
delimits and links two distinct entities.[22] The metaphor of
moonstones drawn from ancient sacred architecture and

developed in Chapter 14, for example, can help us think about the experience of liminality. Another metaphor that might be fruitful is that of a littoral zone (from the Latin *litus*, shore), an intertidal zone where water and land meet, a zone that is constantly shifting from exposed to submerged with the ebbing and rising tides. The constant flow or flux of this between zone supports the greatest biodiversity, suggesting the dynamism and creativity of liminal spaces. And though the concept of a littoral zone or nearshore can be defined, concrete instances of it do not have sharp boundaries; the precise line between a specific body of land and the littoral zone or between a particular body of water and the littoral zone is difficult if not impossible to determine. The focus is on *what lives, what happens* in that "between,"[23] not on drawing its exact boundaries.

A metaphor akin to moonstones and the littoral zone that is also fruitful in imagining the between is that of a *barzakh*, literally "limit," which comes from the work of the philosopher-mystic Ibn 'Arabî (1165-1240 C.E.). A *barzakh* is an isthmus, the place where two seas meet, salt and sweet, but do not touch or mingle. It is an indefinable boundary region or space that separates, distinguishes two defined spaces or realms. The two sides it touches are *distincto non divise*: distinct, not divided. Though neither side touches the other in the *barzakh*, the two are related by the *barzakh*, which means the *barzakh* is a between that paradoxically unifies as it separates.[24]

Ibn 'Arabî uses this term, William C. Chittick explains,[25] to refer to anything that simultaneously divides and brings together two things, without itself having two sides, like the line that separates sunlight and shade. Or the dream world which lies between waking and sleeping. Or the time between death and resurrection. For Ibn 'Arabî, however, a fundamental instance of *barzakh* is the imaginal world, an intermediate world that lies *between* the Real and the impossible, or *between* Nondelimited Being (infinite and absolute, undefined and indefinable being or True Light) and articulated words (all that is defined and limited) a world that is not identified with either yet shares in both. "The imaginal—not imaginary—reality is one that dwells in an intermediate domain between two other realities and shares in the attributes of both sides."[26]

This intermediate world, which Ibn 'Arabî often refers to as the "Breath of the All-Merciful," is the most hidden—like the imperceptible line between dusk and day or dusk and night—and "the vastest of presences," since it "combines the two worlds, the World of the Unseen and the World of the Visible."[27] In this world of the Imaginal or Imagination, which he also calls the world of "compelling power," form becomes meaning and meaning takes form. For Ibn 'Arabî, for example, it is in the isthmus between God's presence and absence that prayer, the converse between the One and human beings, takes place. And, we might add, it is in the isthmus where form becomes meaning and meaning takes form that ritual takes place.

Though it uses very different language, an ancient Yemenite *midrash* on Exodus from the fourteenth or fifteenth century C.E. offers an uncannily similar view of liminality as a *barzakh*, a twilight between, an intermediate state of existence in which two others are distinguished yet linked in the creation of the world. The *midrash* begins by quoting the *Talmud, Pirkei Avot* 5:8: "Our rabbis taught, 'Ten things were created during twilight, and they are these: the mouth of the earth, the mouth of the well, the mouth of the ass, the rainbow, the manna, the staff, the *shamir* [the worm used in divination], the writing, the writing instrument, and the tablets.'" Though *Pirkei Avot* specifies that the twilight occurs on the eve of Shabbat, this is omitted in the Yemenite version, which continues:

> These happened "at twilight" because it was not necessary that these ten things should exist, nor was it necessary that they should not exist. Another item. These actions were associated with twilight because that is an [intermediate] state between two different states. From the aspect of his will (may He be exalted). It [each of the ten things] was possible, but from the aspect of the nature of things it was impossible. Their existence was somewhere

between the impossible and the possible. Their possibility is due to His will (may He be exalted)—which [will] created the whole world as He wanted it to be created. That moment [twilight] is in supposed time, not real time, for time is absolute.[28]

These ten were singled out, the *midrash* explains, because though there are many miracles, the others, the "necessary miracles," were created not at twilight but during the six days of creation. During the days of creation the Creator placed within the breast the power to give milk, within the seed the power to yield fruit, within the sun the power to stand still, and within the nature of water the power to split at the Red Sea. During the nights of creation, the Creator created those things that it is necessary not to exist, of which it is better not to speak. Only in twilight, neither the realm of that which is necessary nor the realm of that which is impossible but a realm between those two creations, a realm of creation that opens to the possible, do these ten exist.

Ontology and miracles aside—whether or not the entire cosmos is a *barzakh* or the twilight creation exists and contains these ten non-necessary miracles—I find the images of *barzakh* and the twilight of creation fruitful for understanding ritual and creativity. I take *barzakh* or twilight to mean that creative space between what is necessary and what is impossible—in other words, the time and field of the possible, the realm between the world that is, the world as we experience it normally, and the world that does not yet exist, the imagination—the place that ritual opens up and where many artists live and work.[29]

A contemporary way to understand this concept of liminality might be to see it as a dynamic third space that alters our perception, or in terms of what philosopher Alva Noë calls "metainstability" in perception. He offers Jastrow's classic ambiguous figure as an example. First you see a duck, then a rabbit (or vice versa). Once you have flipped back and forth between the two, "you experience the figure as actively ambiguous," and a third view comes into play in which you know both the duck and the rabbit are present, even though you see only one. This third view is a new coming into focus after focusing on one or the other image. Your mind doesn't merge or compound the two images. Nor does it simply shift back and forth temporally between the two. Instead, you experience being in a third state, "the experience of unstable ambiguity, which has its own distinct character" and its own unity.[30] The *barzhak* and the twilight of creation, the liminal state, are like that dynamic, distinctive third state of perception in which you leave behind certainty and experience shifting views, an unstable ambiguity, in a new unity: once you've experienced it, it affects everything you see and do.

What one experiences in ritual is like the experience of the *barzakh*, the twilight creation, or the third state of perception, Noë's metastability. It is not a state in which one is acting out of necessity or in one's usual or habitual ways. It is not a state in which one is attempting the impossible or reaching for a state that completely leaves behind ordinary reality. Instead, it is a between state in which one enacts new meaning in a realm of possibility, where new ways of feeling, thinking, acting in our world are imagined and experienced. To cross over an isthmus, to step into the twilight, is to dwell for a moment in a dynamic, transformative space where one's awareness is heightened, expanded, pulsing with possibility. Standing on an isthmus (or on moonstones, an architectural rendering of an isthmus, as described in Chapter 14), resting in the twilight, one is aware of *more*. One does not experience a merging of what lies on either side, visible and invisible, dark and light, profane and sacred. One does not turn first to one side, then the other, and back again. Instead, one is aware of both sides with the pulsing between, and from that awareness arises a sense of new possibilities, a transformation of one's self and one's relation to the world that one carries when reentering everyday reality. This betweenness is the power of ritual as it gives rise to experiences of liminality.

Homo Liminalis and the Power of Imagination

What makes it possible for ritual, in the broad sense we've been using it, to open us to liminal experiences like these? It is our existence as liminal beings, *homo liminalis*.

Ibn 'Arabî uses the term Supreme Barzakh (*al-barzakh al-a'lâ*) as a synonym for Nondelimited Imagination, by which he means the entire cosmos, which is the realm of possible things in his worldview, things which in themselves are neither necessary nor impossible, neither infinite nor finite, neither visible nor invisible. In other words, for Ibn 'Arabî, the entire cosmos, or what we so blithely call "the creation," is a liminal state.

> The Real is sheer Light and the impossible is sheer darkness. Darkness never turns into Light, and Light never turns into darkness. The created realm is the *barzakh* between Light and darkness. In its essence it is qualified neither by darkness nor by Light, since it is the *barzakh* and the middle, having a property from each of its two sides. That is why He "appointed" for man "two eyes and guided him on the two highways" (*Koran* 90:8–10), for man exists between the two paths. Through one eye and one path he accepts Light and looks upon it in the measure of his preparedness. Through the other eye and the other path he looks upon darkness and turns toward it.[31]

Human beings, as microcosm, participate in all three worlds or presences. We are spirit, body, and soul. Though all three belong to the cosmos understood as *barzakh*, with respect to human existence we may say that the soul or imagination is the *barzakh* that joins body and spirit.

Soul or imagination, then, refers to intermediate realm, neither luminous nor dark, neither alive nor dead, neither subtle nor dense, neither conscious nor unconscious, but always somewhere between the two extremes. Through imagination, the high and low interpenetrate, the bright and dark unite. Imagination is neither high nor low, luminous nor dark, spirit nor body. It is defined by its "in-betweenness."[32] Like the image of oneself in a mirror, "imagination is neither existent nor nonexistent, neither known nor unknown, neither negated nor affirmed." And one who sees oneself in a mirror is neither a truth-teller nor a liar in [saying the] words 'I saw my form, I did not see my form.'"[33] Both are true. The person experiences these two different truths in a new unity in the intermediate realm of soul or imagination, similar to Noë's third state of metainstability in perception, in which the image of a duck and a rabbit are both held in by the perceiver in a new unity of unstable ambiguity.

What Ibn 'Arabî calls "soul" and or "imagination" is where spirit and body meet. Again, we need not accept Ibn 'Arabî 's full ontology or anthropology to be inspired by his view of imagination as a between, a distinctive fertile meeting ground, one might say, of the body and mind. It's essential to note here that Ibn 'Arabî, like Merleau-Ponty and many contemporary philosophers, is not a dualist. For him, as Chittick points out, spirit and body are "qualitative distinctions not discrete entities; "one can speak of them as "dimensions of the microcosm."[34] Or, more to my liking, they are powers that enable us to engage the world in different ways. Imagination, for example, is the power of the soul that "bridges the spiritual and the corporeal."[35] It is active, creative. As liminal beings, we are always moving back and forth between the invisible and the visible worlds or presences, bridging the two in fresh ways. Chittick quotes one of Ibn 'Arabî's disciples as saying, "The *barzakh* is a world where the outward becomes inward, and the inward outward."[36] This seems to me a handy way to speak of ritual as well: Ritual is a space where the outward (act) becomes inward (thought) and the inward outward. Perhaps ritual is one of the ways we remind ourselves we are liminal beings and intentionally open ourselves up to the power of transforming ourselves and our way of being in the world.

For though we are gloriously complex creatures, liminal beings, we struggle to live at peace with ourselves. As many philosophers and cognitive scientists have argued, dualistic concepts and images that divide body and spirit or body and mind have tainted and continue to taint our ideas and our experience of ourselves.[37] Many binaries are rooted in the body/mind hierarchy: the inner and outer life, the sacred and the profane, religion or spirituality and the secular world, nature and nurture, women and men, queer and straight, the enslaved and the free, the beautiful and the ugly, Black or Brown and White, the Other and ourself.

One way to resist this perceptual, cognitive, and cultural drag toward dualism is to reflect on our existence as liminal creatures, our experience of *living between*, living in an uneasy, destabilizing tension between two elements, two worlds, two pulls, two forces, two perspectives, two ways of being the same reality, like wave and particle, like the self in the mirror and the self looking at the mirror. Whatever we may name these two— matter and spirit, body and soul, body and mind, instinct and consciousness, outer and inner, nature and culture—it is that tension between them, the tangled existence we find ourselves in that I honor and explore in relation to ritual, for ritual is one of the ways we enact and nourish our existence as liminal beings.

As liminal beings, we're unstable, pulled in two different directions. We find it hard to inhabit or remain aware of that *between*, whether we imagine it as a *barzakh*, or twilight creation, or as Noë's idea of a third state of perception that alters our view of two different images. In our anxiety, we try to resolve the instability we experience, to halt the teeter totter of existence, so we deny that we are liminal, and choose one image of ourselves as the definitive one, the duck or the rabbit, the self in the mirror or the self-looking at the mirror. For some of us, that means landing in our bodies, tending to them, following their lead always, and ignoring anything beyond the realm of the physical because it is beyond our reach or comprehension. For others of us it means living the life of the mind or the ethereal life of the spirit and ignoring the body, giving it its due, but treating it as a second-class citizen at best. Most of the time we find it hard to hold the two together. Rare is the person who doesn't live as if one side of this challenging, de-stabilizing experience we call human be-ing doesn't exist or doesn't really matter. One of the most difficult challenges of being human is learning to live at home in our bodies, to reconcile our bodies and our minds, nature and spirit, which we experience often as irreconcilable.

What if, as many scientists, philosophers, and mystics have argued, matter is coming to consciousness through us, the human creature? What would our task as human beings look like then? Not to give ourselves over to the needs and limitations and desires of our bodies and the physical universe, just sinking into it, whether by addictive behaviors or ordinary habits. Nor to transcend matter by leaping into the spiritual realm, escaping or transcending the limitations of the material world by getting "high" through prayer or meditation or other spiritual disciplines. Our task is much more challenging: It is to live in such a way that these two irreconcilable ways of being are reconciled in our every feeling, thought, and action. Why are we here? For this, says Pir Vilayat Khan: "the materialization of spirit and the spiritualization of matter."[38] Martin Buber says it this way: "In their true essence, the two worlds are one. They only have, as it were, moved apart. But they shall again become one, as they are in their true essence. Man was created for the purpose of unifying the two worlds."[39] This is Ibn 'Arabî's view of the barzakh, liminal human being.

Ritualizing is one of the ways we are nourished and encouraged in this task of unification of our two distinct ways of being, of learning to hold them together in however unstable a whole. Perhaps it is this very anxiety at our difficult two-at-oneness, our dis-ease with the coexistence of incommensurates, our being a problem to ourselves, that gives us a hunger for ritual, in the sense I have described it, as a way to open up a liminal space we can enter to remember and enact our complex, dynamic way of being, to remind ourselves that mystery of our existence cannot be comprehended by reducing our lives to our bodies or our minds, to remind ourselves that we are homo liminalis, the meeting ground where spirit is materialized and matter is spiritualized.[40] Ritual is a powerful way to remember and experience our liminal existence, to nourish ourselves as liminal beings, through the power of imagination.

Ritual as an Invitation to Enter the Holy Between

Even as we forget we are liminal beings, we seem drawn to liminality, liminal moments, and liminal spaces, as many contemporary studies have shown. Across millennia and cultures, we continue to create and participate in rituals, which can open us to liminality. In ritual we experience the conjoining of body and spirit. In ritual, our bodies, gestures, objects, spaces, become portals as it were, openings to a more complex reality that is neither what is, nor what is not, but what may be. Ritual invites us to remember we are liminal beings, body, soul, spirit, and enter a between that may alter how we live.

This view of ritual as an invitation to liminality depends on the view of ritual developed here, with an emphasis on bodies and *action*, not cosmology or cosmogony. The historian of religion Mircea Eliade, for example, focused on ritual as "symbolic reiterations" of the origins of the universe, tying ritual to myth.[41] Jonathan Z. Smith argues against this approach in *To Take Place: Toward Theory in Ritual*. In ritual, Smith says, we are not taking about *symbolizing* place, putting in place, or replacing an original order; we are talking about what it means "to take place." For Smith this means

> [R]itual is, first and foremost, a mode of paying attention. It is a process for marking interest. It is the recognition of this fundamental characteristic of ritual that most sharply distinguishes our understanding from that of the Reformers, with
> their all too easy equation of ritual with blind and thoughtless habit. It is this characteristic as well, that explains the role of place as a component of ritual: place directs attention.[42]

Ritual, then, in the sense of "to take place" rather than as symbolizing or replicating a myth or idea or preexisting order, depends for its meaning on bodies in action in the physical world. This understanding of place in relation to ritual is best illustrated, Smith says, by "built ritual environments—most especially, crafted constructions such as temples." When one enters a "marked-off space," everything, at least potentially, "demands one's attention." In built ritual environments, "[a] ritual object or action becomes sacred by having attention focused on it in a highly marked way."[43] He gives as his example the *Song of Songs*, which, when sung in a tavern is a set of "erotic ditties," but when chanted in a temple (or other ritual space) is sacred. It is not only the content of the song but the location or the use of it that makes it sacred or profane.

Similarly, there is no inherent difference between a sacred vessel or an ordinary one. They *become* sacred if used in a sacred place: "A sacred text is a text that is *used in a sacred place*—nothing else is required." Ritual, then, "is not an expression of or a response to the 'the Sacred'; rather, something or someone is *made sacred by ritual* (the primary sense of *sacrificium*)." That means divine and human, sacred and profane, "are transitive categories; they serve as maps and labels not substances; they are distinctions of office, indices of difference."[44] The Sacred, then, is not a nominative, an unchanging substantive, but an indication of a particular way of *relating* to the world, not our ordinary, everyday way of living. Ritual, as a mode of paying attention, is a *practice* of sanctifying, *making something sacred*. Ritual is *active*, dynamic. By paying attention, we transform the profane into the sacred.

Smith's understanding of ritual as attention is akin to philosopher Alva Noë's view of the aesthetic, which he calls an "attentional discipline." For Noë, the aesthetic interrupts our ordinary way of being in the world. It is a kind of resistance.[45] "The aesthetic is a name for the ever-ongoing process of bringing what there is into an always fragile focus; it is the *movement*, always subject to second-guessing, from not-seeing to seeing, or from seeing to seeing differently. The aesthetic is the fragile, productive (but also entangled) enacting of our consciousness itself." It is "intentionally effortful reorientation."[46] Similar to phenomenologist Edmund Husserl's *epoche* or bracketing of the world, aesthetics or art distances us from the ordinary world in order to see more. Just as our bodies orient us in the world, so ritual, the intentional displacement of our bodies, reorients us.

I understand ritual in this way, as a kind of resistance to getting stuck in the ordinary—the opposite of common views of ritual as nothing more than routine. Ritual is an intentional *reorienting* of ourselves in time and space, through time and space, with our bodies, movement through our bodies and only because of our bodies. Ritual helps us resist the mundane, the profane world, our world of habits, to transform our relation to the world, to see in new ways so we can be in new ways. We do not ritualize to access a Sacred world or dimension "out there" or "up there"or "over there" with authorized acts. Rather, we act in such a way that something may "take place." We perform a sequence of acts that interrupts our habitual way of being and acting in the world, that transforms us and our relation to the world, that enacts meaning and opens up new possibilities for acting within that world. This is what connects ritual to imagination and art, and also philosophy. For Noë, art and philosophy "aim at ecstasy, total release from the states that have pinned us. Though one aims at understanding and the other at pleasure, they both are aesthetic in this sense. Art and philosophy require of us that we work ourselves over and make ourselves anew, individually and ensemble."[47]

Because ritual helps us shift our orientation, our way of being in the world; because it offers us an opportunity for ecstasy, understood as standing apart from or a release from our ordinary ways of perceiving and acting; because it fosters relation rather than separation, within oneself and with others; because it offers radical transformation, I call this between, this realm of the possible that ritual opens up, a "*holy* between." I use *holy* here in the sense of the sacred that arises (or can arise) from ritual, similar to what Durkheim was pointing to when he spoke of "collective effervescence": an experience that goes beyond our ordinary experience of living in the world, our everyday experience of usefulness, productivity, means and ends, practical goals; or as Wordsworth has it: our experience that "[t]he world is too much with us; late and soon,/Getting and spending, we lay waste our powers."[48]

Joas speaks of this sense of the sacred in broad terms as self-transcendence.[49] Because of my focus on liminality, however, and my emphasis on ritual as active and relational, I prefer to use the language of a *holy between*. I understand this phrase in terms of the experience Martin Buber so poetically points to in *I and Thou*. For Buber the between is a place of encounter between self and that which is not self, in which one goes forth from the I-It world of everyday life to meet the You coming toward one, the You that "confronts [one] *bodily*."[50] Every single You one meets is a glimpse of the eternal You. "One does not find God if one remains in the world; one does not find God if one leaves the world. Whoever goes forth to his You with his whole being and carries to it all the being of the world, finds him whom one cannot seek"[51] These holy betweens, these meetings, these glimpses can occur in any of our relationships—with nature, with other human beings, with God. They are not found only within contexts that are intended to be religious and spiritual, and their reality does not depend on their being identified as sacred or holy. This freedom from dependence on a restricted context is true of the rituals that give rise to the liminal, to holy betweens, as well.

For Buber, meeting a You is neither wholly active nor passive. You may prepare yourself for it, be open to it, but you cannot force it. This is true of ritualizing as well. In ritualizing, we may create the conditions for liminal experience, invite a shift in our orientation to the world, but there is no guarantee that this will result from our actions. Ritual is not magic, it is not superstition. In ritual we may step into a holy between, we may be seized by a holy between, we may be lifted into a holy between—or we may remain unmoved, left with our ordinary sense of the world, our I-It relations.

A Note on Liminality and Danger in Ritual

As a place of creativity and imagination, an opening to the new, a clearing that makes way for what is not yet, the between that arises from ritualizing is also holy in the sense of Rudolf Otto's *mysterium tremendum et fascinans*, a disturbing, unsettling, dangerous, at times terrifying place that is paradoxically welcoming and transforming.

This view of the liminal as the holy between and ritual as radical attention and an invitation to the liminal should not be read as glossing over the dangers of liminality. The liminal is a zone of danger. One might react fearfully to it and become paralyzed. On might get lost in it and never emerge. One might emerge only to retreat to the old structures and harden them in order to protect oneself from fear of the new. One might become addicted to the ecstatic state and withdraw from the world or from ordinary action. One might become habituated to a ritual, or addicted to its sequence of acts as an end in itself, depleting it of its power. One might be overwhelmed by fear, or loneliness, or depression, for liminal experiences often require sacrifices—not something most people are eager to embrace or talk about. When one is between, to move forward one might have to give up one's job, one's community, one's place, one's comforting sense of one's self, one's reputation, one's ego. Loss can be painful. At their extremes, liminal experiences can also be felt as a death.

Paradoxically, ritual recognizes the danger of the between and offers ways to help participants move through it to new life. Though I have characterized ritual as interruption of or resistance to our ordinary structures or ways or organizing life, ritual also offers a structure that enables one to bear the uncertainty, the metainstability, of liminal states. This is one of its gifts. In the rites of passage studied by van Gennep and Turner, the young men and women making the passage from childhood to adulthood are required to perform daring acts, not only to prove their worth but to overcome their fear. In secular societies, the transition to adulthood is no less fraught with danger. Not for nothing do sociologists and psychologists speak of adolescence as "a bridge one must cross over," a dangerous bridge with no guarantee of arriving safely or whole on the other side. In the absence of prescribed, sanctioned rituals in the contemporary Western world, teenage dares of jumping into quarries or off bridges may function in a similar way to allay fears and strengthen resolve to make the crossing unscathed.

In the Sundance of Native American tribes, a ritual of healing and transformation, participants sacrifice themselves in many ways. They go without eating from sun-up to sun-down. They dance continuously in the hot sun. Some pierce themselves in the chest and tie themselves to the sacred tree or buffalo robes to tear away their flesh. Others cut away small pieces of flesh from their upper arms. They sacrifice their desires, their flesh, their blood in these ritual ways. They do this not as a transaction, a payment as a guarantee of the outcome of their dancing: If I give this, I will get that. Nor is it an appeasement of an angry God or gods who have inflicted suffering on them or their community. Rather, these acts acknowledge the pain and the sacrifices that are involved in any transformation of an individual or community, for example, from living as an alcoholic to living sober, from despair to radical hope.

Rituals offer a structure, a small, temporary, predictable pattern or container that grounds participants as they dwell in the nebulous and unsettling between, that tethers them as they enter the realm of imagination and possibility on the way to enacting new meaning or creating new structures. Rituals help us to safely make the dangerous journey from what was to what may be.

Invitation: Turn Aside

Throughout these essays, I have presented ritual or ritualizing as a creative, unique embodied way of thinking that can interrupt habitual ways of living and open up a holy between, a liminal space or time for us to enter wherein we can pay attention, standing apart from our ordinary ways of acting and being in order to imagine and envision new ways of being and transform our relationship to ourselves and our world.

Rituals that open to the liminal are not limited to tribal or pre-industrial societies. They are not the domain of anthropologists and ethnographers alone. Nor are they the domain of religious institutions and historians and philosophers of religion alone, for they are not limited to experiences explicitly identified as religious or sacred. Ritual that opens to the liminal may occur anywhere in our lives, in built ritual environments or strange and wild places, at home or abroad, at set times or surprising moments, in ancient orders or unexpected forms.

Not everyone is open to ritual. Some, having experienced ritual as a straitjacket or a weapon wielded to dominate or oppress, may swear off it altogether. Some may simply be ritual blind or tone deaf to ritual. Still, I am persuaded that ritualizing is vital for human flourishing, collectively speaking, and that this way of reorienting ourselves in the world, which enables us to inhabit the world more fully, be more present to it, remains a possibility for all of us. To ritualize is part of our inheritance, connecting us with other animals and with past and future generations of *homo sapiens*. Whether you crave ritual or you avoid it, whether you're familiar or unfamiliar with it, experienced or inexperienced, ritual is an integral part of our life together.

In the end, perhaps the simplest definition of ritualizing as an embodied thinking activity is this: to *move* into knowing, to situate our bodies in a way that enables us to pay attention, to reorient ourselves in the space-time matrix in order to experience and know in the world anew, to *turn aside* from our usual ways of acting to be transformed.

A story of how Moses came to lead the Hebrews out of Egypt begins with Moses out walking in the wilderness of Midian. He was busy tending a flock of his father-in-law's sheep. Suddenly a bush all aflame caught his eye. The bush was burning, but it was not consumed. It was neither alive nor dead, neither necessary nor impossible. It existed in a space between, in the realm of the possible. Moses could have passed by, driven by fear or the urgency of herding skittish sheep. Instead, he chose to enter

that liminal moment and walk toward it. "I will turn aside [אָסֻרָה]
to see this great sight," he said. Only when he had "turned aside"
[סָר] from the path he was on to look [לִרְאוֹת], to pay attention, did
he hear a voice calling him, telling him he was on holy ground.
(Exodus 3:4-5). A voice telling him to return to Egypt, demand the
release of the enslaved Hebrews from their oppressors, and lead
them to freedom.

     Holy betweens await us everywhere, beckoning us to
enter, to turn aside from the cares and ways of the workaday
world in order to pay attention, to open our perception to
something new, and be transformed. If we turn aside, we may
find ourselves on holy ground, readied to act. Let the body lead
the way.

Coda

Minyan, or How to Wear a Prayer Shawl

1. Like a dead man. In the cemetery, kissed by Seattle rain, my friend's father lies on a plank next to his open grave. He is shrouded in white linen and wrapped in the black-striped *tallit* he prayed in all his life, his inescapably human form announcing itself in the curvings of the cloth—rounding over his head and shoulders, flattening and narrowing down his torso and legs, rising again at his feet. The dead body of a human being, fitted with a new skin, clothed in a travelling garment. *This is how a Jew prays.*

2. Like Chagall's praying Jew. In Aramaic, *tallit* means cloak or sheet, a covering. It's the word the rabbis of the Talmud chose for the prayer shawl worn to fulfill the commandment of tying fringes, *tzitzit*, to the four corners of one's garment, as a constant reminder of the Presence. I was nineteen when I first saw a Jew praying in a *tallit.* I was in Paris, at a Chagall exhibition at the Grand Palais. In a room alive with color and crowded with luminous angels, dancing fiddlers, floating brides, and grooms carrying bouquets, a portrait of a lone man in black and white stunned me: a bearded Jew engulfed in a *tallit*—the *tallit* worn by Chagall's father, the catalogue said, worn by a wandering beggar Chagall invited in off the street. The man's face, a face of sorrow, emerged from the opening of the *tallit* like a child being born from a womb of light into the darkness of the world. One long edge of his *tallit* was jagged, the black background devouring his white shelter, enemy incursions into territory set aside for peace. The black stripes too were advancing. They were escaping their woven edges, pushing beyond the boundaries set by the light, threatening to undo creation, threatening chaos, violence, death. Yet the man was not shaken—his body as still and solid as the squared phylacteries on his forehead and arm, his gaze fixed beyond. Trusting in his refuge of wool and its blessing: "How precious is Your kindness, O God! The children of the earth take refuge in the shadow of Your wings…For with You is the source of life; in Your light we see light." (Psalm 36:8, 11) Echoing the prayer of the artist, that he, as he said, might express in his work

"my sigh, the sigh of prayer and of sadness, the prayer of salvation, of rebirth." *This is how a Jew prays.*

The Praying Jew, by Marc Chagall (France, b. Belarus) 1923

3. Like a child afraid of the dark. In my early thirties, while still a Presbyterian teaching in a Christian seminary and guest-preaching in churches, I had recurring visions of being buried in a *tallit*. I flew to New York. In a Jewish shop on the lower east side, the clerk followed me around. "For your husband? Your son?" he asked as I headed for the large wool *tallits* hanging near the back. "For me," I said. He stopped. "Look over here," he said, walking to a rack of narrow rayon *tallits*. He draped one with soft blue stripes and silver metallic stitching over his arm. It was only 12 inches wide and the first three words of the blessing, *Baruch Attah Adonai*, were stitched near the neck. "Try it," he urged. It was slippery and hung weightless around my neck, more like a scarf a woman might accessorize her outfit with or the courtesy *tallits* provided for guests in non-Orthodox synagogues. I handed it back to him. "I want wool," I said, "white with black stripes, no decoration, large." He returned with a traditional 64" X 76" Turkish wool *tallit*. It fell heavily on my head and across my

shoulders, cascaded to my feet. I bent down to grasp the *tzitzit*, which were brushing the floor, and gathered the shawl around me like Chagall's praying Jew. My dream *tallit*. "Let me get you another size," the clerk said. "You don't want it to drag on the ground." "No," I said, feeling its warmth. "This is the one." At home, each night before going to sleep, I spread my *tallit* over my blanket and slept under it, reciting the words of the evening prayer, "Spread over us the shelter of Thy peace." *This is how a Jew in the making prays.*

4. Like a man. When I became a Jew four years later, I began wearing my *tallit* in public, in Shabbat morning services. In my congregation many women, adopting the tradition once reserved for men, wear a *tallit*. Many of them choose not to pray in a traditional *tallit* but in a *tallit* fashioned for their bodies and lives—properly sized; made of pure silk, raw silk, dupioni silks, voile, and organza; hand-woven, hand-painted, hand-embroidered, and hand-appliqued; in pink, coral, peach, purple, teal, and gold; adorned with doves, flowers, pomegranates, stars, flames, and tree of life. They wear them around their shoulders like shawls. Not like the men, who, after draping their *tallit* over both shoulders, fold up one long side over one shoulder, then the other, a tidy sartorial solution for an ungainly garment. My *tallit* is a traditional *tallit*, unmistakably created for a man, and I, ardent feminist, lover of beauty, champion of art and the hand-made life, wear it like a man. *This is how a Jew prays.*

The author's tallit

5. Like a woman. At home I do not decorously fold my tallit over
    each shoulder to pray, as I do in synagogue. When I pray alone, I
    unfurl it, kiss the collar as I recite the blessing, then whirl the wool
    over my head and around my body and let it fall around me like a
    shawl. I gather the *tzitzit* of the four corners in my hands, hold
    them over my heart, and sway, like a mother soothing her baby.
    The black stripes near the fringed ends meet down my front.
    Seven rivers of ink flowing across fertile blankness. Seven rivers of
    letters, out of which the words of my life, the word of my life, my
    past, my present, my unknown, has been written, is being written,
    will be written. Seven lines of text waiting to be read. Our lives,
    too, are texts, say the mystics. It is not enough to expound the
    words of Torah, says Rabbi Leib, one of the Hasids of the Baal
    Shem Tov's circle. We must become entirely a Torah, in our habits
    and our motions and our motionless clinging to the One. Standing
    tall, wrapped in my *tallit*, I become a living text waiting for its
    meaning. *This is how a Jew prays.*

6. Like a desert dweller. Desert peoples, men and women, wear an
    all-purpose outer garment—an *abbaya* or *aba* or *keffiyah*—that is kin

to the four-cornered garment the Torah commands the Hebrews wandering in the wilderness to tie *tzitzit* to, the four fringes that remind one of the surrounding Presence that accompanies one everywhere, fringes of remembrance. One garment—a cloak to shield one from the blazing sun by day and the bitter cold by night, a covering that is armor against sandstorms, a bedsheet, a blanket for the fevered, a carrying sack, a guardian of one's modesty, a baby carrier, a wedding canopy, a winding cloth. Shelter, protection, remedy, blessing. Garment of survival, garment of life. Garment of remembrance, garment of death. *This is how a Jew prays.*

7.   Like Jesus on the cross. At the Chagall exhibition in Paris, after my encounter with the praying Jew, a second painting held me captive: White Crucifixion. A dark scene in blinding white, with Jesus at the center. Not the Jesus I knew, bloodied savior of the Gentiles, wrapped in a loincloth and flanked by two criminals being crucified with him. But Jesus a Jew, hanging on a crossroads of light, wearing a *tallit* and surrounded by Jews. In the heavens, Abraham, Isaac, and Jacob grieving over him, and Rachel weeping for her children. And on earth, Jews fleeing the Nazi extermination, carrying food, babies, menorahs, a Torah scroll, prayers, fear. His suffering their suffering. Their suffering his. The body exposed, the spirit at risk. His *tallit* covering his intimacy, his humanity, his dignity, his awful vulnerability. Theirs. The black and white stripes like waves of sorrow, the fringe like tears. His *tallit* a shield of light against the darkness, spreading light to the cross and the four corners of the world. *This is how a Jew prays.*

White Crucifixion, by Marc Chagall (France, b. Belarus) 1938

8.   Like a *faqir* drunk on the Beloved, a wandering dervish who
     secludes herself in a cave to be alone with the One she loves, to
     remember, to be reborn. Sometimes at home, in the hours before
     dawn, when darkness lingers, hanging heavy on my soul, I kiss
     my *tallit*, swirl it over my head, saying, "My soul, bless the One!
     Wellspring of Life, Fountain of Light, Dwelling of the World, You
     have garbed Yourself with majesty and splendor. You wrap
     Yourself with light as with a garment; You spread the heavens as
     a curtain" (Psalm 104:1- 2), then let it fall over me. I gather the
     tzitzit together and sit cross-legged on the ground, the four
     corners meeting in my lap. Enclosed in my cave, my womb of
     light, I sigh like Chagall, a sigh of prayer and sadness, the prayer
     of salvation, the cry of rebirth. The silence strips me bare. Tears
     fall. Anger flares. Joy rises. Whatever has been hiding. The wool
     traps my body's heat, warming me and giving off a sweet animal
     smell that comforts and arouses me. It lies heavy on my hair, my
     head, my shoulders, arms, back, legs, spirit—a steadying embrace.
     Golden light seeps through the woven threads. I close my eyes
     and the cave expands to the ends of the earth and beyond, into
     nothingness. I am a speck of the universe, but a speck held by

love. My fingers find one of the *tzitzit* to trace the name of God written there, the tetragrammaton, Y, H, W, H, the four letters spelled out by eight threads knotted ten times with thirty-nine wraps of the longest thread to set the name in motion, send it flying beyond the limits of language. The name of the Unnamable. The knotted name of God. The knotty name of God. The fringe of the Unknowable. My fingers rub over each knot, each wrap, following the threads, touching the hem of what is holy. *This is how a Jew prays. With her hands. With her body. With her wild spirit.*

9. Like a dead woman. Like a whirling dervish, one of Rumi's dancers. At home, alone, when I stand to pray with my *tallit* over my head and sway and sway under the weighty wool, arms outstretched, fringes flapping, I dance with the poet and his Mevlevis, who whirl and whirl, like the planets, like the cosmos itself, under their tombstone-shaped hats, their white shroud-skirts spinning wide. A dance to slay the ego, to "die before you die." A dance to be reborn in truth. And when my dancing days are over, when my breath ceases, my body will lie on a plank next to my open grave, alone, shrouded in white linen and wrapped in my black-striped *tallit*, my new skin, my travelling cloak. *This is how a Jew prays.*

10. Like a newborn. Swaddled. Wrapped tight. Head to toe. As if back in the warmth of the womb, once again one with the mother. Womb of mercy. Womb of love. Womb of creation. Womb of light. *This is how a Jew prays.*

Dancing, by Marc Chagall (France, b. Belarus) 1972

Notes

Introduction

[1] Samuel Alexander, *Space, Time, and Deity*. London: Macmillan, 1920. IV:1, p. 345.

[2] In Latin there is no corresponding verb form for the noun *ritus* [rite], precluding a brief Latin phrase for *human the ritualizer* analogous to the other familiar characterizations of *homo sapiens*.

By using the language of *humankind the ritualizer*, I am not implying that ritualizing distinguishes human beings from other animals. Other animals also ritualize, as has been well documented. I am simply highlighting ritualizing as one of the fundamental ways we human beings find our way in the world, a process we may share with other animals but that manifest more complexly in our existence.

Nor am I implying that every human being is tuned to ritual in the same way or with the same intensity. Not everyone is built for ritual. Some people are ritual-blind or tone deaf to ritual. This variation in individuals does not invalidate the general claim.

[3] Arnold van Gennep, *The Rites of Passage*. Tr. Monika B. Vizedom and Gabrielle V. Caffee. Chicago: University of Chicago Press, 1960 (1909).

[4] Victor Turner, *The Ritual Process: Structure and Anti-Structure*. Ithaca, NY: Cornell University Press, 1969, p. 129. See especially chapters 3 and following.

[5] Victor Turner, *From Ritual to Theatre: The Human Seriousness of Play*. NY: PAJ Publications, 1982; *The Anthropology of Performance*. NY: PAJ Publications, 1987.

[6] Ronald L. Grimes, *Beginnings in Ritual Studies*. Waterloo, Canada: Ritual Studies International, 3rd ed. 2013 (1982). In the first four chapters, he summarizes the history of the academic study of ritual and offers his own definition of ritualizing: "Ritualizing transpires as animated persons enact formative gestures in the face of receptivity during crucial times in founded places." (64) Later chapters explore ritual practices such as masking, sitting, eating, and psycho-medical and anthropological theories of ritual.

[7] Catherine Bell, *Ritual Theory, Ritual Practice*. New York: Oxford University Press, 1992, pp. 140-41. Her review and critique of the bifurcation of thought/action that underlies most theories of ritual is especially helpful, as is her emphasis on ritual as a social and cultural *activity* and on the body, especially the social body of ritual.

[8] The theologian Jospeh L. Price investigates ritual spaces and events in baseball in his essays in *From Season to Season: Sports as American Religion* (ed. Joseph L. Price. Macon: GA: Mercer University Press, 2001). See also: "The Psychology of Rituals: An Integrative Review and Process-Based

Framework" by Nicholas M. Hobson, Juliana Schroeder, Jane L. Risen, Dimitris Xygalatas, and Michael Inzlicht, in *Personality and Social Psychology Review*, 2017, pp. 1-25; *Rituals and Practices in World Religions: Cross-Cultural Scholarship to Inform Research and Clinical Contexts*. Ed. David Bryce Yaden, Yukun Zhao, Kaiping Peng, Andrew B. Newberg. New York: Springer, 2020; James W. Jones, "How ritual might create religion: A neuropsychological exploration," in *Archive for the Psychology of Religion* 2020, Vol. 42(1) 29 –45. For an interdisciplinary approach using a broad conception of ritual, see Ronald Grimes, *Beginnings in Ritual Studies* (CreateSpace Independent Publishing Platform; 3rd ed. Edition. October 4, 2010). For current work in Ritual Studies, see the *Journal of Ritual Studies* (founded 1987) and the special issue of *Religions Journal*: *Exploring Ritual Fields Today* (Issue 12, ed. Martin Hoondert and Paul Post.)

[9] In *Beginnings in Ritual Studies*, Ronald L Grimes notes that Turner's image of a *limen* or threshold was and continues to be fruitful for further study of ritual, but he doesn't develop this. He also suggests that Ritual Studies would benefit from new or additional metaphors but adds that no one metaphor has yet appeared that has the generative power of *limen*. (p. 136.) See Chapters 14 and 18 of this book for several metaphors that may be helpful for understanding liminal experiences.

[10] *From Ritual to Theatre*, pp. 52-55 *et passim*. It's important to note here that the use of *liminal* in cases of rites of passage in pre-industrial societies is also metaphorical.

[11] Scheler's philosophical attitude and interests were key to the early formation of my thought, particularly these works: *On the Eternal in Man* (Tr. Bernard Noble. London: SCM Press. 1960); *The Nature of Sympathy* (New Haven: Yale, 1954); *Ressentiment* (Tr. William W. Holdheim. New York: Schocken. 1972); and *Man's Place in Nature* (Tr. Hans Meyerhoff. Boston: Beacon Press, 1961).

[12] Maurice Merleau-Ponty, *Phenomenology of Perception* (Tr. Colin Smith. New York: Routledge & Kegan Paul, 1962) and *The Visible and the Invisible* (Tr. Alphonso Lingis. Evanston, IL: Northwestern University Press, 1968); Gaston Bachelard, *The Poetics of Space* (Tr. Maria Joas. Boston: Beacon Press, 1969) and *Water and Dreams: An Essay on the Imagination of Matter* (Tr. Edith R. Farrell. Dallas: Dallas Institute for Humanities and Culture, 1999); Alva Noë, *Strange Tools: Art and Nature* (NY: Hill and Wang, 2016) and *The Entanglement: How Art and Philosophy Make Us What We Are* (Princeton: Princeton University Press 2023).

[13] Tim Ingold, *Correspondences*. Cambridge: Polity, 2021: p. 8.

[14] Tim Ingold, *Making: Anthropology, Archaeology, Art and Architecture*. NY: Routledge, 2023. Throughout this book, Ingold's critique of the dualistic hylomorphic model of form and matter, in which form precedes and is imposed on matter (pp. 20ff., 41ff., 69ff.); his view of "emergent form" in which the essential relation is not between form and matter, but *forces* and *materials* (p. 45); and his view of "correspondence" rather than interaction with material things are compelling and engaging.

[15] Ingold, *Correspondences*, p. 11.

[16] Ibid. pp. 13, 14
[17] Ingold, *Making*, pp.11, 94.
[18] Paul Klee, *Pedagogical Sketchbook*. Tr. Sibyl Moholy-Nagy. NY: Prager, 1972 (1925): p. 16.

Chapter 1: Between Chaos and Light: Calvin, Card Playing, Comic Books, Sex, God, and Dancing

[1] Friedrich W. Nietzsche, *Thus Spoke Zarathustra*. Tr. Thomas Common. New York: Dover, 1999, p. 24.
[2] Andrew Jacobs, "China Puts a Hitch in the Step of 'Dancing Grannies.'" New York Times, March 24, 2015.
[3] Ibid.
[4] Gabrielle Roth, *Sweat Your Prayers: Movement as Spiritual Practice* (New York: Tarcher/Putnam, 1998), p. 4.
[5] Robert Bellah, *Religion in Human Evolution: From the Paleolithic to the Axial Age*. Cambridge, MA: Belknap Press of Harvard University Press, 2011), pp. 12 and 13.
[6] Ibid. pp. 13, 36.
[7] Ibid. p.17.
[8] Ibid.
[9] Translation by Everett Fox in *The Five Books of Moses: Genesis, Exodus, Leviticus, Numbers, and Deuteronomy* New York: Schocken, 1997.
[10] Max Picard, *The World of Silence* (Wichita, Kansas: Eighth Day Press, 2002 reprint edition. Originally published in Switzerland: Eugen Rentsch Verlag, 1948), p. 53.
[11] Yitzhak Buxbaum, *The Light and Fire of the Baal Shem Tov* (New York: Continuum, 2005), p. 151. Another version of this story appears in Martin Buber, *Tales of the Hasidim* (New York: Schocken, 1947), I: 53.

Chapter 2: Because We Are Bodies: Bread, Wine, Rice, Water

[1] "Service for the Lord's Day," in *Book of Common Worship* (Louisville, KY: Westminster John Knox, 1993), pp. 68–69.
[2] Book of Order 2015–2017: *The Constitution of the Presbyterian Church (U.S.A.)*, Part II (Louisville, KY: Office of the General Assembly, 2015), W-2.4011.a.
[3] Although Augustine often discusses sacraments in these terms, this exact wording comes from the Catechism of the Council of Trent for Parish Priests, trans. John A McHugh and Charles J. Callan (New York, NY: Joseph F. Wagner, 1947), p. 143.
[4] Howard Thurman, *With Head and Heart: The Autobiography of Howard Thurman* (New York, NY: Harcourt Brace and Company, 1979), p. 68.
[5] Ibid. p. 68.
[6] Augustine, "On the Catechizing of the Uninstructed," trans. S. D. F. Salmond, in *A Select Library of the Nicene and Post-Nicene Fathers of the*

Christian Church, ed. Philip Schaff, vol. 3, St. Augustin: On the Holy Trinity, Doctrinal Treatises, Moral Treatises (Buffalo, NY: Christian Literature Company, 1887), p. 312.

[7] John Calvin, *Institutes of the Christian Religion*, Tr. Henry Beveridge, *Institutes of the Christian Religion*. Tr. Ford Lewis Battles. Ed. John T. McNeill. Philadelphia: Westminster Press, 1960, 2 vol.: 2:1281 (4.14.6). Calvin refers to Augustine's Treatise *Against Faustus* 19.16 to support his view of "visible word."

[8] Ibid.

[9] See Jonathan Edwards, *Images or Shadows of Divine Things*, ed. Perry Miller (Westport, CT: Greenwood, 1977), a posthumously published collection of observations Edwards recorded in his personal journal.

[10] Maurice Merleau-Ponty, "Faith and Good Faith" (1946), in *Sense and Non-sense*. Tr. Hubert L. Dreyfus and Patricia Allen Dreyfus. Evanston, IL: Northwestern University Press, 1964, pp. 168-71.

Chapter 3: When Bones Are Not Bones

[1] Martin Bucer, *Ground and Reason* XI: 178. See *Martin Bucer's Ground and Reason: A Commentary and Translation* by Ottomar Frederick Cypris. Yulee, Florida: Good Samaritan Books, 2016.

[2] John Calvin, *Treatise on Relics.* Tr. Count Valerian Krasinski. Edinburgh: Johnstone, Hunter & Co., 1870. https://www.gutenberg.org/files/32136/32136-h/32136-h.html

[3] Ibid.

[4] Mihaly Csikszentmihalyi and Eugene Rochberg-Halton, *The Meaning of Things: Domestic Symbols and the Self.* Cambridge: Cambridge University Press, 2000, p. 17.

[5] Ibid. pp. 16-17, 37, 26-27.

[6] Ibid. p. 15.

[7] Ibid. p. 247.

[8] Peter Brown, *The Cult of the Saints: Its Rise and Function in Latin Christianity.* Chicago: University of Chicago Press, 1981.

Chapter 4: The Story of a Hollowed-Out Bone

[1] Alexandra David-Neel, *Magic and Mystery in Tibet.* New York Dover, 1971 (1931).

[2] Ibid. p. 112.

[3] Ibid. p. 113.

[4] "The Dalai Lama and Arthur Brooks: All of us can break the cycle of hatred." https://www.washingtonpost.com/opinions/2019/03/11/dalai-lama-arthur-brooks-each-us-can-break-cycle-hatred/

[5] David-Neel, *Magic and Mystery*, p. 115.

[6] Charlie Campbell, "The Dalai Lama on Donald Trump, China, and His Search for Joy." http://time.com/longform/dalai-lama-60-year-exile/

Chapter 5: The Liminal Work of Sacred Clowns

[1] Paul Radin, *The Trickster: A Study in American Indian Mythology*. New York: Schocken, 1988. See his discussion of this figure in Winnebago culture in Part 3.
[2] Lewis Hyde, *Trickster Makes This World: Mischief, Myth, and Art*. New York: North Point Press, 1999, pp. 7, 8.
[3] Paul Mattick, "Hotfoots of the Gods," review of Lewis Hyde's *Trickster Makes This World: Mischief, Myth, and Art. New York Times on the Web*, February 15, 1998.
[https://archive.nytimes.com/www.nytimes.com/books/98/02/15/reviews/980215.15mattict.html]
[4] Dominique Godrèche (interviewer), "Speaking With Clay, Mud and Clowns: Pueblo Potter Roxanne Swentzell." *Indian Country Today*, November 26, 2013.
[https://ictnews.org/archive/speaking-with-clay-mud-and-clowns-pueblo-potter-roxanne-swentzell].
[5] Lewis Hyde, *Trickster Makes This World*, p.13.

Chapter 6: A Gathering of Different Lights: Invitation to Enter the Between

[1] Martin Buber, *The Legend of the Baal Shem Tov*. Tr. Maurice Friedman. Princeton: Princeton University Press, 1995 (1955), p. 36.
[2] Hayim Nachman Bialik, "Cedars of Lebanon: Revealment and Concealment in Language," in *Commentary* February 1950. Tr. Jacob Sloan. https://www.commentary.org/articles/hayim-bialik/cedars-of-lebanon-revealment-and-concealment-in-language/
[3] Martin Buber, *I and Thou*. Tr. Walter Kaufman. New York: Charles Scribner's Sons, 1970, pp. 62, 124, 123.

Chapter 7: Feeding the Spirit: Dwelling in the Space Between Religious Traditions

[1] Harvey Cox, *The Future of Faith*. New York: Harper One, 2009, pp. 18-19.
[2] Peter L. Berger, *Heretical Imperative. Contemporary Possibilities of Religious Affirmation*. New York: Doubleday, 1980.

Chapter 8: Ever Becoming, Never Being: Dwelling in the Sukkah

[1] Psalm 103:13, New Living Translation.
[2] Leviticus 23: 42-43.

[3] Marc-Alain Ouaknin, *Symbols of Judaism*. New York: Assouline Publishing, 2000, p. 72.

[4] Ibid.

[5] Gaston Bachelard, *The Poetics of Space*. Tr. Maria Joas. Boston: Beacon Press, 1969, pp. 17, 21, 18, 48.

[6] Ibid. p. 206.

[7] Ouaknin, *Symbols*, p. 72.

[8] Ibn 'Arabî, *Seven Days of the Heart: Prayers for the Days and Nights of the Week*. Tr. Pablo Beneito and Stephen Hirtenstein. Oxford, UK: Anqa Publishing, 2000, pp. 37, 41.

[9] John Calvin, *Institutes of the Christian Religion*. Tr. Ford Lewis Battles. Ed. John T. McNeill. Philadelphia: Westminster Press, 1960, 2 vol.: 1:223 (1.17.10).

[10] Ibn 'Arabî, *Seven Days*, p. 30.

[11] Martin Buber, *The Legend of the Baal Shem Tov* (Princeton: Princton University Press, 1995 [1955]), p. 19.

Chapter 9: By the River of 1000 *Lingas*

[1] Heraclitus, Fragment B49A, in Kathleen Freeman's *Ancilla to the Pre-Socratics: A complete translation of the Fragments in Diels, Fragmente der Vorsokratiker*. Oxford: Basil Blackwell, 1948, p. 28.

[2] Heraclitus, Fragment DK 8,in Freeman, *Ancilla*, p. 25.

[3] Ibn 'Arabî, *Seven Days of the Heart: Prayers for the Days and Nights of the Week*. Tr. Pablo Beneito and Stephen Hirtenstein. Oxford, UK: Anqa Publishing, 2000, p. 47.

[4] This is a refrain in Ibn 'Arabî. See James Winston Morris's "Ibn 'Arabî's 'Short Course' on Love," which includes his translation of several chapters from Ibn 'Arabî's *al-Futuhat* (*Journal of the Muhyiddin Ibn Arabi Society*, Vol. 50, 201ff, reprinted as https://ibnarabisociety.org/ibn-arabi-short-course-on-love-james-morris/).

[5] Maurice Merleau-Ponty. *The Visible and the Invisible*. Ed. Claude Lefort. Tr. Alphonso Lingis. Evanston: Northwestern University Press, 1968, pp. 138ff.

[6] Tim Ingold, *Correspondences,* Cambridge: Polity Press, 2020, p 9.

Chapter 10: Between the Living and the Dead

[1] Rainer Maria Rilke, *Duino Elegies and the Sonnets to Orpheus*. Tr. A. Poulin, Jr. Boston: Houghton Mifflin, 1977, pp. 10-11.

Chapter 14: Standing on Moonstones: The Art of Dwelling Between

[1] Fernando Pessoa, *The Book of Disquiet* (New York, N.Y.: Penguin Books, 2003), p. 11.

[2] Emile Durkheim, *The Elementary Forms of the Religious Life*. Ed. and tr. Karen E. Fields (New York, N.Y.: The Free Press, 1995 [1912]). See all of Chapter 1, but especially pp. 36–42.

[3] Victor Turner, *The Ritual Process: Structure and Anti-Structure* (Abingdon and New York: Routledge Press, 2017 [1969]), 95.

[4] Ariel Dorfman, quoted by Andrew Madigan in his Interview, "Ariel Dorfman: 'Not to Belong Anywhere, to Be Displaced, Is Not a Bad Thing for a Writer,'" *The Guardian* 9 May 2018.

[5] Karl Jaspers, *The Origin and Goal of History* (London: Routledge and Kegan Paul, 1953 [1949]), 1. See the entirety of Chapter 1.

[6] Quoted by *Robert Bellah in his Religion in Human Evolution: From the Paleolithic to the Axial Age* (Boston: Harvard, 2011), p. 268.

Chapter 15: Playing in the Between: The Power of Ritual in Art

[1] *The Five Books of Moses*, Tr. and commentary Everett Fox. New York, Schocken, 1997: pp. 11, 13.

[2] Ibn 'Arabî, The *Bezels of Wisdom*. Tr. R.W.J. Austin. New York: Paulist Press, 1980, p. 123.

[3] *Yemenite Midrash: Philosophical Commentaries on the Torah*. Tr. Y. Tzvi Langermann. HarperSanFrancisco, 1996, p. 20. The *midrash* is found in the Talmud, *Pirkei Avot* 5:8.

[4] Edmund Jabès, *The Book of Questions*. Tr. Rosemarie Waldorp. Middleton, CT: Wesleyan University Press, 1972, p. 39. This quote is from a commentary by one of the many fictional rabbis in the novel, Reb Ab.

[5] https://www.poetryfoundation.org/articles/69384/selections-from-keatss-letters

[6] I find Arthur Koestler's view more amenable to mine, and less dualistic than Keats's: "To recapitulate: ordered, disciplined thought is a skill governed by set rules of the game, some of which are explicitly stated, others implied and hidden in the code. The creative act, in so far as it depends on unconscious resources, presupposes a relaxing of the controls and a regression to modes of ideation which are indifferent to the rules of verbal logic, unperturbed by contradiction, untouched by the dogmas and taboos of so-called common sense. At the decisive stage of discovery the codes of disciplined reasoning are suspended—as they are in the dream, the reverie, the manic flight of thought, when the stream of ideation is free to drift, by its own emotional gravity, as it were, in an apparently 'lawless' fashion." (*The Act of Creation*. London: Hutchinson, 1964, p. 178.) Koestler developed a view of the creative act that he calls "bisociation," by which he means "the independent, autonomous character of the matrices which are brought into contact in the creative act," in contrast to "associative thought [which] operates among members of a single pre-existing matrix." (p. 654) This bringing together of two *different* matrices ("any ability, habit, or skill, any pattern of ordered behaviour governed by a 'code' of fixed rules," p. 38) can result in collision, synthesis, or juxtaposition, leading to a new way of thinking.

[7] Edmund Jabès, *The Book of Questions*, p. 169.

[8] Maurice Merleau-Ponty, *The Visible and the Invisible*. Tr. Alphonso Lingis. Evanston, IL: Northwestern University Press, 1968, p. 259. For a discussion of the complex relationship of freedom, will, imagination, and repetition in art, see Susan Stewart, *The Poet's Freedom: A Notebook on Making*. Chicago: University of Chicago Press, 2011.

[9] Clarice Lispector, *The Foreign Legion: Stories*. Tr. Giovanni Pontiero. New York: New Directions, 1986, p. 172.

[10] Alva Noë, *The Entanglement: How Art and Philosophy Make Us What We Are*. Princeton: Princeton University Press, 2023. He makes a similar argument in *Strange Tools Art and Nature* (NY: Hill and Wang, 2016).

[11] Arthur Koestler, *The Act of Creation*, p. 96.

[12] In *The Act of Creation*, Koestler acknowledges that "[T]here are two ways of escaping our more or less automatized routines of thinking and behaving. The first, of course, is the plunge into dreaming or dream-like states, when the codes of rational thinking are suspended. The other way is also an escape—from boredom, stagnation, intellectual predicaments, and emotional frustration—but an escape in the opposite direction; it is signalled by the spontaneous flash of insight which shows a familiar situation or event in a new light, and elicits a new response to it. The bisociative act connects previously unconnected matrices of experience; it makes us 'understand what it is to be awake, to be living on several planes at once' (to quote T. S. Eliot, somewhat out of context)." (p. 45) Neither dreaming nor flashes of insight, however, are the result for him of intentional sequences of actions, unlike ritual, which may be an intentional preparation for or invitation to interrupting our habits to experience the liminal. In fact, he classifies ritual with lower forms, "rigid, automatized, and compulsive, petrified habits of unknown phylogenetic origin." (pp. 485-86)

Koestler does acknowledge that when one "thinks aside" one can escape habit, but this, too, comes intuitively for him and has no connection to ritual: "The period of incubation represents a *reculer pour mieux sauter*. Just as in the dream the codes of logical reasoning are suspended, so 'thinking aside' is a temporary liberation from the tyranny of over-precise verbal concepts, of the axioms and prejudices engrained in the very texture of specialized ways of thought. It allows the mind to discard the straitjacket of habit, to shrug off apparent contradictions, to un-learn and forget—and to acquire, in exchange, a greater fluidity, versatility, and gullibility. This rebellion against constraints which are necessary to maintain the order and discipline of conventional thought, but an impediment to the creative leap, is symptomatic both of the genius and the crank; what distinguishes them is the intuitive guidance which only the former enjoys." (p. 208)

[13] This may be similar to athletes performing rituals to put them "in the zone," to enter "flow" before they perform or compete. Watching Minnesota Twins Kirby Puckett cross himself and move his bat through the same sequence of actions before hoisting it in position over his

shoulder always fascinated me. This is just one of countless examples in sports.

[14] Twyla Tharpe, *The Creative Habit*. New York: Simon & Schuster, 2003, pp. 18, 19.

[15] Ibid.

[16] Interview in *The Paris Review: Art of Fiction*, No. 182, Summer, 2004: https://www.theparisreview.org/interviews/2/the-art-of-fiction-no-182-haruki-murakami.

[17] Tim Ingold, *Making: Anthropology, Archaeology, Art and Architecture*. NY: Routledge, 2023., p. 72. Emphasis added.

[18] Ibid.

[19] Ibid. It is one of the paradoxes of art, that the artist distances their self from their subject in order to draw closer.

[20] Victor Turner, *From Ritual to Theatre: The Human Seriousness of Play*. New York: PAJ Publications, 1982.

[21] Johan Huizinga, *Homo Ludens: A Study of the Play Element in Culture*. Kettering, OH: Angelico Press, 2018 (1938). For his discussion of play and ritual, see pp. 5, 14-27.

[22] Huizinga, *Homo Ludens*, pp. 1, 3. In *Religion in Human Evolution: From the Paleolithic to the Axial Age* (Cambridge, MA: Belknap, 2011), the sociologist Robert Bellah demonstrates how play and ritual are closely related in evolution. (pp. 80ff.)

[23] Ibid. p. 1.

[24] Ibid. p. 158.

[25] Ibid. p. 4. See also p. 19, where he sums up: "[O]ne of the most important characteristics of play [is] its spatial separation from ordinary life," a characteristic of ritual as well.

[26] Ibid. pp. 25, 27.

[27] Ibid. p. 119.

[28] Ibid. p. 122.

[29] Ibn 'Arabî, Proem to *The Universal Tree and the Four Birds* Tr. Angela Jaffray. Oxford: Anqa, 2006, p. 25.

Chapter 16: Strange Tools: Art as Holy Possibility

[1] Kevin McIlvoy, *Is It So? Glimpses, Glyphs, and Found Novels*. WTAW Press, 2023, p. 123.

[2] Alva Noë. *Strange Tools: Art and Human Nature*. Hill and Wang, 2015, p. 100.

[3] Ibid. pp. 10, xiii.

[4] Ibid. p. 17.

[5] Ibid. p. 44.

[6] Antonio Damasio, *The Strange Order of Things: Life, Feeling, and the Making of Cultures*. New York: Vintage, 2018, p. 196.

[7] McIlvoy, *Is It So?*, p. 12.

[8] Clarice Lispector. *The Complete Stories*. Translated by Katrina Dodson. Edited by Benjamin Moser. New Directions, 2015.

[9] Ibid. p. 475

[10] Clarice Lispector, *Discovering the World*. Tr. Giovanni Pontiero. Paris: Carcanet, 1993.

[11] Clarice Lispector, *The Hour of the Star*. Tr. Giovanni Pontiero. New York: New Directions, 1992., p. 8.

[12] Lispector, *Complete Stories*, p. 485.

[13] McIlvoy, *Is It So?*, p. 91

[14] Ibid. p. 571.

[15] Noë, *Strange Tools*, p. xi.

[16] Lispector, *Complete Stories*, p. 276.

[17] McIlvoy, *Is It So?*, p. 100.

[18] Ibid. pp. 393-94.

[19] Ibid. pp. 359, 361.

[20] McIlvoy, *Is It So?*, p. 110.

[21] Ibid. p. 115.

[22] Ibid. p. 84.

[23] "A Conversation with Kevin McIlvoy," in *Willow Springs Magazine*, January 25, 2021. [https://inside.ewu.edu/willowspringsmagazine/a-conversation-with-kevin-mcilvoy/]

[24] Clarice Lispector, *A Breath of Life*. Tr. Johnny Lorenz. New York: New Directions, 2012, p. 141.

[25] Clarice Lispector, *The Stream of Life*. Tr. Elizabeth Lowe and Earl Fitz. Minneapolis: University of Minnesota Press 1989.

[26] Clarice Lispector, *The Foreign Legion: Stories and Chronicles*. Tr. Giovanni Pontiero. New York: New Directions, 1992, p. 114.

[27] Noë, *Strange Tools*, p. 102.

[28] McIlvoy, *Is It So?*, p. 99.

Chapter 17: In a Crisis, Call in the Poets: The Need for Liminal Leaders

[1] Gaston Bachelard, *The Poetics of Space*. Tr. Maria Joas. Boston: Beacon Press, 1969, p. 208.

[2] Gaston Bachelard, *Water and Dreams: Essay on the Imagination of Matter*. Tr. Edith R. Farrell. Dallas: Dallas Institute for Humanities and Culture, 1999, p. 16.

[3] Jonathan Lear, *Radical Hope: Ethics in the Face of Cultural Devastation*. Cambridge: Harvard University Press, 2008, p. 2.

[4] Ibid. p. 84.

[5] Ibid. p. 51.

[6] Ibid. p. 146.

[7] Willa Cather, *Death Comes for the Archbishop*. New York: Vintage Press, 1990.

Chapter 18: The Body Leads the Way: Ritual, Liminality, and Imagination

[1] Ronald. L Grimes makes a point of this in *Beginnings in Ritual Studies* (Waterloo, Canada: Ritual Studies International, 2013. 3rd ed. [1982], as does Catherine Bell in *Ritual Theory, Ritual Practice* (New York: Oxford University Press, 1992).

[2] Midrash on Exodus 5:9 found in *Genesis Rabbah*. See the translation by William G. Braude in *The Book of Legends: Sefer Ha-Aggadah: Legends from the Talmud and Midrash*, eds. Hayim Nachman Bialik and Yehoshua Hana Ravnitzky. New York: Schocken, 1991, p. 80:40.

[3] Gershom Scholem, *The Messianic Idea in Judaism and Other Essays in Jewish Spirituality*. New York: Schocken, 1971, p. 296.

[4] Maurice Merleau-Ponty, *Phenomenology of Perception*. Tr. Colin Smith. New York: Routledge & Kegan Paul, 1962, p. xi.

[5] Merleau-Ponty, *Phenomenology of Perception*, p. 100. Emphasis added.

[6] Maurice Merleau-Ponty, *Phenomenology of Perception*, p. 184.

[7] Mark Johnson, *The Aesthetics of Meaning and Thought*. Chicago: University of Chicago Press, 2018, pp. 86-87. See also his argument in *The Meaning of the Body: Aesthetics of Human Understanding* (Chicago: University of Chicago Press, 2007) for "mind" and "body" not as two separate "things" but "aspects of one organic process." (p. 1)

[8] Marc-Alain Ouaknin, *Symbols of Judaism*. New York: Assouline, 2000, p. 10. His definition of gestural memory as "the concrete textual memory expression and objectification of myth in the human body and gesture" could be read as Cartesian, but I believe it's more accurate to understand his notion of gestural memory along the lines of Merleau-Ponty's view of gesture as enacting meaning, in which meaning is inseparable from the act.

[9] Catherine Bell, *Ritual Theory, Ritual Practice*. New York: Oxford University Press, 1992; *Ritual: Perspectives and Dimensions*. New York: Oxford University Press, 1997. Ronald L. Grimes, *Beginnings in Ritual Studies*. Waterloo, Canada: Ritual Studies International, 2023 3rd ed. [1982]. Grimes offers this definition: "Ritualizing transpires as animated persons *enact* formative gestures in the face of receptivity during crucial times in founded places." (p. 64, emphasis added). Though I came to Bell's and Grime's work only after I had formulated the view of ritual described here, and while there are clearly differences, there is a great deal of overlap, including a focus on: action as a way of thinking, gesture and body, the generative or transformative power of ritual.

[10] Tim Ingold, *Making: Anthropology, Archaeology, Art and Architecture*. NY: Routledge, 2023. See Chapter 2, especially pp. 25 and 31; and p. 94.

[11] Robert Bellah, *Religion in Human Evolution: From the Paleolithic to the Axial Age*. Cambridge, MA: Belknap, 2011, p. 86.

[12] Quoted in Alva Noë, *The Entanglement: How Art and Philosophy Make Us What We Are* (Princeton and Oxford: Princeton University Press, 2023, p. 3. Emphasis added.) Collingwood also argued that art was fundamental to the human species and present at the emergence of *homo sapiens*, a

view that Noë supports. Ellen Dissanayake develops this view in her book *Homo Aestheticus: Where Art Comes from and Why* (Seattle, WA: University of Washington Press, 1995).

[13] Quoted in Robert Bellah, *Religion in Human Evolution*, p. xvi. Emphasis added.

[14] Bellah, *Religion in Human Evolution*, p. 17.

[15] Ibid.

[16] Emile Durkheim, *The Elementary Forms of the Religious Life*. Tr. Joseph Ward Swain. New York: Collier, 1961, pp. 249-50. See also pp. 361ff., 389-91, 469 ff.

[17] Hans Joas, *The Power of the Sacred: An Alternative to the Narrative of Disenchantment*. Oxford: Oxford University Press, 2021, pp. 59, 89, and all of Chapter 3, "Ritual and the Sacred."

[18] Ibid. p. 67. See also pp. 85, 242. Joas's examples of other self-transcending experiences beyond the boundaries of religion are: "falling in love and of love, of the opening of the self through successful dialogue or through shattering empathy, as well as euphoric experiences of the dissolution of boundaries in response to nature" and "sacramental experiences." (p. 242)

[19] Ibid. p. 85.

[20] This Durkheim-inspired view of ritual, which emerged from my observations over many years, shares some similarity with Hans Joas's Durkheim-inspired summary of ritual and the sacred in his 2021 book *The Power of the Sacred*: "Ritual creates a controlled environment that temporality suspends the mechanism of everyday life. Ideal states can thus be rendered experienceable, in such a way that individuals remember them as intensive experiences when they have returned to the realm of the quotidian." (p. 87) Joas does not speak of liminality however, but "self-transcendence," which he describes in terms of "shattering events," "shattering of the symbolic boundaries that make up the self." (p. 241) His criticisms of the limitations of Durkheim's theory of ritual and of scholars who judge ritual to be "archaic" are incisive and welcome, as is his assumption of "the persistence of ritual and the sacredness to which it gives rise." (p. 86)

[21] I do not find the image of "marginality," which is often used when speaking of liminality, to be as resonant. Margins suggest the edges of one thing, the boundary of one entity, rather than a space between, and they do not evoke bodily action, the way the image of a threshold does.

[22] Metaphors are not window-dressing or an accommodation for those who have difficulty with abstractions. Metaphor is inevitable for us, because of embodiment, and much of our reasoning depends on metaphor. See the work of George Lakoff and Mark Johnson: *Metaphors We Live By* (Chicago: University of Chicago Press, 1980) and *Philosophy in the Flesh: The Embodied Mind and Its Challenge to Western Thought* (New York: Basic Books, 1999, pp. 45-132). See also Chapter 9, "From Embodied Meaning to Abstract Thought," in Mark Johnson's *The Meaning of the Body: Aesthetics of Human Understanding* (Chicago: University of Chicago Press, 2007). Metaphors are essential to abstract

thinking in general and helping us understand the complex experience of liminality.

[23] Using the word *between* as a noun in addition to using it as an adjective or adverb runs the risk of implying that it a substance and that it is static. I hope the context will make it clear that this "state" or "moment" of "meeting" of finding oneself between or dwelling between that I call "a holy between" is relational and dynamic.

[24] Ibn 'Arabî's understanding of *barzakh* is distantly echoed, I believe, in Maurice Merleau-Ponty's notion of *chiasm* in his later ontology. Chiasm, for Merleau-Ponty, is a third way. Neither dialectic nor intuition, *chiasm* is an "intertwining," a structure of mediation that combines unity-in-difference with reversal and circularity or bi-directionality. This mediation occurs between sentient and sensed, body and world, perception and language, and others, with the ultimate ontological chiasm being that between the sensible and the intelligible. See *The Visible and the Invisible* (Tr. Alphonso Lingis. Evanston, IL: Northwestern University Press, 1968), pp. 130 ff.

[25] William C. Chittick's entry *Ibn 'Arabî* in *Stanford Encyclopedia of Philosophy* [https://plato.stanford.edu/entries/ibn-arabi/#Bar] is a clear and concise summary of Ibn 'Arabî's ontology. For an in-depth presentation of the *barzakh*, the imaginal world, the cosmos, the soul, and the multiple ways Ibn 'Arabî understands imagination, see his *Imaginal Worlds: Ibn al-Arabî and the Problem of Religious Diversity*. Albany, NY: SUNY Press, 1994. *Barzakh* is also translated as *barrier* or *limit*, emphasizing that though the two sides meet they remain separate. For this essay I use the translation *isthmus* to focus on *barzakh* as a meeting place. I am not fool enough to think I understand the work of Ibn 'Arabî; I claim only to be captivated by his vision of life and his writing, including his poetry.

[26] Chittick, *Imaginal Worlds*, p. 25.

[27] *The Meccan Revelations*, Ed. Michel Chodkiewicz. Tr. William C. Chittick and James W. Morris. New York: Pir Press, 2002, 172. This translation of parts of *al-Futûhât al-makkiyya*, focuses on the *barzakh* as the intermediate time between death and the final resurrection. Ibn 'Arabî speaks of the *barzakh* in both spatial and temporal terms, both as world and a presence. This seems to me to accurately point to the complex reality experienced in liminal states, and why I choose to use both kinds of terms as well.

[28] *Yemenite Midrash: Philosophical Commentaries on the Torah*. Tr. Y. Tzvi Langermann. HarperSanFrancisco, 1996, p. 20.

[29] Being or what exists and the imaginary are not objects, Merleau-Ponty argues, but fields. I find this description of the imaginary as a field useful, though I still use the words *space* and *moment*. For me, time and space cannot be separated in these threshold experiences of the imagination; they are two ways of speaking about the same experience, like particle and wave, two sides of one reality, like body and mind, body and soul. *The Visible and the Invisible*. Ed. Claude Lefort. Tr. Alphonso Lingis. Evanston, Northwestern University Press, 1968, p. 267.

[30] Alva Noë, *The Entanglement: How Art and Philosophy Make Us What We Are*. Princeton and Oxford: Princeton University Press, 2023, pp. 219-23.

[31] Ibn 'Arabî, *al-Futûhât al-makkiyya*, 1911 edition, 3:274.28. Tr. and quoted by William C. Chittick, "Ibn 'Arabî" in *Stanford Encyclopedia of Philosophy*. (2008/revised 2019) [https://plato.stanford.edu/entries/ibn-arabi/#Bar].

[32] Chittick, *Imaginal Worlds*, p. 25. For a full discussion, see Chapter 7, "The In-Betweenness."

[33] Ibn 'Arabî, *al-Futûhât al-makkiyya* I:304. Quoted in William C. Chittick, *Imaginal Worlds*, p. 112.

[34] Ibid. p. 25.

[35] Ibid. pp. 71-72.

[36] Ibid. p. 106.

[37] See George Lakoff and Mark Johnson, *The Philosophy of the Flesh: The Embodied Mind and Its Challenge to Western Thought* (New York: Basic Books, 1999).

[38] Pir Vilayat Inayat Khan, *The Call of the Dervish*. Sante Fe, NM: Sufi Order Publications, 1981, p. 155.

[39] Martin Buber, *The Way of Man According to the Teachings of Hasidism*. Chicago: Wilcox & Follett, 1951, p. 44.

[40] This is perhaps an example of Hans Joas's statement about the "creativity of action" in *The Power of the Sacred*: that "in her relationship to her environment, the human being as organism experiences problematic tensions that must be dealt with and that this forms the point of departure for new variants of action that are then incorporated into a routinized repertoire of action." (p. 238)

[41] Mircea Eliade, *Myth and Reality*. New York: Harper Torchbooks, 1963, p. 49 and all of Chapter 3.

[42] Jonathan Z. Smith, *To Take Place: Toward Theory in Ritual*. Chicago: University of Chicago Press, 1987, p.103.

[43] Ibid. p. 104. It's essential to point out that he is saying that this notion of ritual as paying attention is "best illustrated" by built ritual environments, *not* that it applies only to such environments. Time-based rituals performed in no specific location, for example, or any ritual that may take place regardless of a designated location, like the whirling of Sufi dervishes, the celebration of a Passover seder, keeping kosher or halal, and many of the ritual practices in this book, also share this quality of calling the participant to heightened attention.

[44] Ibid. p. 105. Emphasis added.

[45] Noë, *The Entanglement*, pp.188, 22.

[46] Ibid. p. 100. Emphasis added.

[47] Ibid. p. xii.

[48] William Wordsworth, "The World is Too Much With Us." This famous sonnet published in Wordsworth's collection *Poems, in Two Volumes* (London: Longman, Rees, and Orme, 1807).

[49] Hans Joas, noting the difficulties associated with interpreting "sacred," says that he uses the term "to designate a complex of affective qualities that rises from experiences of self-transcendence," a complex that may

not be identified as "sacred" by those who experience it. *The Power of the Sacred*, p. 246.

[50] Martin Buber, *I and Thou*. Tr. Walter Kaufman. New York: Charles Scribner's, 1970, p. 58. Emphasis added. It's significant that Buber's philosophy is neither static nor abstract but rooted in the physical world, in dynamic relationships between *bodies*.

[51] Ibid. p. 127.

www.ingramcontent.com/pod-product-compliance
Lightning Source LLC
Chambersburg PA
CBHW060913120626
46553CB00001B/308